T0244621

Soldiers of Revolution

Soldiers of Revolution

The Franco-Prussian Conflict and the Paris Commune

Mark Lause

VERSO

London • New York

First published by Verso Books 2022
© Mark Lause 2022
Illustration on page 184, *Illustrated London News*, October 1, 1870

1 3 5 7 9 10 8 6 4 2

Verso
UK: 6 Meard Street, London W1F 0EG
US: 20 Jay Street, Suite 1010, Brooklyn, NY 11201
versobooks.com

Verso is the imprint of New Left Books

ISBN-13: 978-1-78873-054-9
ISBN-13: 978-1-78873-057-0 (US EBK)
ISBN-13: 978-1-78873-056-3 (UK EBK)

British Library Cataloguing in Publication Data
A catalogue record for this book is available from the British Library

Library of Congress Cataloging-in-Publication Data

Names: Lause, Mark A., author.
Title: Soldiers of revolution : the Franco-Prussian Conflict and the Paris
    Commune / Mark Lause.
Other titles: Franco-Prussian Conflict and the Paris Commune
Description: London ; New York : Verso Books, 2022. | Includes
    bibliographical references and index. | Summary: "A study of the
    momentous military developments during the Franco-Prussian War, which
    shaped the nature of civilian insurrection as well as presaging the
    events of the Great War that would follow in the next century"—
    Provided by publisher.
Identifiers: LCCN 2021042930 (print) | LCCN 2021042931 (ebook) | ISBN
    9781788730549 (hardback) | ISBN 9781788730570 (ebk)
Subjects: LCSH: Franco-Prussian War, 1870–1871. | Paris
    (France)—History—Commune, 1871. | Military history, Modern. |
    Revolutions and socialism—France—History—19th century.
Classification: LCC DC293 .L378 2022 (print) | LCC DC293 (ebook) | DDC
    943.08/2—dc23
LC record available at https://lccn.loc.gov/2021042930
LC ebook record available at https://lccn.loc.gov/2021042931

Typeset in Minion Pro by Hewer Text UK Ltd, Edinburgh
Printed and bound by CPI Group (UK) Ltd, Croydon CR0 4YY

Contents

Part III
WAR FOR THE REPUBLIC

Part IV
WAR FOR THE PEOPLE: THE REVOLUTION

Introduction

This study revolves around several concerns, the first rooted in issues around the development of society and the concept of revolution. After all, from one perspective, the most hellish and dramatic incidents in the history of the Butte de Warlencourt represented relatively short punctuation points in its long and interesting history. Clearly, from time immemorial, those working the land around Butte de Warlencourt have sought shelter under its trees, a rest from labors or a refuge for rural lovers hidden from the prying eyes. For the better part of two thousand years, merchants and their servants making the peaceful commercial trek along the nearby road found the butte a well-positioned point of rest. So did the exhausted and footsore journeyman walking hopefully toward the next job. Nearby, the locals or travelers could find something to help appease their hunger, a supplement to the cheap bread picked up at the last village and dropped into a satchel for just such a sumptuous repast. Nobody remembers the site because of the human associations that filled the vast bulk of its history.

What happened in 1916 overshadowed its entire history. That July 1, the "Big Push" began just to the southwest at Albert. Protected by trenches and machine guns, the Germans made that day the bloodiest in the history of the British Army, and the slaughter in the Somme continued into November. The British made it halfway to Bapaume, to what was left of the village of Le Sars, beyond which loomed the Butte de Warlencourt. With great effort and despite tremendous losses, the British took the butte, then lost it and retook it many times. In the aftermath of this fighting, soldiers from Australia and New Zealand finally had it long enough to fortify it for the Allies, though the Germans retook it in their spring offensive of 1918, forcing the Allies to retake it for a final time in August. Thereafter, unexploded munitions and the grisly remains of casualties from around the world made it an unmarked monument to a war to end all wars—or the American version, a war to make the world safe for democracy.

What raged about the Butte de Warlencourt in the twentieth century virtually obliterated what took place in 1871 when French horsemen clambered up its icy slopes, to scan the frozen fields around them for Germans. It cast the war of 1870–1 as far into the shadows as it had the Roman victory over a Frankish invasion in 448 CE. Indeed, the butte itself was no natural formation but likely the burial mound of a long-forgotten prehistoric chief.

In this layered history, the Franco-Prussian War rested roughly halfway between Napoleon's wars and the *Götterdammerung* of 1914–18. The brevity of the war belies its importance, and its chroniclers tend to present a truncated version of an already brief war. On August 4, 1870, armies of the Prussian-led German federation began pouring into France, and, by September 2, destroyed or neutralized the major French armies, captured Emperor Napoleon III himself, and brought down the French government. This destroyed the Second Empire of France and placed the Confederation around the leadership of Prussia on the fast track to becoming a new German Reich, toppling a balance of power established in the wake of the first Napoleon.

The war continued for another five months, through a bitter winter into February 1871.[1] In terms of numbers, organization, and technology, it brought the standards of a modern total war to the European heartland. The new industrial conflict focused the priorities of the entire civilization on itself. Society and its masters gained the power to bend everything to its concerns, including those older stabilizing structures, rituals, and ideologies. This new kind of modern, total war transformed the economy, strained the coherence of the social order, and often disrupted the functioning of the political structure. Moreover, it required

---

1   Indeed, a British documentary, *The Franco-Prussian War 1870–1871* (2007) abbreviates the conflict in just this fashion, albeit with a brief concluding nod to developments in Paris.

the persistent and coherent engagement of the civilian populations, creating the focus and social discipline that Karl Marx and others had ascribed to industrialization generally.

Marx may have also been correct in suggesting that the new class structures created identities that transcended narrow national interests, but, similarly, wars—the most dramatic celebrations of national madness—were events of global importance. The origins, waging, and impact of the Franco-Prussian War not only created Germany and remade France, but also had a major impact on neighboring countries, as well as North Africa and the Balkans. Over time, the shifting balance of power affected Great Britain and Ireland and the transatlantic community, as well as the fate of Africa and Asia.

Individual entanglements in the war reflected this kind of cosmopolitanism, particularly among those who fought for France. As an imperial power, it fielded an army that included its colonial subjects. Then, as a new republic, it inspired politically motivated volunteers from across the Western world, including Germans.

At the same time, the new kind of total war that produced a modern, centralized militarized state with unprecedented authority also vested it with unprecedented responsibility. Its exercise of that expanded and invasive power required the cooperation of its subjects, who could also hold government responsible more directly, regardless of their older institutional subjugation. The Great War and its detonation of the Russian Revolution of 1917 dramatically demonstrated this relationship between war and revolution, but it also reiterated what had been established half a century earlier, in the Franco-Prussian War and the Paris Commune, as with the American Civil War and the destruction of African slavery.

After a preliminary view of nineteenth-century Europe and the mid-century crisis of mass republicanism, this brief work sketches, I hope, enough of that experience to provide a clearer approach to the outbreak of the largest armed insurrection of the nineteenth-century working class.

Certainly, the popular revolts of 1870–1, like those of half a century later, grew from deep roots. As later in Russia, republican discontent had simmered for decades, frustrated by the unrelenting rule of empires and monarchies. Between 1848 and 1871, new centralized nation-states struggled to incorporate older national republican aspirations. Also, the class nature of that rule—unapologetically allied to the new hierarchies of capital—increasingly shaped the practical meaning of republicanism. The rise of the Commune and its kindred movements across France reflected presistent if different efforts to define the republic for which they contended, a model defined by the vocabulary of the "social republic," social democracy and socialism, or anarchism. Scholars have also focused on the people behind the new ideas, from Karl Marx to Mikhail Bakunin, battling over the future of the International Workingmen's Association and its legacy.

Nevertheless, however compelling the innovative thinking about class and class revolution, however persuasive its advocates, and however secure their organizations, revolutionary circles would never have been able to topple the dominant structures of power. The upheaval that established the Commune—as surely as the 1917 revolution in Russia—grew from conditions that the revolutionaries themselves never shaped. Of course, the masters of war themselves take great pains to plead their innocence, asserting the irrelevance of war to revolution, or even emphasizing its overt hostility to mass revolt. With reactionaries of all sorts, they attribute mass revolt to the work of a consciously revolution-ary clandestine current, as they had done so from its beginning. A contemporary self-confessed ignoramus on the Paris Commune managed to squeeze out a book on the subject; he found it "difficult to assign a correct cause for the insurrection in Paris, but the agents and ringleaders of the International Working Mens' Association were supposed to be implicated with the rising."[2] As happens in such cases, the International and allied revolutionaries were not so much leading as running to catch up with developments.

Disconcerting to the power structure, Paris had been an acknowledged high point of Western society, and the war demonstrated just how vulnerably low that pinnacle might be brought. The immediate aftermath of the war inspired a full-blown social revolution, so long dreaded and much discussed. This was neither confined to Paris nor particularly or uniquely French. It expressed the aspiratoins of a new working class, functioning internationally and facing a transnational experience. Elements of it had begun to act as history's replacement for the

---

2 H. Allnutt, *Historical Diary of the War between France and Germany, 1870–1* (London: Estates Gazette Office, 1872), 417.

self-interested bourgeoisie. This raw class sensibility transformed an older revolutionary tradition.

That required the kind of social turmoil and chaos that only the ruling class itself could conjure. Their decision to go to war put the nation on just such a path. War, with its cheapening of life, risks becoming an act of institutional suicide by the nation-state. In the broadest sense, a peoples' history of the Franco-Prussian conflict underscores the basic relationship of war and revolution. Most sobering, perhaps, revolutions owe more to the implosion of the old order than to the agitation of revolutionaries, though that may well be a major factor in shaping the character of a new order.

Indeed, even under those circumstances, the radical bid for a more substantive kind of alternative republic—socialism, anarchism, or whatever any particular Communard chose to call it—continued to come to naught. As late as October 31, the elder statesman of the Parisian Left, Auguste Blanqui, attempted to lead a force of determined radicals to power in order to proclaim a commune in the French capital. The authorities had no serious problems dealing with it as they had others over the previous twenty years.

What changed between the end of October 1870 and March 1871, when the Commune successfully declared itself?

The experience of the war changed the nature of much of the army itself. The original imperial *casus belli* had been a dynastic squabble with national "honor" at stake. On its behalf, they sent thousands uniformed and trained for Napoleonic warfare into a conflict of trenches, long-range firearms, heavy artillery, and machine guns.

More horrifically, perhaps, the transformation of France into a "republic" fueled expectation in, as well as out of, uniform about the nature of the new government. Since its general policies seemed to differ little from those of the old empire, sharp debates took place, particularly among those fighting to secure its survival.

While I thoroughly sympathize with the sentiments of an old friend who barely deigned to teach anything that might encourage the mystification of martial glory, not only is war an integral reality of human history but also, without coming to grips with it in this case, we risk mystification of the revolutionary process. At the most basic level, France faced a seemingly hopeless military situation, and the same spirit that inspired the mutineers of 1918–19 moved their grandsires.

Simply put, the experience of the war created a soldiery more willing to challenge officers and officers more inclined to confront generals.

This deep crisis of legitimacy within the army itself—as well as that of the military in the wider society—produced the most important precondition for something such as the Commune. This realization, in turn, fueled the motives for the gratuitous slaughter that accompanied the defeat of the Commune.

That brutal repression of the Commune—inseparable from that crisis in the military—casts a long, dark shadow of the subsequent history of the modern world. The ruling elites monopolize both how republicanism is to be defined and the extent to which critics can act, organize, or even speak and write in opposition. Robert Tombs oddly argued that the Left exaggerated how many civilians were murdered by the army in an attempt blacken the reputation of capitalism . . . as though the world stood still after 1871 rather than repeatedly offer those lessons in greater and greater amounts of blood.

This systemic imbalance of power has made war a perennial feature of modern history. From this perspective, the hell periodically visited on places such as the Butte de Warlencourt dramatized the incredible willingness of people to engage in acts of heroic sacrifice to the point of self-destructiveness. In it, we see how modern, cultivated Western civilization has retained much that would be recognizable to the prehistoric tribes that entombed their dead there. And the Commune offers hope in the possibility of an alternative.

PART I
Republic and Nation

1

Civilization and Its Old Mole: Visions of Republican Revolution

In its rapid development, the nineteenth century defined what came to be called Western civilization on many levels. In March 1868, work crews on an access road to the train station shared by the village of Les Eyzies and neighboring Tayac began using gravel and landfill from a low-ceiling horizontal cleft in the bluffs overlooking the Vézère river. As they reached the floor, they found shaped stones similar to the artifacts of the "primitive" peoples of the Americas, sub-Saharan Africa, and the Arctic. They telegraphed for expert advice, and a well-dressed associate of the Muséum national d'histoire naturelle, Louis Lartet, arrived quickly by train. After proceeding more carefully into the enclave, they found themselves staring into the eyeless sockets of an empty skull.

So it was that the civilized European world came face to face with what was then the oldest of their immediate ancestors. Those who grappled with the past acknowledged a certain unevenness in the process, but believed in a progress that had carried us from stone tools to a world of railroad industrialists, road crews, academics, bohemians, and peasants. They also understood that the recent past had exponentially expanded productivity, population, and prosperity—at least for some— creating new problems that mandated further change. The eighteenth- and nineteenth-century effort to supersede what seemed to be the legacy of a dark and superstitious antiquity turned on two insights, the first relying on the rise and strengthening of the modern nation-state as a vehicle with the power to change the world. Additionally, they generally seemed to understand that power and stability, resting on the consent of the governed, recast a version of classical republicanism. Republicanism became the focus for the broad and diverse libertarian, egalitarian, and fraternal aspirations throughout society, some acknowledging a tension between nationalism and republicanism.

Civilization and Its Challenges

Nineteenth-century people understood that civilization had emerged slowly through a series of complex processes. A fortunate few of the wandering hunter-gatherers of the Stone Ages found a particularly fertile microclimate like the Vézère valley, suitable for regular foraging and through which prey animals regularly passed. These permitted some to enjoy a more sedentary life than most of their contemporaries, and the warming after the last Ice Age later gave rise to agriculture and the domestication of animals.

Lartet and his contemporaries had a hard-won understanding of the long past that had brought civilization to the crises of the mid-nineteenth century. Only a few thousand years before Lartet found the remains of some of those lucky few, people elsewhere began more regularly cultivating certain plants and domesticating animals, eventually using plows to break the soil along the Nile, Indus, Tigris, and Euphrates, as well as in China and in the valley of Mexico. Better nutrition extended individual lifespans, while leaving people increasingly toil-worn. The overwhelming majority of the population lived and labored on the land and would do so for generations, for centuries.

Viewed down the nose of the literate and learned, these country people seemed homogeneous in their inferiority, parochialism, and incompetency in anything beyond dirt and sweat. In his *Leviathan* of 1651, Thomas Hobbes famously described such primitive lives as "solitary, poor, nasty, brutish, and short." The absence of commerce and order, he reasoned, meant the "warre of every man against every man." For thousands of years, the exhausting—even backbreaking—demands of the land were anchored by the annual ordeal of the plow.

Yet the broad brush of this memorably poetic stroke did not do the subject justice. Different plows drawn by different draught animals cultivated what had been ancient Roman territory and the more recently wooded lands to the east or north. They owned, loaned, managed, and borrowed the means of production to produce different kinds of crops, in different combinations, aimed at different kinds of consumption. They divided lands differently, and attributed differing importance to those divisions.[1]

Those who came after Hobbes observed what he had not. They knew, for example, that farming became more complicated and required greater cooperation. Villages grew larger, and the family evolved to suit the practical needs of the land. Moreover, peasants in some places as a group gained access to land by renting or providing services to a manor presided over by a lord or church official. They might also hold some of the unused lands and forests as commons.

Trial and error had already taught farmers the value of rotating between planting cereals and legumes, periodically leaving the land to regenerate, and using animal dung to assist the process. An open-field agriculture spread, particularly in the colder, wetter world of Northern Europe, with many pragmatic modifications. By the close of the first millennium CE, European farmers began adopting a three-field system, planting cereals in one, vegetables in another, and leaving the third fallow. Starting in the fourteenth century, the Black Death began a series of visitations that left its fortunate survivors with more land and their scarce labors more valued. In many places, as demands grew greater on the tools and draught animals, relatives, neighbors, and entire villages learned to refine and share them.

These changes expanded the range of individual destinies. This meant greater personal opportunities—more in some places than others—but imposed heavier economic demands on the peasantry. As old feudal relations weakened, growing numbers of peasants got greater responsibility for—and sometimes even ownership of—the lands they worked. Still, any unexpected development—too much rainfall or too little—could threaten the well-being of even successful peasants.

A new "scientific revolution" among "the learned" also cultivated a "scientific agriculture," and new rural elites enjoying various relationships with the old aristocracies came to the fore. A little property could

1   Eric J. Hobsbawm, "Peasants and Politics," *Journal of Peasant Studies*, 1 (October 1973), 3–22. Eric R. Wolf, *Peasants* (New York: Prentice-Hall, 1966), and his *Peasant Wars of the Twentieth Century* (New York: Harper & Row, 1969).

provide a household with a life markedly superior to that of most of the peasantry. Their children benefited the most from what schooling the communities or churches established to meet the need for literacy and technical training. These, in turn, provided the possibility, if not the promise, of a more distinctive and specialized life.

The expansion of property and of its privatization changed the nature of the family. Sons and daughters felt pressures to accept marital arrangements, but increasingly resisted them. Generally, as tasks became more complicated and physically demanding—and healthy children more plentiful—the young took up the less demanding chores, particularly the care of the smaller domesticated animals.

These very real changes took place unevenly and sometimes indirectly. Older practices lingered in places such as the Pyrenees and on the plains along the Baltic, even as prehistoric slash-and-burn agriculture continued in parts of the far north. In the east, Junkers and Boyars still exercised lordly control over their peasants. Only in 1861 did Russia officially end serfdom, but many peasants remained on their families' traditional ground for years, decades, and even generations. Indeed, fishermen, shepherds, and those who tended ducks, geese, chickens, sheep, goats, swine, and cattle continued to lead largely ancient, virtually biblical lives. Older standards and practices of all sorts persisted, as they always had, where they found ways to fit into a changing social and economic order.[2]

Nevertheless, the overall trend grew networks of new roads and canals—later supplemented by railroads, such as that running through Les Eyzies—which created new mass markets for some products. These growing markets naturally tended to extend their branches along lines of cultural and linguistic affinity. New political institutions imposed standards creating common weights, measures, and currencies—along with language and cultural awareness—that shaped a national identity beyond the farm, the village, and the smaller community.

New institutions and authorities emerged to manage the functioning of these markets and infrastructure. Religion had long provided the sense of community and identity necessary to the functioning of these villages. For centuries, the Roman church had rooted itself in the needs of that collective life, with special sacramental functions focused on the

_____

2   Wolf, *Peasants.*

individual's place in a community of faith. Local and regional patron saints deepened this association, and Christianity proved remarkably flexible in assimilating preexisting religious beliefs and practices, along with feasts, festivals, games, and rituals. Seasonal celebrations of the predictability of the moon and the sun marked the passage of the year. As the persistent importance of midwives and "wise women" helped the community to function, though only up to a point. Also, the general exclusion of Jews from the mechanisms of rural European society and the centuries-long struggle to exclude Islam had been frighteningly thorough. Theological conflicts often tended to blur almost seamlessly into vehicles for peasant discontent.

Secular authority increasingly emerged as the final arbiter defining the relationships of individuals in these communities and of communities with other communities. Affinities and hostilities defined one hamlet from another. Appeals to external authorities could tilt these tensions in the favor of one side or the other. Concerns about being identified as somehow deviant from the outside made these communities sensitive to external pressures.

That kind of authority became essential. Mechanical and chemical innovations augmenting agricultural production not only permitted rapid population growth but also made much of that population superfluous to its needs. It compelled many, often unwillingly, to seek a living elsewhere. In the end, these vast new numbers of individuals, no longer tied to the networks of extensive rural kinships, would remain governable only by their consent.

In the course of this process, writers and thinkers across the Western world had turned to the rediscovery of the pre-Christian idea of the republic. A representative system would ensure that those subjected to centralizing rule would themselves be rulers of sorts. While the Enlightenment generally expressed a great deal of optimism about the power of reason in establishing republics, it became clear that those holding power would not yield it without a revolution. The Dutch in their revolt against Spain, the English in their civil war, the colonists in America, and finally the French subjects of their monarchy took steps toward this. Aimed at institutions governing nations, the revolutionary processes would themselves be inherently national.

France demonstrated just how difficult realizing the promise of the republic could be. Louis XIV had established the predominant position of the centralized French state generations before. This essential national identity survived the Revolution of 1789, the Revolutionary and Napoleonic Wars, and the Restoration of the Bourbon monarchy in 1815. Over the half a century after the defeat of Napoleon, the lingering vision of the republic persisted through the "July Revolution" of 1830 that replaced the Bourbon dynasty with Orleanists, and the short-lived republic of 1848. However, it had hardly triumphed.

The mid-nineteenth century stumbled through the metaphorical rubble of these upheavals seeking evidence to sustain a faith in the ultimate transformative triumph of republicanism. The more the republican faith spread among the people generally, the more those in power tended to offer little more than lip service.

They certainly had good reasons for this.

The National Framework of the Republican Revolution

The institutions of power had always been in the best position to take up and implement the national promise of republicanism without much more than a nod toward the concept of a representative political order. This represented a time-honored approach, while new concentrations of wealth required strong central governments and the armies to sustain them.

France, the country with the clearest revolutionary traditions on the continent, reached mid-century as an empire. Louis Bonaparte, the nephew of the great conqueror, offered his leadership as the lowest-common-denominator opposition to the Orleanist and the older "legitimist" Bourbon monarchists. His coup of 1851 seized both the crown and the title of Napoleon III. Critics scoffed at the attempt to smother real problems with pretentious flummery, but the Second Empire played well enough to last for twenty years.

As the promise of 1789 terrified the surrounding monarchies, who mobilized their military responses, they predisposed the French Revolution to becoming the kind of centralized military state that required a Napoleon. The Napoleonic experience, including the experience of his enemies in mobilizing for his defeat, set the Western nations on the road to a modern technocratic military. This, in turn, needed governments centered on the mystique of past battlefield glories. Across the continent, an officer caste developed a new voice with highly specialized preoccupations and concerns, to which the other institutions of power tended to defer uncritically. These formed a new element in the nuts and bolts of state formation.

Beyond the military—or the residual feudal obligations—no new state exercised a more rationalized central authority than France. It had thirty-two provinces governing eighty-nine departments, each administered by *préfet* and *sous préfets* appointed by the central government. Within these were several hundred arrondisements, several thousand cantons, and several tens of thousands of communes, but local autonomy was virtually nonexistent.[3]

Modern nations evolved out of older networks of political power. Because the new governments standardized language, it is tempting to read a common language back into the formative period of the nation-building enterprise when it did not exist. Even so, the populations of Alsace, the Basque country, the Languedoc, Savoy and Brittany used regional languages, as did those in Swabia or Hanover. In places, local communities had their own patois that could even vary from village to village.

Then, too, nation-states were built on bones of older identities, whether codified into a state or not. Implicit in the matrix of the modern states was the systemic frustration of national aspirations. Britain embraced Ireland, Scotland, and Wales, while groups such as the Bretons in France or the Basques there and in Spain arguably represented stateless nations. Further east, scores of nationalities had similar aspirations, even as Romania, Serbia, and Montenegro strained for more autonomy under the Russian, Austrian, and Ottoman states. The Germans and Poles strove without success to attain national states; the Italians had only recently done so. This inherent contradiction of nationalism as the most serious obstacle to its own realization became even more pronounced with its extension beyond Europe.

Those who rooted the legitimacy of the state in the voluntary popular identification of its subjects with a common national identity saw this as

3   F. Ansart, *Petite géographie moderne a l'usage des écoles primaires* (Paris: Librairie Hachette et Cie, 1871), 153–78; for French departments, see John J. Lalor, ed., *Cyclopedia of Political Sciences, Political Economy, and of the Political History of the United States*, vol. 2 (Chicago: Rand, McNally & Company, 1881), 265–6; and Maurice Block, "France," in ibid., 263.

essential to the idea of republicanism, a vital mesh of identity between the lived community and the intangible Church Triumphant. In the end, they believed, the need to legitimate the bourgeois state required not only the baubles and geegaws of monarchy but the trappings of republican government as well.

After Napoleon, European rulers had sustained a delicate balance of power that would foster economic development and related progress. Still, Europe remained dominated by imperial power structures that had no direct connection to issues of nationhood. At the edges of the continent, antiquated old monarchies—Spain, Austria–Hungary, Russia, and the Ottoman Empire—still clung to power. In contrast, Britain and France had revolutions of sorts in the seventeenth and eighteenth centuries that had restructured those institutions. Prussia, Spain, Sweden, Norway, and Denmark had minor roles, the last reeling from a crushing defeat by Prussia. Still smaller and less powerful states—Switzerland and the Netherlands—had even less importance, with Belgium operating within limits imposed by the Great Powers as the price of its independence. Treaties constrained the position of Greece, and left Portugal virtually a protectorate of Great Britain.

The weight of the Second Empire rested heavily on a carefully constructed myth of military prowess that belied both its past and its present. Despite having been dismissive of imperial ventures by his predecessors, Napoleon III never forgot his ultimate dependence on the army and realized the advantage of cheaper labor and raw materials and an ever-sharper definition of nationality and race. France maintained its international prominence, in large part, through the globalization of its power. Claiming the dual virtue of monarchist legitimacy and progress, it carried the tricolor out into a world not quite ready for it.

Napoleon III painted imperial ambitions on a global canvas. France had established itself in North Africa, and its army fought in a Second Italian War of Independence. The regime intervened in Senegal, a Second Opium War, and the Indochina campaign, even as it intervened around China's Taiping Rebellion, and Japan's Boshin War, as well as against Korea. Most recently, the French attempted to resolve the problem of Mexico's debt by placing the Archduke Ferdinand Maximilian Joseph of Habsburg–Lorraine on the throne as Emperor Maximilian I, a particularly bloody and brutal attempt that had ended in disaster by 1867.

Eager to place himself at the head of Christian Europe, Napoleon III demonstrated that the Ottomans cede France sovereignty over the Holy Land. When the Russia asserted its historic role as the protector of the Orthodox Church, the French sent a warship into the Black Sea and won an Ottoman agreement to take the Church of the Nativity from the Orthodox Church and cede it to the Roman Catholics. The Russians then advanced into the Danube principalities of Moldavia and Wallachia, and the British, who saw the Turks as a buffer against Russian expansion, found themselves drawn into what became known as the Crimean War of 1854–6.

Imperial expansion paradoxically opened the door for a national assimilation of the outsiders. Forty years before 1870, the Irish provided over 42 percent of the British Army. In 1868, after famine and migration had depleted the resident population, their proportion had fallen almost to 30 percent, but this figure was still far out of proportion to their civilian numbers.[4] Military training—in both the British Army and in American forces in the war of 1861–5—could backfire.

Just as the British imperial military recruited the Irish and the Indians in service to the empire, the French relied on colonial people of color. The empire reached beyond North Africa into sub-Saharan Africa as well. In 1857, for example, the governor general of French West Africa, Louis Faidherbe, lacked enough troops to control the territory and got authorization to raise Senegalese *tirailleurs*, a sub-Saharan extension of North African practice. The new corps included slaves bought from West African owners as well as prisoners of war. Rather famously, black conscripts kidnapped by Egyptian allies aided the French imperial venture in Mexico, earning the men French citizenship.[5]

Africans—black Africans—could even attain a military commission, despite all customs in dealing with all Africans. If an Arab became a captain, the rank would be "purely nominal . . . as he was under the control of a French lieutenant, and had nothing to say." There was once

4   Peter Karset, "Irish Soldiers in the British Army, 1792–1922: Suborned or Subordinate?", *Journal of Social History*, 17 (Autumn 1983), 36. See also Paul Huddie, "British Military Recruitment in Ireland during the Crimean War, 1854–56," *British Journal for Military History*, 2 (November 2015), 34–55.

5   Jean-Michel Deveau, "Esclaves noirs en Méditerranée," *Cahiers de la Méditerranée*, 65 (2002), online 15 October 2004, accessed 9 May 2010, at revues.org; and Richard L. Hill and Peter C. Hogg, *A Black Corps d'Élite: An Egyptian Sudanese Conscript Battalion with the French Army in Mexico, 1863–1867, and Its Survivors in Subsequent African History* (East Lansing MI: Michigan State University Press, 1995).

a "Jussuf, who became a general." The army even had some talk about ceding overall command to Emir Abd-el-Kuda, but, even had they done so, the regiment would have remained "under the control of a French colonel." Still, black soldiers could win a commission among them, as did a "civilized and intelligent negro" named Salem ben Guibi, who entered the *tirailleurs algériens* and rose through the ranks. After distinguishing himself at San Lorenzo in May 1863, when a Mexican force attempted to break the French siege of Puebla, he won promotion and, finally, an officer's commission.[6]

The expansion of global power also had a direct and detrimental impact on the prospects for self-government at home. In the aftermath of 1848, authorities relied on repression to marginalize the criticism of the propagandist and the agitator. While never entirely successful, their efforts established an institutional monopoly over the power to legitimate and sustain the idea of France around the pageant of Napoleonic ambitions, even as others sought to build the idea of Germany around the priorities of Prussia and the Hohenzollerns.

This new institution needed someone—a Napoleon, even if he had to be *Napoléon le Petit*, as Victor Hugo called him. The army had raised him to power, and he, in turn, wore the uniform and embraced the identity of the military, as did Herr Wilhelm Hohenzollern in Prussia. This symbiotic relationship of Napoleon III and the army extended to the choice of General Charles Auguste Frossard to personally direct the education of Napoleon Eugene ("Loulou"), the young prince imperial, which would be a military education, as it was for the Hohenzollern sons.

Many members of this expanded and bureaucratic fraternity had known each other from youth. They attended the same schools, notably Saint-Cyr, and shared monarchist predilections. A graduate there, the elderly General Paul de Ladmirault, remained the devout son of a counterrevolutionary who had fled the country during the French Revolution.[7] The solid career of his fellow alumnus Maréchal François

---

6   Heinrich von Maltzan, Baron zu Wartenburg und Penzlin, "The Turcos," *Appleton's Journal of Literature, Science and Art*, 5 (March 11, 1871), 102–3; Mariscal Bazaine, *La Intervencion Francesa en Mexico según el archivo del Mariscal Bazaine* (Mexico: Libreria de la Vda. de C. Bouret, 1907), 136 n.; Douglas Fermer, *Sedan 1870: The Eclipse of France* (Barnsley: Pen & Sword Military, 2008), 156.

7   Jacques de La Faye (pseudonym of Marie de Sardent), *Le général de Ladmirault (1808–1898)* (Paris: Bloud et Barral, 1900); and Maguy Gallet-Villechange, *Le général*

Marcellin Certain de Canrobert included the direction of troops against the republican "mobs" of 1848 and the coup of 1851 that raised the emperor to power.

Of course, the relatively recent expansion of the military had left the door open to commissioning relative outsiders, who had proved themselves in North Africa, Crimea, Italy, China, Indochina, and Mexico. Marshal Patrice de MacMahon had studied at the Petit Séminaire at Autun before continuing on to the Lycée Louis-le-Grand at Paris. Marshal Françoise Achille Bazaine had joined the army as a private but found service in the Foreign Legion to his liking and not only fought in the battles of France but in Spain's Carlist Wars, before taking charge of Napoleon III's debacle in Mexico. With the responsibility for that fiasco easily deflected onto the dead Emperor Maximilian, Bazaine returned to France with a greater reputation than before.

This rapid construction of modern military institutions did produce renegades. The undisguised inequalities and injustices of the system fueled discontent among the thoughtful who seriously wanted to be of service to society. In the Russian Empire, officers and lesser nobility organized the abortive effort of the Decembrists. By mid-century, the military wing of the post-Napoleonic state had produced an August Willich or a Joseph Weydemeyer in Prussia, a Gustave Paul Cluseret in France, and even a William DeRohan in the US.

In the face of the rapidly expanding repressive institutions of the emergent state, articulating the old vision of a republican transformation sounded increasingly utopian. Giuseppe Mazzini compared the nation to a family, wherein its health and success would be measured by the well-being of its most disadvantaged peoples. Abraham Lincoln came to evaluate the success of the American union and its members in terms of its utility as a liberating force for laboring people. An essential component of the appeal of republicanism had been its promise to elevate the base of society.

Then, too, republicanism had always claimed that its triumph in any nation would be the triumph of reason over parochial superstitions and prejudices. The continental character of the uprisings of 1848 inspired hope that "the springtime of nations" might set the world on the course to a universal republic, to be most immediately in a United States of

---

Paul de Ladmirault, un enfant du Poitou sous les aigles impériales (Parçay-sur-Vienne : Anovi, 2008).

Europe. Benito Juarez, the indigenous president of Mexico, explained, "Among individuals, as among nations, where there is respect for the right of others, there is peace."[8] As republicanism would prevail in country after country, it would eliminate the monopoly of power by the elites and the brutal superstitions that allowed those elites to go to war.

Depending on national and local conditions, various republicans could carry their concerns to revolutionary conclusions. Generally, the more repressive the existing government, the more tightly organized would be any revolutionary organization. In places, this distilled into a very small but important cadre of organized professional revolutionaries. If earlier reversals left those cadres divided, muddled, or inconsistent ideologically, they still remained remarkably united in their general hostility to the institutions of power.

Louis Auguste Blanqui embodied the continuities of a series of secret societies launched by their most prominent progenitor, Philippe Buonarroti, who had participated in the original French Revolution of 1789 and assisted the first attempted "communist" revolt of 1796. Back in his student days, Blanqui became involved in Buonarroti's associations, and built a lifelong career around insurrectionist plots and attempted abortive rebellions. In May 1839, his Société des saisons took up arms to find almost no real support, though émigré Germans in their Bund der Gerechten joined them. Blanqui continued to envision a revolutionary seizure of power by a tiny cadre organization that would temporarily establish a Jacobin-like revolutionary dictatorship, to make essential changes before handing over power to the people.[9]

It was a perspective largely shared—with all its contradictions and ambiguities—by Giuseppe Garibaldi. A sea captain born in Nice, he joined Mazzini's La Giovine Italia, seeking to unify the Italian peninsula as a republic, and the even more secret Carbonari. Implicated in an abortive rising, he fled to Latin America, where he adopted what became his distinctive red shirt, poncho, and sombrero; raised an immigrant "Italian Legion"; and learned guerrilla tactics from local slave rebels. Returning in 1848, he aided revolts in several places, most notably the

---

8 "The Triumph of the Republic, 1867," in Gilbert M. Joseph and Timothy J. Henderson, eds., *The Mexico Reader: History, Culture, Politics* (Durham, NC: Duke University Press, 2002), 272.

9 Doug Enaa Greene, *Communist Insurgent: Blanqui's Politics of Revolution* (Chicago: Haymarket Books, 2017).

insurgent and beleaguered Roman Republic. On July 2, 1849, after the negotiation of a truce, he and several thousand volunteers slipped from the city, and, reinforced by the column of the former English officer Hugh Forbes, tried unsuccessfully to reach Venice, still holding out against the Austrians.[10] Like Blanqui, Garibaldi saw the function of a revolutionary movement as the destruction of the old order, though he had actually built armies around the idea.

That said, the wispy web of secret societies and clandestine networks linked functioning revolutionary circles distinct from established national institutions, which provided an internationalist substance to the idea of a universal republic. When the institutions of the nation-states met the risings of 1848–9 with a common repressive response, it created a milieu of the generally like-minded proscribed and the émigré. London became the principal center for large numbers of French, German, Italian, Polish, and other revolutionaries, with New York providing a key secondary site.

These early internationalist bodies reflected the experienced reality of those who adhered to them.

The Revolutionary Legacy Refreshed

The frustrated national aspirations of the Italians and Irish refreshed the revolutionary movement from the mid-1850s into the late 1860s, with both assuming international proportions on their own. In the aftermath of their detention in 1849, Forbes and Garibaldi wound up in the US, with Alberto Mario and his English wife, Jesse White Mario. Forbes and the Marios remained long enough to advocate the abolition of slavery. Garibaldi headed back to Latin America in the spring of 1851, then crossed to China with side trips to the Philippines and Australia, before returning to Europe. When an associate of Garibaldi's took a potshot at Napoleon III in April 1855, and another lobbed a bomb at him in January 1858, the International Association rallied to their support.[11]

---

10   Robert L. Scheina, *Latin America's Wars: The Age of the Caudillo, 1791–1899* (New York: Random House, 1992), 120, 121–2, 153, 171; James H. Billington, *Fire in the Minds of Men: Origins of the Revolutionary Faith* (New York: Basic Books, 1980), 151, 486.

11   Mark A. Lause, *A Secret Society History of the Civil War* (Urbana and Chicago:

Garibaldi's circle went beyond such acts to revitalize faith in the prospects of a revolution won by the masses of people themselves. In 1859 and 1860—even as his old comrade Forbes became entangled with John Brown's plan to liberate American slaves—the Kingdom of the Two Sicilies, with its capital at Naples, orchestrated the brutal repression of risings in Messina and Palermo. Garibaldi responded by raising a thousand volunteers at Genoa on May 5, and landing them at Marsala six days later. Taking such a small force onto an island against a massive professional army entailed a great act of faith in the power of a popular *levée en masse* as a revolutionary tool. In vindication, locals flocked to the revolutionary army in large enough numbers to win an impressive victory at Calatafimi and drive the Neapolitans from Palermo. Toward the end of July, they won a fierce battle at Milazzo and had all of Messina but the citadel. When they crossed the strait to the mainland, Garibaldi continued north, greeted along the way as a liberator. They entered Naples on September 7, and defeated the Neapolitans at Volturno toward the end of the month.[12] Garibaldi and his "Thousand" exemplified the viability of the old union of mid-nineteenth-century revolutionary republicanism and nationalism.

On October 5, he began organizing an International Legion comprising different national divisions of volunteers, with a view of not only finishing the liberation of Italy, but fostering republicanism in their own countries. Back from America, Forbes took charge of English-speaking volunteers already turning up in Sicily. Garibaldi sent William De Rohan—the pseudonym of William Theodore Dahlgren, the brother of US admiral John Dahlgren—to London to organize another. This effort included not only many old Owenites and Chartists, but prominent freethinkers such as Bradlaugh. It also enjoyed the tacit support of elements in the British government and assistance from the deep pockets of the American adventurer and entrepreneur George Francis Train.[13]

University of Illinois Press, 2011), 41–4, 44–8; Elizabeth A. Daniels, *Jessie White Mario: Risorgimento Revolutionary* (Athens: Ohio University Press 1972), 6–7, 79, 109, and 74–87 *passim*.

12   George Macaulay Trevelyan, *Garibaldi and the Thousand* (London: Longmans, 1919), covers the essentials. Alexandre Dumas, *Les garibaldiens, révolution de Sicile et de Naples* (Paris: Michel Lévy, 1861).

13   Marcella Pellegrino Sutcliffe, "British Red Shirts: A History of the Garibaldi

The French Legion followed a former officer, Gustave P. Cluseret. A native of the Paris area then in his mid-thirties, he had joined the army in 1843 and even helped to suppress the 1848 revolution. His subsequent service in Algeria and Crimea left him increasingly disaffected until he left to join Garibaldi's volunteers. Coming from a far less martial background was the small but lively figure of Philippe Joseph Bordone, formerly a surgeon in the Crimean War, who had later had a series of minor civil suits over debt, earned by carelessness in money matters.[14]

German volunteers also cast a long shadow. Aged nearly forty, Wilhelm Rüstow had already theorized about the potential of a "people's militia" before 1848, and faced a prison sentence for high treason in its wake. From his Swiss exile, he wrote a number of military-historical and military-theoretical works before hurrying to join Garibaldi. Johann Philipp Becker, an old friend of Karl Marx and Friedrich Engels, also hurried to the banner of Garibaldi.[15]

Marx and Engels usually remained skeptical of the adventurism associated with international legions. Engels recalled how the Bonapartists had used this call in Paris to recruit some the most radical of the Spaniards, Italians, Belgians, Dutchmen, Poles, and Germans to get them out of the city. More deeply, such ventures seemed to provide

---

Volunteers (1860)," in Nir Arielli and Bruce Collin, eds., *Transnational Soldiers: Foreign Military Enlistment in the Modern Era* (London and New York: Palgrave Macmillan, 2013), 202–18; George Francis Train, *My Life in Many States and in Foreign Lands* (New York: D. Appleton & Co., 1902), 317, 302; David Tribe, *President Charles Bradlaugh* (London: Elek, 1971), 63, 68–9, 75, 77–8, 81, 83–4, 88.

14   Florence Braka's new biography *L'honneur perdu du Général Cluseret: De l'Internationale au nationalism* (Paris: Maisonneuve & Larose nouvelles éditions–Hémisphères éditions, 2018) supersedes everything on the subject, but see the appended note on sources. Also see Ferdinand Boyer, "Les volontaires français avec Garibaldi en 1860," *Revue d'histoire moderne et contemporaine*, 7 (April–June 1960), 123–48; Émile Maison, *Journal d'un volontaire de Garibaldi* (Paris: A. de Vresse, 1861); Ulric de Fonvielle, *Souvenirs d'une chemise rouge* (Paris: E. Dentu, 1861); and Clément Caraguel, *Souvenirs et aventures d'un volontaire de Garibaldi* (Paris: G. Paetz, 1861).

15   see Karl Marx and Friedrich Engels, *Collected Works*, trans. Richard Dixon and others. 50 vols. (Moscow: Progress Publishers; New York: International Publishers; and London: Lawrence & Wishart, 1975–2004) (hereafter *MECW*), vol. 26, 421–3. See also Ferdinand Nicolas Göhde, "German Volunteers in the Armed Conflicts of the Italian Risorgimento 1834–70," *Journal of Modern Italian Studies*, 14(4) (November 2009?), 461–75; Tristam Hunt, *Marx's General: The Revolutionary Life of Friedrich Engels* (New York: Metropolitan Books and Henry Holt and Company, 2009). "La levée en masse," *La Mascarade*, November 13, 1870, 2.

substitutes for a rebellion rooted in the local population. "We opposed this playing with revolution most decisively," insisted Engels. A military expedition tended "to import the revolution forcibly from outside," which would "undermine" the mass revolution and wind up strengthening the governments. Nor did they trust the political grasp of characters such as Harro Harring, who had joined Garibaldi abroad "to further the idea of the future of the nations by establishing a United States of South America."[16]

Nevertheless, the romanticism of the age affected even the most hardened materialists. Even as Garibaldi battled to save the Roman Republic in 1849, similar international legions rallied in the Baden-Palatinate to defend the last bastions of the German revolutions. Engels himself gathered valuable military experience there, fighting alongside Willich and Becker. Indeed, Marx and Engels were not above enthusiastically exchanging news about the successes of Garibaldi's later volunteer legions. As late as 1863, their close comrade Wilhelm Liebknecht reported efforts to raise a German legion in London to aid the Poles, an idea Forbes also then publicized among the English.[17]

Cluseret's career reflected the extent of that international republican revolutionary tradition. After Italy, he went to America, taking a commission and rising to the rank of brigadier general in the Union Army, gaining particular fame at Cross Keys in defeating Stonewall Jackson's men. He resigned to enter journalism and helped to boost the more overtly abolitionist presidential campaign of John C. Fremont in 1864. In addition to these associations, Cluseret developed close ties among Irish war veterans.

British efforts to drive out Irish nationalists or deport them to Australia encouraged republicans to flee overseas. John O'Mahony and James Stephens had spent years in France before passing on to other pastures.

---

16   Engels, "On the History of the Communist League," *MECW*, vol. 26, 324; Karl Marx, "The Great Men of the Exile," *MECW*, vol. 11, 288; and Göhde, "German Volunteers in the Armed Conflicts of the Italian Risorgimento"; Simon Sarlin, "Fighting the Risorgimento: Foreign Volunteers in Southern Italy (1860–63)," *Journal of Modern Italian Studies*, 14(4) (November 2009), 476–90.

17   For various comments by Engels on this, see *MECW*, vol. 9, 151, 426–7; vol. 10, 45–146; vol. 14, 460; vol. 16, xxii, 149–50; vol. 19, 232; vol. 33, 171–238; vol. 37, 22. See also "End of the Garibaldian Movement," *Herald of Progress*, September 13, 1862, p. 4; and "Noble Words from Garibaldi," *Herald of Progress*, November 1, 1862, p. 5.

Stephens started the Irish Republican Brotherhood at Dublin, and O'Mahony the Fenian Brotherhood in America. Though factionalized, the Fenians drew thousands of exiled Irish in fund-raising and organizing efforts.[18]

Both currents focused on the potential of the US as a base for armed invasions of Canada, the most vulnerable of the English colonies. In New York, Colonel Thomas J. Kelly had worked as a printer and a member of the Typographical Union before joining the Union Army, after which he became a deputy to Stephens of the IRB. On the night of May 31–June 1, 1866, between 800 and 1,500 Fenians from Buffalo seized Fort Erie and defeated a Canadian force at Ridgeway. Over the next week, US officials broke up other groups gathering along the St. Lawrence Valley, but gave the would-be raiders their railroad tickets home. Partly owing to the Fenian threat on its southern border there, the British readily acceded to the formation of the new Canadian confederation. Canada would prove to be no Sicily.

Like the Italian national movement, that of the Irish became transnational in its sources and influences. The Fenians in the US involved Train and Cluseret, veterans of Garibaldi's venture. In addition, they recruited the former secretary of Louis Riel, leader of the Métis people in Canada, and a former officer in the army of Juarez in Mexico. Stephens had strong connections to the "reds" among the French, Italians, and other elements of the International Workingmen's Association (IWA) at New York. "Jenny Williams," actually Jenny Marx—the daughter of Karl—publicized the imprisonment of Jeremiah O'Donovan Rossa among French readers.[19]

At the 1868 convention, an estimated 6,000 armed men in uniform escorted 400 delegates through the streets to the hall. There they heard a major address by Train, then also bankrolling *The Revolution*, the paper of Elizabeth Cady Stanton and Susan B. Anthony. At the same

---

18   Leon Ó Broin, *Fenian Fever: An Anglo-American Dilemma* (London: Chatto & Windus, 1971), 19, 25, 31, 46, and 183; but see also his *Revolutionary Underground: The Story of the Irish Republican Brotherhood, 1858–1924* (Totowa, NJ: Rowman and Littlefield, 1976). Reflecting more recent preoccupations, see Brian Jenkins, *The Fenian Problem: Insurgency and Terrorism in a Liberal State, 1858–1874* (Montreal: McGill-Queen's University Press, 2008).

19   Peter Edwards, *The Infiltrator: Henri Le Caron, the British Spy inside the Fenian Movement* (Duboyne: Maverick House, 2010), 89–90, 90–1, 95.

time, the inspector general of the Brotherhood's army—a British agent named Henri Le Caron—reported on further military preparations along the Canadian border between Ogdensburg, New York and St. Albans, Vermont.[20]

Nevertheless, the Fenians had already planned to initiate operations back home. They offered Cluseret command of their scheduled insurrection and he arrived in London just after the Reform League's Hyde Park demonstration on May 6, 1867. Cluseret met with Bradlaugh and a dozen members of the league in the White Horse in Rathbone Place, and suggested a coordinated rising in England with the support of 2,000 sworn members of the local Fenian body. With the exception of George Odger of the IWA, the league rejected the call, some even leaving in hopes of avoiding their mention by the press, a desire with which *The Times* did not comply.

Some English radicals continued to admire Cluseret. William Linton, another old associate in the Italian struggle, described the general as "a moody, white-faced, black-bearded international freedom fighter." A gadfly himself, Linton also favored land nationalization, complained of the US subjugation of Indians, and came to believe that the Americans were repeating the same mistakes as Britain, albeit on a larger scale and with effects less correctable.[21]

Later, when the Fenians produced a mere fraction of the numbers they had promised to supply, Cluseret disassociated himself from an operation he saw as doomed, and slipped from the country. Nevertheless, the British authorities condemned him *in absentia*.

Through these years, Cluseret maintained close ties to the short-lived

---

20   William D'Arcy, *The Fenian Movement in the United States, 1858–86* (Washington: Catholic University of America Press, 1947); Hereward Senior, *The Fenians and Canada* (Toronto: MacMillan, 1978); Senior, *The Last Invasion of Canada* (Toronto and Oxford: Dundurn Press, 1991); Senior, *The Battles of Ridgeway and Fort Erie, 1866* (Toronto: Balmuir Book Publishing, 1993). Brian Jenkins, *Fenians and Anglo-American Relations during Reconstruction* (Ithaca, NY: Cornell University Press, 1969).

21   Francis B. Smith, *Radical Artisan* (Manchester: Manchester University Press, 1973), 167. See also Frederick W. Hoeing, "Letters of Mazzini to W. J. Linton," *Journal of Modern History*, 5 (March 1933), 55–68, with a brief note on Cluseret at 66 and 66 n.; and Linton's "The Paris Commune," *The Radical: A Monthly Magazine Devoted to Religion*, 1 (September 1871), 81–104. Marx urged the IWA in America to engage with Cluseret. Timothy Messer-Kruse, *The Yankee International: Marxism and the American Reform Tradition, 1848–1876* (Chapel Hill and London: University of North Carolina Press, 1998), 67.

abolitionist plans to end slavery in Cuba, and these new radicals generally included members of the African diaspora. One of Cluseret's associates, Sainte Suzanne Melvil-Bloncourt, a mixed-race republican journalist, had played a prominent role back in 1848 in abolishing slavery in the French colonies.[22] Born on Guadeloupe, he had enough ties to the island's elite to wind up in Paris studying at the Lycée Louis-le-Grand. As a law student there, he took up the pen and became associated with Charles Baudelaire and Henri Murger, the author of *La vie de Bohème*, as well as Gaspard-Félix Tournachon, the photographer known as Nadar.

Melvil's political work associated him with other radicals known to Cluseret. These included Louis Charles Delescluze, Felix Pyat, and Elisle Reclus, as well as Hughes Felicité Robert de Lamennais, a pioneering Christian socialist, and Alexandre Auguste Ledru-Rollin. He also wrote for Pierre-Joseph Proudhon's *Le Peuple*. When the revolution of 1848 established a new republic, Melvil pressed tirelessly and successfully for an end to slavery in the colonies, doing so alongside Adolphe Crémieux, an advocate of Jewish emancipation and equality. In turn, the former slaves there elected Melvil their deputy to the constituent assembly, and he suffered brief incarceration after the coup of Napoleon III.

By the late 1860s, then, active proponents of revolution—anticipating a repeat of 1848, albeit with a successful conclusion—had adopted politics as a career.

Marx is often quoted to have said, "We recognize our old friend, our old mole, who knows so well how to work underground, suddenly to appear: the revolution." At that point, the old mole of revolution still burrowed deep through republican soil. A genuinely representative system of power would have to acknowledge the reality that the vast majority of society

22   Nelly Schmidt, "Slavery and Its Abolition: French Colonies, Research and Transmission of Knowledge," posted in UNESCO's *The Slave Route Project*; Jacques Adelaide-Merlande, "La Commission d'abolition de l'esclavage," *Bulletin de la Société d'histoire de la Guadeloupe*, 53–4 (1982), 3–34; Augustin Cochin, *L'abolition de l'esclavage*, rpr. (Fort-de-France: Dsormeaux, 1979; first published 1861); and Gaston Martin, *L'abolition de l'esclavage, 27 avril 1848* (Paris: Presses universitaires de France, 1948). Gerald Bloncourt, "Melvil-Bloncourt: Mon grand oncle Communard. Biographie extraite du dictionnaire des parlementaires français de 1789 à 1889 (Adolphe Robert et Gaston Cougny)," in *Le blog de Gerald Bloncourt*, at bloncourtblog.net.

consisted of the laboring classes. By the middle of the century, massive new cities, new industries, and new kinds of laboring people transformed ideas spawned in the parlors of the Enlightenment. Even the old ideal would require mobilizing those new layers, and that would have its own dynamic.

In reality, though, national republican aspirations had already assumed different meanings. Among the yet disunited German states, it remained bound to the hope for national unification. It had done so among the recently unifying Italians and among the Americans, where a new Republican Party had battled primarily for the establishment of a stronger union. In contrast, among the subjects of the centralized French state, the idea of representative government seemed to demand popular revolution.

A general crisis was coming to a head across the Western world.

2

New Peoples, New Visions: Industrialization, Workers, and Internationalist Revolution

As 1860 warmed into early summer, forces fighting for the national liberation and unity of Italy and autonomy took the field against all odds in Sicily, and marched to victory there and across southern Italy. An industrial worker born in the north of France, Adolphe Assi had joined the army as an alternative to mechanical labor. After years of service, he left his job to go and fight under the banner of Giuseppe Garibaldi, alongside people from across the Western world who had taken up arms to fight for Italy. Returning to take a job in the industrial town of Le Creusot, he became a key organizer of both local strike movements and the local section of the International Workingmen's Association.[1] The older utopian republican vision continued to move workers, and workers, in turn, certainly moved the utopian republican vision.

By the middle of the nineteenth century, recent generations had experienced transformative change in their economic, social, and cultural lives, unmatched by political processes. In large part, the weakening of the old monarchies and oligarchies permitted the rise of new masters who ruled through their control of capital, though once they attained sufficient authority, this new capitalist class functioned in alliance with the older elites. In part, ideas of republicanism evolved accordingly, the more persistently revolutionary interpretations

---

1 Bernard Noël, *Dictionary of the Commune* (Paris: Flammarion, Collection Fields, 1978).

increasingly describing its goals as a more specific "social republic" or even as socialist. That version of the "universal republic" had already begun to inspire ambitiously international efforts to rally the workers of all nations. Moreover, these intellectual distinctions had growing importance among the new working-class communities, such as that of Assi at Le Creusot.

New Cities and Industrial Communities

The most obvious and visible recent changes in society assumed the forms of bricks and mortar. For generations, larger hamlets, villages, towns, and cities provided so much more than growing markets for what the countryside produced. People became part of the necessities that made their way into population centers over the roads, canals, and, later, railroads. Most of the individuals who did leave for larger communities did not do so by train or by stage, or even mounted. Walking into the nearest big town or village—perhaps with the occasional lift in a wagon or cart—allowed migrants to ease into how the wider economic and social world worked. If fortunate, one could also build up what one needed to move on to an even larger or more distant city.

Moreover, *die Stadtluft macht frei*, even for those who did not directly breathe it. The very knowledge that such an option existed provided a safety valve of sorts for individuals who had not actually taken that road. City lights cast rural life into an increasingly claustrophobic shade, culturally and socially. Many came to imagine a large world beyond the village with opportunities for economic advancement or just a more interesting life. The cities provided a market for what the countryside produced, whether grain or coal, but also for the labor of people who preferred to live there. Trade, the primary engine of this process, fueled itself. Towns and cities became successful by generating more commerce, which fostered the growth of similar communities.

The cities presented the most obvious demonstration of the explosive growth, technological development, and social expansion that followed the Napoleonic wars and the crop failures and famines after the 1816 eruption of Mount Tambora. Buffered by the English Channel and sustained by a massive and lucrative empire, London claimed to have reached nearly 3.5 million people in its metropolitan area. This also reflected the peculiar status of Britain as the preeminent naval power and imperial force in the Western world.

Though smaller, Paris emerged as the jewel of the European continent. With roots in an age-old Celtic and Gallo-Roman community, the population of medieval Paris reached a quarter of a million people, which then doubled during the reign of Louis XIV, and it had nearly a million by the mid-nineteenth century. At that point, the government began a thorough reconstruction of the city that expanded its limits, cultivating unprecedented growth to roughly 2 million by 1870.

Despite a much slower start, Berlin dogged the progress of Paris, though at some distance. The city emerged from the union of a Slavic town where Nikolaiviertel in Alt-Berlin now stands and a medieval German settlement called Cölln, on what became the Museum Island in the Spree. The emergence of authoritarian tendencies in other states benefited the quality and quantity of the peoples seeking to make a home in the Prussian capital, about a fifth of whom were French Protestants by the late seventeenth century. Under the active sponsorship of Frederick the Great, Berlin's population reached around 100,000 people, and it had approached half a million by the middle of the nineteenth century. By 1870, the capital—with additional numbers in adjacent Charlottenburg—approached a million.

Alongside these capitals grew a spate of secondary cities that exploded in population, often within living memory. Eight French cities had between 100,000 and 900,000 people. Lyon and Marseille probably hovered around 335,00 and 310,000 respectively, while Bordeaux topped 200,000, Lille nearly 160,000, Toulouse 130,000, and Nantes nearly 120,000, with Rouen, Saint-Étienne, and Strasbourg over 100,000. The decentralized nature of the German states fostered even more and larger secondary cities—thirteen of them. The busy port of Hamburg had roughly 350,000 in its metropolitan area, and Breslau (now Wrocław in Poland) had a quarter of a million. Munich approached 200,000, and Dresden around 180,000, with Cologne, Leipzig and Königsberg hovering between 120,000 and 130,000, and Bremen, Hanover, Stuttgart, Frankfurt am Main, and Danzig clustering around 100,000.[2] By then, hundreds of communities in Central Europe topped 10,000 and dozens had passed the 50,000 mark.[3]

---

2   On French cities see Lalor, *Cyclopedia of Political Sciences*, vol. 2, 266.

3   *Statistisches Jahrbuch für das Deutsche Reich* (Statistical Almanac for the German Reich); 1881, 3 ff. (for 1875); 1893, 9 ff. (for 1890); 1914, 12 ff. (for 1910).

Hobbes's description about life being nasty, brutish, and short perhaps best describes the lot of the urban poor eking out an existence. What newcomers to the cities found often failed to meet even their most minimal hopes. To some extent, the cost of living increased with the size of the city and the demand for real estate, and poverty increased with scale as well. Even those who arrived with a bit of money in their purses found that it did not last as long on the city's cobblestones as it did the dirt lanes of home.

Steady work in an established trade best defined success. For generations, skilled artisans had been more citizens of their craft than of anything else. Entering the craft proved terribly difficult for outsiders. One began as an apprentice, theoretically spending years learning "the art and mystery" of a craft. At eighteen, the apprentice left the master's shop to work as a journeyman—that is, for a daily wage in other workshops. After creating one's masterpiece, a craftsman applied for, and hopefully gained, admission to a guild as a master in his own right. Masters enjoyed the privilege of opening their own shop, but the prospect of this receded for many, even as ownership increasingly belonged to people from outside the craft.

In this increasingly complex economy, the nature of their product created a hierarchy in the crafts. Goldsmiths and, earlier, wig makers rode atop the heap, while cordwainers and tailors, whose customers included almost everybody in the cities, occupied the broad base. General utility ceded place to creators of the more monetized commodities. On the one hand, this posed new problems for newcomers to the city too old to get into an apprenticeship. On the other, all these trades had to expand to keep up with demand, which opened possibilities to slip into the process even without an old-fashioned apprenticeship.

If cities still promised a freer life, it would be a freedom increasingly defined by what could be earned and purchased. Money defined where you lived, what you ate, and with whom you could live. An accident or an illness or even the simplest of human vicissitudes could leave you at the door of the church, a life of petty larcenies, or a quiet death, leaving the husk of a human being drained of life by the despair of the new world.

Labor entailed more repetition and persistently longer hours performed under bosses much less likely to be kith or kin, and increasingly likely to be someone who did not actually know the work or do the work. Also, the cycle of work ran hourly, daily or weekly more than

seasonally or annually, which meant that many workers had to repeatedly scrounge the job market. It left little leisure to build human relationships in the absence of the sort associated with village life.

In the cities and towns particularly, elites maintained their virtual
monopoly of power not just by force of arms but by force of ideas. Power,
pulpit and press repeatedly asserted the idea of France, a Second Empire,
and the regime of Napoleon III, just as it elsewhere proclaimed the
merits of Prussia and the Hohenzollerns. While eager to marginalize the
propagandist and the agitator, those elites often resolved factional
rivalries by trying to mobilize and control the public, which did run the
risk of detonating the explosive pressures of these deeper social tensions.
When this happened, laboring people poured into the streets of Paris,
Berlin, Vienna, and other cities, as the shock troops of a social revolution.

In these decades, new industrial communities grew, turning out not
only new kinds of products but also new class formations and relations.
Depending on the time and place, a peasant fleeing from the countryside might find more opportunities in the smaller communities that
formed the matrix of what came to be called "the Industrial Revolution."[4]
Le Creusot in France and Essen in Central Europe represented this new
order and its potential.

What became Le Creusot had a long industrial history. Three
centuries earlier, people around the village of La Charbonnière had dug
coal and iron from the surrounding hills. However, the 1786 opening of
a glass factory opened the way for the latest foundries, furnaces, and
workshops. Iron mines, eight miles from town, were connected by railroads, so Le Creuzot could compete with any such community. It not
only still excavated coal—20,000 tons a day, by some accounts—but also
produced all sorts of machinery, including the necessities of the railroad
that carried their products across the country.

By the mid-1830s, Adolphe and Joseph-Eugène Schneider gained

---

4   See, in general, Bernard H. Moss, *The Origins of the French Labor Movement: The
Socialism of Skilled Workers, 1830–1914* (Berkeley: University of California Press, 1976);
Alain Cottereau, "The Distinctiveness of Working-Class Cultures in France, 1848–1900,"
in Ira Katznelson and Aristide R. Zolberg, eds., *Working-Class Formation: Nineteenth-
Century Patterns in Western Europe and the United States* (Princeton: Princeton
University Press, 1986), 110–54; and Ronald Amizade, *Ballots and Barricades: Class
Formation and Republican Politics in France, 1830–1871* (Princeton: Princeton University
Press, 1993).

ownership of both the mines and these nascent industries. They added new forging mills and foundries, and turned to manufacturing everything for the railroads, from engines to rails. With the cooperation of the government, the Schneiders won political appointments and carried elections as a matter of course. Napoleon III—after Eugène Schneider suffered defeat for elected office—invited him into the cabinet in 1851. When the emperor decided to establish a new Chamber of Deputies in 1867, Eugène Schneider rose to chair of the *corps législatif*, leaving his son Henri in charge of the business, which included the schools, mutual relief fund, and housing on which the working-class families depended.[5] Like others of their class, the Schneiders stood to gain from the war and the French armies boldly carried their weaponry into defeat after defeat.

Within living memory, a small rural village had become a modern industrial city. From 1836 to 1866, the population grew from 2,700 to 24,000, with the number of workingmen going from 1,700 to around 10,000. They came from across much of Europe, and constituted a community that lacked the usual associations of family and familiarity associated with the term. Atomized and relatively powerless, they seemed to be as much at the mercy of the Schneider dynasty as had the peasants been subject to their feudal masters.

The Krupps—who ruled their community at Essen like the Schneiders in Le Creusot—had entered business when the family arrived from the Netherlands around 1587. The clan sold everything from ironware and wine to food, livestock, and real estate, before Friedrich Krupp decided to launch a cast-steel works early in the nineteenth century. Such projects required intense long-term investments of capital, and Krupp went deep into debt. The operation had only begun to show substantial promise before his death in 1826.

Friedrich's son Alfred Krupp reshaped the business into a dynamically innovative mid-century enterprise. Early on, he developed a method for

---

5   On Creusot and its influence. Edmund Ashworth to the editor, "The Injurious Effect of Trades Unions," *The Times*, January 8, 1870, 7; Jessie White Mario, "Garibaldi in France," *Fraser's Magazine* (new series), 16 (October 1877), 602; Schneider, Le Creusot de Dominique Schneidre, Caroline Mathieu, Patrice Notteghem, Bernard Clément (eds.), Schneider, Le Creusot, une enterprise, une ville (1836–1960) (Paris: Fayard, 1995); Jean Jolly, ed., *Dictionnaire des parlementaires français: Notices biographiques sur les ministres, sénateurs et députés français de 1889 à 1940* (Paris: Presses universitaires de France, 1960–1977), 1548.

casting seamless railroad carriage wheels that required no potentially
vulnerable welding points. Krupp's steel wheels sold across the world.

Such communities not only made products for public use, but also
built machines necessary to construct such machines. Both Essen and Le
Creusot cranked out locomotives, remarkably complex machines requiring the precise manipulation of several hundred tons of metal. This
required a heavy mechanized forge hammer to shape parts that would
then be drilled with precision to take the rivets and bolts to fit them
together. Foundry work made the cylinders to heat the water more easily
in the boiler, and to forge the large wheels for the drivers. For the
undercarriage, workers hammered a compound of wet sand into metal
casts, with more skilled workers setting these into a larger cast, like pieces
of a puzzle. Skilled hands fit it all together. Increasingly powerful and
efficient overhead cranes put together the pieces of this massive new
artifact.

The complexity of these highly engineered products—from steam
engines to locomotives to the powerful new rifled artillery—required
making parts that fit precisely. This meant increasingly specialized tools
with the hands and minds necessary to their use. All of this would be as
distinctive of their own world as had been the stone tools unearthed
near Les Eyzies.

The Persistent Shadow of Internationalism

Industrialization changed not only the nature of power but also what a
representative exercise of that power could mean. A generation or so
earlier, the old romantic dream of the universal republic blended a militant nationalism with a radical internationalism. Over time, this had
become increasingly plebeian, divorced from any association with
governmental power. Often small organizations, albeit part of much
larger networks, carried those ideals into a later age.

In the aftermath of 1848, unrepentant revolutionists—particularly
those who had fought to the last around Rome or Venice or in Baden—
found themselves in exile. In London—but also in New York and
elsewhere—they naturally gathered periodically to celebrate
revolutionary anniversaries and act in solidarity with contemporary
efforts.

Radicals of various nationalities in London decided to greet the visit of Napoleon III to the city with a grand festival in October 1854. The following January, the new London Chartist Organizing Committee reached out to French, German, Belgian, Polish, Italian, Hungarian, and Spanish societies, along with a few Russians and others. Despite their skepticism, Karl Marx and Friedrich Engels became increasingly involved in an emerging "International Committee." On May 6, 1856, this launched the new International Association.[6] It limped along for a few years before being overwhelmed by events, notably the reemergence of the revolution in Italy.

French visitors to the 1862 International Exposition in London met with English workers and decided to make another attempt. On September 28, 1864, émigré circles in London joined local radicals at Freemason's Hall in London to launch the IWA. Adherents saw the same idea expressed in different languages—the Association internationale des travailleurs (AIT) or the Internationale Arbeiterassoziation (IAA)— but it remained to be seen what might be lost in the translation. Most famously, the effort enjoyed the active leadership of Marx, an exiled Rhenish journalist, and Engels, the son of a German industrialist in Britain, former spokesmen for the old Communist League. For years, these two brilliant figures had developed a partnership centered on their urging an anticapitalist class agenda on the international radical movement.

As in most countries where the IWA amounted to any kind of force, the organization in France represented a conglomerate of various socialist currents. Followers of Charles Fourier and Étienne Cabet still looked to the possibilities of launching socialist communities, and the advocacy of worker cooperatives by Pierre-Joseph Proudhon—who essentially confined his rabid anti-Semitism to his diaries—had broad interest and support. Most radically, Auguste Blanqui had nurtured the old dream of Gracchus Babeuf that the rising of small armed groups might detonate social revolution.

On the other hand, German radicals launched an Allgemeiner Deutscher Arbeiterverein (ADAV—the General German Workers'

---

6   Arthur Lehning, "The International Association, 1855–1859," in Lehning, *From Buonarroti to Bakunin: Studies in International Socialism* (Leiden: E. J. Brill, 1970), esp. 198–201 for the American branches; "Universal Democratic Republicans," *New York Daily Tribune*, March 7, 1855, 7. See also Billington, *Fire in the Minds of Men*, 326, 328.

Association) on May 13, 1863. Its leading theorist and organizer, Ferdinand Lassalle, like Marx, described capitalism as a centralizing force. However, Marx saw socialism as the result of a class struggle to replace the bourgeoisie with the proletariat as a new, majoritarian ruling class. Lassalle had an abiding faith that the process of centralization itself created a natural dynamic toward socialism. This established a particularly dangerous predisposition in the German context, where the most obvious dynamic toward centralization turned on Prussian efforts to unite the country. Still, Lassalle's organization spread among workers in Germany at a pace that should have discomfited their bosses.

Other organizations were closely related to the International. Many of the leaders of the International, especially among the French, also held membership in a Loge des Philadelphes. Other members included Garibaldi, Giuseppe Mazzini, and Charles Bradlaugh, as well as Louis Blanc, Ledru-Rollin, and others. In 1867, Garibaldi and other democrats set up the international Ligue de la paix et de la liberté to promote the idea of the "United States of Europe." The *ligue* had close, but complex, relations with the IWA.

For their part, Marx and Engels persuaded the IWA's General Council meeting of August 13 to extend its nuanced support of the Ligue de la paix et de la liberté without affiliation. The Brussels Congress suggested that IWA members participate as individuals and declared itself in favor of joint action by the working class and all the progressive anti-war forces. However, the involvement of Mikhail Alexandrovich Bakunin in the *ligue* left many unwilling to assume any responsibility for what might be done in its name. By September 1868, when the *ligue* declined to accept Bakunin's wish that it declare for an "equalization of classes," he simply turned his attention to his own Alliance internationale de la démocratie socialiste.[7]

Bakunin took his alliance into the IWA. He joined the Romande section at Geneva, and the rest followed him into the organization. None of that endeared Bakunin to Marx, who called him not only "an old acquaintance of mine" but also "Pope Michael." Bakunin understood politics as an abstract profession of faith—as with his equalization-of-classes resolution—or as something conducted by secret societies, conspiracies, and power struggles within them. Most importantly, he

7   *MECW*, vols. 20, 23, 24, 43, 44, 45, 47.

never saw political leadership as fundamentally a team effort and tended to go off on this own with little consultation with his comrades or even consideration of the chances of success. Still, his approach attracted those influenced by the Italian struggle. Marx and Engels bemoaned Bakunin's seduction of Johann Philipp Becker—"brave old Becker"— whom they thought to be "an enthusiast like Garibaldi, easily led away."[8]

Regardless of its concerns about class issues, the IWA everywhere tapped into deeply rooted republican impulses. By July 1870, the Paris organization had grown from ten to thirty-six affiliates, largely through their focus on mass work. The principal vehicle for this called itself the Légion garibaldienne.[9]

In Southern Europe, this dimension of the IWA became particularly evident. Many of Garibaldi's followers tended to see the IWA as the culmination of the universal republic, and Garibaldi himself became increasingly friendly. Hugh Forbes and Gustave Cluseret shaped the IWA's prehistory as far away as the US, the latter returning to plunge himself into the movement in France. Becker contributed to shape the IWA in Switzerland, Germany, and Britain.

Another peripatetic Garibaldian, Giuseppe Fanelli, took the message to Spain, the same way the ideas of Fourier, Cabet, Robert Owen, and other critics of capitalism had gotten there. Through the influence of the IWA at Marseille and Lyon, Spanish workers formed affiliates in Catalonia and elsewhere. Although Bakunin's allies around La Federacion prevailed, their section at Madrid faced stiff competition from a rival section with Solidaridad under Paul Lafargue. By 1870, when the IWA in Spain held its first public congress at Barcelona, an

---

8   Karl Marx, "The Alliance of Socialist Democracy and the International Working Men's Association," *MECW*, vol. 23, 454–580; Karl Marx to Paul and Laura Lafargue, February 15, 1869, *MECW*, vol. 43, 218; Marx to Engels, March 5, 1870, *MECW*, vol. 43, 445; Karl Marx, "The International Working Men's Association and the International Alliance of Socialist Democracy," *MECW*, vol. 21, 34–6. On anarchism in the IWA, see Robert Graham, *We Do Not Fear Anarchy, We Invoke It: The First International and the Origins of the Anarchist Movement* (Edinburgh and Oakland, CA: AK Press, 2015; Ulrich Peters, *Kommunismus und Anarchismus: Die Zeit der ersten Internationale* (Cologne: PapyRossa, 1997).

9   "The Minute Book of the General Council of the International Working Men's Association" (July 19, 1870), hereafter "G. C. Mins," in *Documents of the First International* (hereafter *DFI*), 5 vols. (Moscow and London: Progress Publishers andLawrence & Wisehart, 1963–6), 29–30.

orientation distinctly more focused on the masses than that of the secret societies began to emerge.[10]

The conspiratorial schemes of these kinds of clandestine society seemed to Marx and others in the IWA to be a diversion from mass organization. Mazzini's secretary, Major Luigi Wolff—later exposed as a French police agent—tried without success to get the IWA to adopt the organizational structure of Mazzini's secret societies. After this defeat, Mazzini persistently attacked the IWA. Also, the growth of Bakunin's groups in Italy confirmed that "the working classes, in the towns at least, were rapidly abandoning Mazzini," a hopeful development.[11]

Everything attempted by the Internationalists took place against a backdrop of repression. The Spanish authorities had "arrested, undressed, searched, kept in prison for 28 days, then discharged" two members of the organization. One lost his job in the arsenal and his pension and the other expected the same fate. The last maker, Auguste Serraillier, reported half a dozen cases involving fines and imprisonment imposed on IWA members there.[12] This denial of basic rights to plebeian militants—common across the Western world—wedded the IWA and kindred organizations to the struggle for essential republican standards, even as the class nature of their constituency became increasingly evident to the most persistent and consistent republicans.

All of this might have remained an abstract footnote to nineteenth-century intellectual history had it not been for the grounding of this debate in the concrete problems of laboring people across the Western world.

---

10   On Spain, see Ferran Aisa, *La Internacional: El naixement de la cultura obrera* (Barcelona: Editorial Base, 2007); Luis E. Esteban Barahona, *La I Internacional en Castilla-La Mancha* (Madrid: Celeste Ediciones, 1998); Rafael Flaquer Montequi, *La clase obrera madrileña y la 1. Internacional (un análisis de prensa)* (Madrid: Editorial Cuadernos para el Diálogo, 1977); Carlos Díaz, *La Primera Internacional de Trabajadores* (Madrid: Mañana Editorial, [1977]); and Murray Bookchin, *The Spanish Anarchists: The Heroic Years, 1868–1936* (New York: Free Life Editions, 1977), 15.

11   Engels, Giuseppe Garibaldi's Statement and Its Effects on the Working Classes in Italy: Engels' Record of His Report at the General Council Meeting of November 7, 1871, *MECW*, vol. 23, 43, 44. Engels to Carlo Cafiero, July l[–3], 1871, *MECW*, vol. 44, 164.

12   G. C. Mins., *DFI*, 4 (July 19, 1870) 30; (July 26, 1870), 31–2.

Class Militancy

The views of the masses on such concepts as class would determine what importance, if any, an organization such as the IWA might have. A peasant—or the artisan of a generation before—would have found the emergence of a working class around them quite intimidating. Large numbers of men scrambled about furiously to perform very specific tasks, incomprehensible to those who watched them. Their work required not only precision components but the carefully calibrated cooperation of hand, eye, and hammer. The process differed little from place to place, and it forged similar values among people of all sorts of backgrounds.

Workers themselves, though, rarely appreciated being made into a working class. People did prefer to migrate to growing towns near their villages rather than strike out across the country for someplace entirely unknown to them or their families. Indeed, mobility among country people varied widely across France. Still, as late as 1861, only 11.7 percent of the population lived outside the department of their birth.[13] That did not mean that many had not ventured beyond and returned.

Industrial labor is physically draining, psychologically demanding, and generally unpromising of a better future. So workers came and stayed as long as they had no better alternative, and any alternatives tended to look better the longer they stayed. As a result, turnover was tremendous. In fact, only about a tenth of the work force became permanent.

Jean-Baptiste Dumay, the son of a worker who had lost his life in an accident in a Schneider mine, began his long personal rebellion against the brave new world of the Schneiders though his voracious reading habits. At thirteen, he left school for an apprenticeship in the factory only to confront the definitive source of the mind-numbing, soul-deadening tedium of life under capitalism. Having retained his taste for reading, Dumay looked beyond the factory.[14]

---

13 Timothy B. Smith, "Public Assistance and Labor Supply in Nineteenth-Century Lyon," *Journal of Modern History*, 68 (March 1996), 10.

14 Pierre Ponsot, "Dumay, Jean-Baptiste" in Jean Maitron, ed., *Dictionnaire biographique du mouvement ouvrier international*, 12 vols. (Paris: Les Éditions Ouvrières, 1974); and Pierre Ponsot, *Les grèves de 1870 et la Commune de 1871 au Creusot* (Paris: Éditions socials, 1958). René-Pierre Parize also studied a later period in *Le Creusot, 1898–1900: La naissance du syndicalisme et les mouvements sociaux à l'aube du XXe siècle*

Informally he continued his studies under a teacher who had been deported after the ascendency of Napoleon III in 1851, and officially barred from teaching. At eighteen, Dumay finished his apprenticeship and left to study metallurgy at Paris, Dijon, Lyon and Marseille. In 1860, the government selected Dumay for military service by lot, and he served his time at Cherbourg, Rennes, Lyon and Saint-Étienne, but, in 1868, returned to Le Creusot.[15]

From 1868, a group of young workmen, craftsmen, and small shopkeepers sustained a circle of militant republicans. Dumay rather quickly fell in with a number of other dissatisfied residents, most notably Adolphe Assi, the military veteran with strong radical credentials, having fought alongside Garibaldi.

In 1869, Dumay, Assi and their comrades ripped the mask of paternalism from the Schneiders. Six years before, Eugène Schneider had won election with but one vote against him, but this time the workers rallied behind a rather moderate liberal who wound up with about 800 votes in the city. Schneider responded by firing 200 workers he suspected of having voted for his opponent. At the end of the year, a referendum over the future of the mutual relief fund returned a strong majority for worker management, which would theoretically allow for its use as a strike fund.

On January 17, 1870, a strike movement elected Assi president of a provisional committee. Three days later, the prefect brought to town 3,000 to 4,000 soldiers who killed half a dozen workers and took measures to cripple the strike and, by January 24, broke it. Schneider then complained that troops had been necessary because "some foreign leaders" had misled his otherwise contented local workers.

In March, the workers—angrier and more determined than ever—launched what they later called the "long strike." Eugène Varlin, the Parisian printer and leader of the International at the capital, came to Le

(Le Creusot: Les Nouvelles éd. du Creusot, 2009); as well as Jean-Baptiste Dumay, *Mémoires d'un militant ouvrier du Creusot*.

15   Heinz-Gerhard Haupt, *Social History of France since 1789*, trans. Francoise Laroche (Paris: Editions of the House of the Social Sciences, 1993), 42. See also René-Pierre Parize, "Savoir de soumission ou saviors de révolté? L'exemple du Creusot," in Jean Borreil, ed., *Les sauvages dans la cité: Auto-émancipation du peuple et instruction des prolétaires au XIXe siècle* (Seyssel and Paris: Champ Vallon and Presses universitaires de France, 1985), 92–4. Dumay, *Mémoires d'un Militant Ouvrier du Creusot*.

Creusot and organized a local section of the IWA on March 18 with Dumay as its secretary. Three days later, 1,500 miners walked off the job because of a pay cut, but the lack of coordination left them largely isolated from the movement in town. On March 23, three regiments arrived, an act of crude repression that had the most immediate effect of revitalizing the strike movement. Workers in Le Creusot itself made an impressive march south to Montchanin, drawing more strikers into action as it went.[16]

The arrogance of the Schneiders made the strikers more combative. The women of the community turned out to drive the few strikebreakers off the job, clashing with the gendarmes. When the authorities arrested three of the women, the rest brought their children to the fore and chanted for the police themselves to feed them. Finally, they forced the release of the arrested women by blocking the train scheduled to take them north to court at Autun. In the course of the strike, Benoît Malon, another member of the IWA from Paris, helped organize the growing movement, even as the threat of repression drove Assi into hiding.[17]

The bosses, backed by the government and the authorities, crushed the movement. After twenty-three days, though, the strike in Le Creusot itself imploded. In the countryside, the Schneiders fired a hundred miners. On April 25, the magistrates' court at Autun sentenced twenty-five strikers to prison terms of up to three years. Though defeated, the strikers and republicans remained unrepentant.

Political action followed. In early May, Napoleon III's plebiscite sought public ratification for the imperial reforms, including a dutifully loyal National Assembly. Dumay, Assi, and the workers threw together a committee to campaign against it, and, on May 8, Le Creusot delivered the government a massive defeat, voting 3,400 to 1,500 against the government measures. Only the vote reported from the countryside tilted the final result in its favor. In the subsequent election to fill the local seat in the National Assembly, Dumay took the field against Henri Schneider.[18]

---

16   On Varlin, see Michel Cordillot, *Eugène Varlin: Chronique d'un espoir assassiné.* (Paris: Editions de l'Atelier, 1991).

17   Mira Adler-Gillies offers a recent look at Malon in "Reform or Revolution: Benoît Malon and the Socialist Movement in France, 1871–1890," *George Rudé Society, French History and Civilization*, 6 (2014 Seminar papers), 172–88.

18   Jolly, *Dictionnaire des parlementaires français*, p. 1548.

Even as the strike movement took its course at Le Creusot in 1870, workers in the Krupp factory at Essen made similar efforts and faced a similarly brutal response, with the same kind of backing by the government. When Alfred Krupp heard about a strike of highly skilled workers constructing the machines needed to make locomotives and other highly specialized products at Essen, he left orders that "neither now nor in the future" would his works employ anyone involved, regardless of how badly they may need hands. He also suggested that the mood of their workers be "secretly observed," so that they could respond quickly, he himself determined to make a personal appearance, dismiss the troublemakers "without regard to dispensability," and stifle any unionist impulses in the bud.[19]

Wilhelm Hasenclever emerged at the head of the movement at Essen. He belonged to a Protestant family who had moved to predominantly Catholic Arnsberg, where he took up his father's trade as a tanner. At around the age of twenty in 1857, he found himself compelled into a year of military service; and 1859 brought further service in the Prussian Army at Düsseldorf and Cologne. As suited a traditional artisan, Hasenclever took to the road when not in uniform, attempting to squeeze the traditional *Wanderjahr* into his working tour through shops located in Switzerland, Italy, and France, as well as the North German Confederation. Through social and gymnastic associations, he began organizing meetings, speaking, and writing in the interests of the working class. He gained even greater prominence after taking an editorial post at Hagen for the republican *Westfälische Volkszeitung*.

There, Hasenclever came into contact with socialism of Lassalle. He and his followers gathered at Leipzig to found the ADAV. It spread quickly among workers in Germany. Almost immediately, Hasenclever encountered the paradox of the ADAV in organizing workers around a strategy that did not grow from fostering working-class organization.

However, worker self-organization had its own paradox, in that the bosses ultimately found them manageable. The management of these

---

19   Alfred Schröter and Walter Becker, *Die Deutsche Maschinenbauindustrie in der industriellen Revolution* (Berlin: Akademie-Verlag, 1962), 249; Ulrich Engelhardt, *"Nur vereinigt sind wir stark": Die Anfänge der deutschen Gewerkschaftsbewegung 1862/63 bis 1869/70*, 2 vols. (Stuttgart: Klett-Cotta, 1977), 1096–97, 1097 n. 137, citing Wilhelm Berdrow, ed., *Alfred Krupps Briefe 1826–1887, im Auftrage der Familie und der Firma Krupp* (Berlin: R. Hobbing, 1928), 243.

early industries faced horrific turnover in the workforce—to the point where they could rely persistently on only about a tenth of those workers. The Krupp works tried to improve conditions with training programs, medical care, schools, and libraries for its most reliable workers. In the long run, cooperation with workers' associations provided a vehicle for maintaining social peace in the industry. A significant network of Catholic workers grew in the Krupp factory, serving not only to divide workers, but to provide a safe mechanism for negotiating over such innovations.[20]

As an old crisis concerning Schleswig-Holstein erupted, Prussia sought to rally other German states to get the provinces out from under Denmark. At a meeting of the local ADAV in Hagen, Hasenclever posed the problem entirely in Prussian terms. Thereafter, he also reentered the army for the Second Schleswig War of February to October 1864. When mustered out, though, he wrote a piece for the *Rheinische Zeitung* that earned him a sentence of six weeks in prison for insulting the majesty of Wilhelm I, though he won an acquittal on appeal.

With this ordeal behind him, Hasenclever joined the ADAV, and wrote regularly for the *Social Demokrat*. That said, though, the militarism of their society posed the question whether the centralization of state power would be innately positive for the working class. Indeed, in 1866, when Prussia went to war with Austria, Hasenclever once more had to provide military service.

These overarching issues aside, though, the ADAV faced a serious crisis in its leadership. Lassalle had been killed in 1864, in the self-indulgent and pointless bourgeois affectation of a duel. This left a dearth of experienced figures, and his successor, Bernhard Becker, had little base in the organization and no clear idea of how to build one. Hasenclever's friend Carl Wilhelm Tölcke had strong support in Westphalian affiliates of the ADAV and a strategy heavily reliant on building a party press. When Tölcke came to power, he brought Hasenclever with him into the political committee of the ADAV, eventually serving as the secretary while running the family tannery in Halver, then belonging to his sister. In the jostling that eased Tölcke out of office, Hasenclever also found himself briefly nudged from office.

---

20 Fostering the organization of Catholic workers as a means of supplanting class organization. Johann Paul, *Alfred Krupp und die Arbeiterbewegung* (Düsseldorf: Schwann, 1987), 161–71.

Nevertheless, Hasenclever had emerged as a crucial leader in constructing the public face for the movement. He did this not only as a writer but also by running for office in 1867 at Altena, just southeast of Hagen. The following year brought him back into a national office for the ADAV, managing its finances from 1868 to 1870 under chairman Johann Baptist von Schweitzer. Moreover, in 1869, he won election to the North German Reichstag from Duisburg.[21]

Significantly, Hasenclever became an important figure in drawing the ADAV close to the Verband Deutscher Arbeitervereine (VDAV— Assembly of German Worker Associations), also a relatively loose body with no organizational discipline over its membership. In contrast to Lassalle's confidence in the logic of the centralization of government, the VDAV tended to be much friendlier to Marx's emphasis on the potential power of working-class self-organization. The development of capitalism had given rise to more labor organizations increasingly interested in trade union concerns. For a dozen years before 1870, workers in the new industries organized by the hundreds and went on strike over wages and working conditions.[22] Yet the more prominent ADAV seemed to be the public face of German socialism.

However, the political development of the state tended to draw elements of the VDAV into political action. Some of its adherents wandered into the new Deutsche Volkspartei (German People's Party) formed in 1868, but others in the Kingdom of Saxony had tried to build a left wing of the Sächsische Volkspartei (Saxon People's Party), the Saxon People's Party. In August 1869 they convened at Eisenach to help launch the Sozialdemokratische Arbeiterpartei (SDAP—Social Democratic Workers Party). Contrary to the ADAV, the SDAP followed a strict anti-Prussian position and worked toward *Großdeutsche* (greater German) unification, including Austria and a federal structure, with the goal of constricting the hegemony of Prussia, which was considered

---

21   Ludger Heid, "Wilhelm Hasenclever in der deutschen Sozialdemokratie," in Ludger Heid, Klaus-Dieter Vinschen, Elisabeth Heid, Wilhelm Revel, eds., *Wilhelm Hasenclever: Reden und Schriften* (Bonn: J.H.W. Dietz Nachf, 1989), 28–30, "notoriously one of the most outstanding leaders of the Social Democratic Party." See also Andrew Bonnell, "Between Internationalism, Nationalism and Particularism: German Social Democrats and the War of 1870–71," *Australian Journal of Politics & History*, 38 (December 1992) 375–85.

22   Schröter and Becker, *Die Deutsche Maschinenbauindustrie*, 245–9.

reactionary and militaristic by the SDAP. However, two of the key leaders of the VDAV, August Bebel and Wilhelm Liebknecht, contributed to the campaign of Hasenclever, who became a strong voice for the unification of the movement.

Hasenclever won a seat in the Reichstag of the North German Confederation, where he served in 1869 and 1870. After his election, he moved to Berlin, placing him at the center of the ADAV, along with the other ADAV representatives—Schweitzer and Friedrich Wilhelm Fritzsche. Schweitzer, the long-standing president of the organization, coined the term "democratic centralization" to define the character of his party.

While governments, churches and civil society could adapt to many changes in society, the emergence of these new kinds of people with their new concerns as majorities in the new urban communities posed serious problems. Nor were these simply theoretical matters, but involved very practical considerations, essential to the orderly function of the capitalist order.

The two decades leading to 1870 remade the people of the Western world. They radically transformed the peasantry and unavoidably shaped a new kind of workforce. The appearance of artisans and laborers in the streets of Paris and Berlin or the actions of the industrial workers of Le Creusot and Essen heralded the arrival of a permanent new force in the shaping of Western civilization. Most had come to those activities from the countryside, carrying with them the ideas and assumptions of their backgrounds and bearing the burden of that past.

Yet the rise of modern nation-states and the subsequent production of mass politics and public opinion became part and parcel of these transformations. The same expanded literacy that allowed plebeian readers to peruse Marx also defined their perceptions by languages and institutionally monopolized sources of information. The new demands of nationhood and the Napoleonic scale of military life also offered a new option for men eager to escape the workaday world. The demands of industry alone did not shape the lives of people such as Dumay, Assi and Hasenclever.

Nor did they shape the lives of their class and their countrymen. This set the stage for the tragedy of their generation.

3
The Health of the State:
War and Secular Faith in the Nation

In late July 1870, the troops of Prussian crown prince Friedrich Wilhelm gathered in growing numbers around the market square of Rastatt. They did what nervous soldiers do in such circumstances. They regularly meandered over the grounds of the adjacent palace of the grand duchy and sang traditional patriotic airs such as "Die Wacht am Rhein" and "Das Lied der Deutschen," saluting "Germany over all." There, twenty-two years before, the German patriots who proclaimed that idea sparked what became the most long-lived of the popular risings in Germany in 1848–9.[1] In a fundamental way, what they wanted had been a different Germany.

Nothing demonstrated the general implosion of republican nationalism into the armed and authoritarian nation-state as clearly as this strange resolution of "the German problem." Like all nations, Germany would be born in war, though few approached the task with a more clinical cold-bloodedness than its leaders. Despite the global scope of the French military experience, the course of the war bloodied and unraveled all the schemes and plans of both armies.

---

1 George F. R. Henderson, *The Battle of Spicheren: August 6th 1870* (Solihull: Helion & Company, 2009; first published 1891), 37.

The German Problem from Republicanism to Nationalism

The upheavals of 1848 reminded rulers of all sorts that their own people might well hold them to account for their rule. In many places, such as Ratstatt in Baden, mostly moderate reformers shuttled forward to speak for the people, though some represented radical and anti-monarchist ideas. Similarly conservative, bourgeois fears of serious change informed the concerns of most of the nascent national assembly sitting in the Paulskirche at Frankfurt, which proposed national unity with few democratic requirements and a common crown over the Germanies going to Prussia. This left participants such as Friedrich Hecker and Gustav von Struve utterly disillusioned.

Hecker, the Mannheim democratic spokesman in the lower chamber of the parliament of Baden hoped to bypass those invested in the status quo. Nearly fifty popular sports clubs had formed around Joseph Fickler's radical *Seeblätter*. On March 26, these reorganized as an armed militia. When the authorities arrested Fickler on April 8, Franz Sigel, a former officer, raised a force of 400 men and invited Hecker to take charge. Only a minority of those present proved willing to take the field against the combined might of the coalition of states headed by Prussia. So Hecker's effort failed, as did an attempted putsch by Gustav von Struve at Lörrach.

The situation continued to simmer until the most reactionary of the German nobles flatly rejected the proposal from Frankfurt in May 1849. By then, the confederation troops in the fortified city of Rastatt mutinied, inspiring an armed campaign in Baden.[2] Hecker returned, followed by a succession of revolutionary marriages—Struve with his wife Amalie, Georg Herwegh and his wife Emma, and Fritz and Mathilde Anneke. Carl Schurz served under Anneke in the artillery. Hecker, Anneke, and Schurz became US generals in the Civil War, as did August Willich. Future socialist leader Wilhelm Liebknecht served as Struve's adjutant and Friedrich Engels as aide-de-camp to Willich. They assigned Johann Philip Becker to organize them into a *Volkswehr*, a people's army. In

---

2   Charles W. Dahlinger, *The German Revolution of 1849: Being an Account of the Final Struggle, in Baden, for the Maintenance of Germany's First National Representative Government* (New York and London: G. P. Putnam's Sons, 1903); and Wolfgang Dressen, *1848–1849: Bürgerkrieg in Baden—Chronik einer verlorenen Revolution* (Berlin: Klaus Wagenbach, 1975).

June, command of the army went to Ludwik Mierosławski, the French-born Pole then under a death sentence for his political work.

Local groups, such as at Freiburg, also rose against their occupation, only to be crushed. By June 20, the authorities seem to have dissipated what remained of the revolution. The revolutionary constituent assembly—armed and on the run—reassembled at Freiburg and, on June 28, voted to continue the war against the enemies of German freedom and unity. The next day, Prussian and Hessian troops crushed the rebels in the battle of Gernsbach. Leaving Major Gustav Tiedemann, one of Struve's people, to serve as governor of the military base at Rastatt, Mierosławski fell back into southern Baden, while Sigel, with several thousand supporters, held Freiburg until July 7, when the Prussians arrived.

The bulk of the armed revolutionaries escaped into Switzerland on July 12 and asked for asylum, though the Prussians still besieged the radicals in the fortress of Rastatt. When, after three weeks, they surrendered, the military authorities spared nothing in their reprisals against the soldiery that had sided with the people. They sent twenty-seven men to the firing squad and many more to long prison sentences.

In the absence of action by the people, the German question required resolution from the top. Giuseppe Garibaldi, it should be remembered, found national unity under a crown preferable to disunity. Just as Italian unification took place under the auspices of a regional monarchy in the Piedmont, Germans continued to look to their most powerful state, Prussia. Teutonic knights crusading against the Slavs had created the Duchy of Prussia, which acquired the Margraviate of Brandenburg and moved the combined capital from Königsberg to Berlin. In the next century, Friedrich der Grosse—"great" in luck as well as talent—made the ruling Hohenzollern dynasty a significant power through military strength. Voltaire famously quipped that while other states had armies, in Prussia the army had a state.

Napoleon's rampage across Europe deepened these predispositions early in the nineteenth century. He crushed the military autonomy of the German states, irretrievably so for the smaller ones, and ended the thousand-year-old fiction that had been the Holy Roman Empire. All of this brought Prussia to the fore, alongside Austria, as leading powers in Central Europe. By mid-century, emergent republican and national aspirations aimed at the idea of a *Großdeutschland*, a common nation of all German-speaking peoples likely centered on Austria and the

Habsburgs or the *Kleindeutschland* dream of a unification without Austria, implicitly centered on Prussia.

These experiences created a ruthless team of nationalists in Prussia, committed to a rigorous realpolitik. When Crown Prince Wilhelm came to the throne in 1861, he found interest in a larger German national identity useful primarily as a means to justify a military buildup in Prussia that would strengthen the power of the monarchy within it. In contrast, the reactionary Junker political leader, Otto von Bismarck, saw national unity as essential to the survival of the monarchy and the ruling elites across the German states. "The great questions of the time," he instructed members of the Prussian Chamber of Deputies, "will not be resolved by speeches and majority decisions—that was the great mistake of 1848 and 1849—but by iron and blood."

His ally in these plans, Helmuth Karl von Moltke, had been a child when the French burned out his family at Lübeck. He had grown up tough and entered the Danish military before returning to cast his lot with the Prussian Army, though he took leave to help reorganize the Ottoman forces and study such matters across Europe. Like Bismarck, Moltke saw 1848–9 as not so much the top-down betrayal of German national aspirations as the suppression of internal revolts in the interest of the order necessary to securing a common national government.

These allies saw national unity as coming from the centralization of power, in which conflict and military action could be decisive. They deplored Denmark's success against adjacent German allies of the Prussians to keep control of Schleswig-Holstein in the First Schleswig War of 1848–51. That conflict—with the Crimean War—rattled the continental balance of power. The Prussians happily gave it a bigger shake with the Second Schleswig War. Rallying neighboring German states, Prussia led allied columns into the disputed territory in February 1864, winning victory in October.

Prussia then delivered a terminal blow to the idea of a *Großdeutschland*. Austria remained preoccupied with working out that peculiar dual monarchy with Hungary, and retaining its holdings in Italy and the Balkans. By the spring of 1866, though, their Prussian rivals had woven another network of mutual defense alliances, even with Italy. It even made a cynical bid for republican support by proposing a national constitution with an elected national diet and universal manhood suffrage. In May, Prussia constructed another set of alliances and moved into the south, inflicting a severe defeat on Austria on July 3 at Königgrätz near Sadová in the present Czech Republic.

In these years, Prussia annexed Hanover, Hesse-Kassel, Nassau, and the city of Frankfurt am main. It also gained some territory from Hesse Darmstadt, and drew Baden, Württemberg, and Bavaria into alliances with Prussia. It also created another means for unification by transforming the old north German customs union, the *Zollverein*, into a tighter organization with greater authority. The Prussia's *Augustbündnis* of 1866 forged an alliance of twenty-two states, which became the Norddeutscher Bund the following year, coaxing into membership the Kingdom of Saxony (with its capital at Dresden). The following February, allied German states elected—based on local suffrage arrangements—a common *konstituierender Reichstag* that made major changes in the proposed republican constitution, and ratified it in June, authorizing its promulgation on July 1, 1867.[3]

Many saw this drive for German unification as a prerequisite for the creation of the kind of European federation that Mazzini and other European republicans had been promoting for more than three decades: Italian patriots had fought as allies of the Prussians a few years earlier and naturally sympathized with the Germans over the thwarting of their national aspirations. The old republican warrior Garibaldi took Italian troops into the Austro-Prussian War in 1866. When Italy allied itself with Prussia in hopes of wresting Venetia from Austria–Hungary, he gathered a force said to be of some 40,000 men, and won the only major Italian victory of the conflict, defeating the Austrians at Bezzecca. Prussian arms secured an armistice rewarding its allies in what they

---

3   "Population of France and Prussia," *Sacramento Daily Union*, July 30, 1870, 4c2. In addition, there were *Großherzogtümer* or grand duchies: Mecklenburg-Schwerin (Schwerin), Mecklenburg-Strelitz (Neustrelitz), Oldenburg (Oldenburg), and Saxe-Weimar-Eisenach (Weimar). The *Herzogtümer* or duchies were Anhalt (Dessau), Brunswick or Braunschweig (Braunschweig), Saxe-Altenburg or Sachsen-Altenburg (Altenburg), Saxe-Coburg and Gotha or Sachsen-Coburg und Gotha (Coburg), and Saxe-Meiningen (Meiningen). Smaller *Fürstentümer* or principalities were Lippe (Detmold), Reuss-Gera (Gera in east Thuringia), Reuss-Greiz (Greiz), Schaumburg-Lippe (Bückeburg), Schwarzburg-Rudolstadt (Rudolstadt), Schwarzburg-Sondershausen (Sondershausen), and Waldeck and Pyrmont (Arolsen). Finally, there were the *Freie und Hansestädte*—Bremen, population 102,532; Hamburg, population 264,675 (the second-largest in what became Germany); and Lübeck, population 44,799—as well as the *Reichsländer* or imperial territories.

called a "Third War for Italian Independence." Of course, nothing like a United States of Europe could have happened under the continental leadership of France nor would it be likely to do so. "The progress of humanity seems to have come to a halt," wrote Garibaldi, in hopes of a Germany that "would rally to its cause all those who are suffering wrong or who aspire to a better life, and all those who are now enduring foreign oppression."[4]

Still, Prussian plans still faced some resistance in the south. Well-developed local governments and institutions prevailed in the *Mittelstaaten* of Bavaria, Württemberg, the *Großherzogtümer*—the grand duchies—of Baden and Hesse), which represented between 9 million and 10 million Germans. In the elections, anti-Prussian parties showed with considerable strength. The unification of Germany required another Napoleon.

That specter of a new Napoleon came from a crisis in Spain. The revolutionary turmoil of 1848 had largely bypassed that country, leaving many old issues festering. Twenty years later, rebellions in Cuba threatened the last of its New World empire. Observers from abroad, such as the French republican journalist Louis Blairet, took heart at the prospect of abolishing slavery in Cuba, as a natural outcome of the triumph of abolition in the US.[5] Ruling circles in Spain came to agree on the removal of Queen Isabella II and her ministers. In 1868, Spain had its own "Glorious Revolution."[6]

Like the similarly named event in English history two centuries earlier, this palace coup had to look abroad for a successor. As the dispute staggered into 1870, one faction of the movers and shakers in government suggested leaping over the usual rivalries among themselves to place the crown on the head of a Hohenzollern. Of

---

4   Denis Mack Smith, ed., *Garibaldi: Great Lives Observed* (Engelwood Cliffs, NJ: Prentice Hall, 1969), 76. Friedrich Engels, who had a much longer and closer experience with Prussia, remained skeptical. See *MECW*, vol. 23, 47–8.

5   Blairet wrote *Le Général Prim* (Paris: A. Lacroix, Verboeckhoven et Cie, 1868), *Le général Prim et la situation actuelle de l'Espagne* (Paris: Achille Faure, 1868), and *Espagne et Cuba* (Paris: Imp. de C. Schiller, 1869), as well as *Le Mexique historique, géographique, politique et social* (Paris: Périnet, n.d.).

6   Robert C. Binkley, *Realism and Nationalism, 1852–1871* (New York: Harper & Row, 1935, Harper Torchbook edn, 1963), 138, 286. See also Isabel María Pascual Sastre, *La Italia del Risorgimento y la España del sexenio democrático (1868–1874)* (Madrid: Consejo Superior de Investigaciones Científicas, 2001).

course, the Second Empire of Napoleon III would never accept having the two major countries east and west of France under the same dynasty.

The French minister left Berlin to confront the Prussian king vacationing at the Ems spa, on July 13. Even though the German candidate for the throne had already declined the offer, the French wanted a formal statement assuring them that the Spanish crown would never rest on a Hohenzollern head. Wilhelm assured the French that the Hohenzollerns had no interest in the Spanish crown, but ruled out any permanent commitments. The king then left the tedious work of documenting the exchange to Prime Minister Bismarck.

Bismarck understood how foreign conflicts had unified the German states around Prussia. He also saw post-Napoleonic France as a prisoner of an exaggerated sense of national honor. In what became the infamous Ems telegram, he stuck to the facts but presented them in a way that implied that the Prussians had been dismissive of the French. To make sure it had the desired effect, he also arranged for its release on Bastille Day in July.

On July 19, the French government responded with a declaration of war, though even Napoleon III himself had reservations. A broad opposition to war extended from the shrewder pragmatists among his military advisers through republicans of various stripes and into the working classes, from Paris artisans to the new kind of industrial workers at Le Creusot.

Still, nobody with enough principles of *noblesse oblige*—no bishops or clergy, no professors of ethics—cared to ask how much French honor would be worth in terms of lives forever snuffed out or truncated in body and soul.

Preparations for War

The highly professional army of imperial France remained, at heart, an institution apart. It grew from decades of experience far from France. This left it a legacy of pride and confidence that hardly equipped it for a European war. "The Minister says the army is ready," quipped General Louis Jules Trochu. "And I believe him. In this year of Our Lord, 1870, it is ready for the Crimean War of 1855 or the

Austrian War of 1859. Our army, it appears, is always ready for a war of the past."[7]

Those on both sides who favored war promised a quick and easy victory, as they usually do. The French Army had around 400,000 men and needed only 50,000 for territorial and domestic policing. They expected that they could quickly raise a million men, of which they could get half east to the frontier for a speedy seizure of the Rhine valley, supplemented with over 417,000 Garde mobile, also called the Garde nationale mobile (not to be confused with the Garde nationale).

The *mobiles* theoretically armed every man of military age not otherwise engaged. Historically, the government supplied them only fourteen training days annually, and these nonconsecutively, so each man could sleep at home. They had lacked standard military uniforms and made do with whatever weapons could be spared. Much of the *mobiles* resembled a loose militia, not useful for much beyond the immediate locality in which they were raised. The government also quickly found that it had based its estimates on projections made years before, and exemptions shrank the numbers.[8]

On paper, the regular army of Prussia seemed deceptively inferior to that of France in point of numbers. In fact, very different numbers lurked behind the regulars. Every man of military age faced conscription and service for three years, after which they served another four in the reserves and still another five in the Landswehr. So while the Prussians could field only 382,000 under arms, they had massive reserves on which to draw. Also, their allied states adopted—along with a common postal and passport system, equality among the denominations, and metric weights and measures—a common military system. The German Confederation, then, had nearly a million in the Landswehr alone.

A French soldier served in a squad of ten soldiers headed by a corporal or sergeant. Eight of these constituted a company of roughly 120 or 130 men under a captain, lieutenant, *sous-lieutenant*, sergeant major,

---

7   Irving Werstein, *The Franco-Prussian War: Germany's Rise as a World Power* (New York: Julian Messner, 1965), 41.

8   L. Thiriaux, *La garde nationale mobile de 1870* (Brussels: L'expansion Belge, 1909). The French authorities conscripted people in a very limited and focused way, and benefited from the payments of those buying their release. Michael Howard, *The Franco-Prussian War: The German Invasion of France 1870–1871* (London: Routledge, 1988).

and *fourrier* or quartermaster, as well as with a drummer, a bugler, and an underage aide, an *enfant de troupe*. Half a dozen of these formed a battalion of roughly 800 men. On a larger scale, three battalions formed a regiment of 2,200 to 2,500 men. Two of these formed a brigade and two brigades, or possibly three in the case of cavalry, formed a division. Each division also had a regiment of *chasseurs* and three batteries of artillery, including one with the new *mitrailleuse*. Three or four divisions constituted a corps, which had roughly 28,000 to 37,000 men. The size of the army would ultimately depend on how many corps the army received.

Their German counterparts served in a section, three of which formed a company averaging around 220 men. Four companies made a battalion, three of which constituted a regiment of roughly 3,000 men. Beyond this, two regiments made a brigade, two of which became a division, each of which had its own company of pioneers. Two divisions made a corps, which also had six batteries of artillery and its own independent rifle battalion, but ran to a smaller size range compared to a French corps. Each of the eleven provinces of Prussia had its own corps, and the acquisitions of 1866 added three more.

Prussian soldiers on the march sometimes carried loads of as much as a hundred pounds. Something over ten pounds of that was a state-of-the-art breech-loading bolt-action Dreyse *Zündnadelgewehr* or "needle gun" developed almost thirty years before. The trigger released a spring that shot the firing pin, penetrating the paper cartridge like a needle to strike a percussion cap. It could fire as many as a dozen shots per minute at an effective range of 800 to 1,200 yards. They had a million and a half of these ready for use in 1870.

The French had a significant edge in terms of practical technology. Their newer *chassepot* rifle could fire eight to fifteen rounds per minute. It also had an effective range of 1,300 to 1,500 yards, a bit longer than the principal Prussian weapon, the Dreyse. Not all of the *mobiles*, of course, had to make do with refurbished older firearms. By 1864, their *tabatière* system converted old muzzle loaders into breech-loading rifles, in a process similar to that of the Snider-Enfield in Great Britain. The name *tabatière* comes from the fact that the breech-loading mechanism looked like a snuffbox. France also had a little over 200 of the new *mitrailleuse*, a machine gun that could spit out a hundred rounds a minute across 2,000 yards.

Thanks to the superb works at Essen, the Krupp family had already begun to roll out tremendously accurate steel cannons. Alfred Krupp himself knew which side of his bread was buttered—and by whom. When the liberal forces in the parliament reasonably balked at the cost of feeding the Prussian military machine, Krupp offered the government 2 million talers in credit. Not without reason, his role in securing Germany's military superiority earned him the nickname "Krupp, the cannon king."

Also, the French proved remarkably slow to adopt better communication techniques, along with, moving, arming, equipping, and maintaining large numbers of forces in the field. Much later, Thomas Augustus Le Mesurier later wrote *The Feeding of Fighting Armies*, a book-length whitewash of the institutional buck-passing central to the functioning of the old imperial army. He cited Ludwig Lohlein to imply that the Germans faced the same hardships in their periodic shortages of salt and tobacco, particularly when supply trains became "stuck fast in the snow at or between the different stages." The horses, even for the officers, sometimes had to subsist on "half rations, and later on only quarter rations." They had to resort to using ambulances to haul ammunition.[9]

Yet these proved to be minor issues compared with those afflicting the entire French war effort. Eager to understate the incompetence of the high command and its government, Le Mesurier whined dismissively that it had become "too much the fashion to condemn the supply or transport when there are any privations," while acknowledging that logistical problems in that corner of the war had been "very indifferently administered." The authorities lacked reliable rail transport north of Lyon, where they had concentrated the food and forage, and staff officers gave priority to reinforcing the front, which "often sent forward more men to starve and to incommode the already over-taxed resources of the supply and transport. If men cannot be fed, neither can they fight. The consequence was that the ranks were filled with men lacking stamina, who were unfit either to march or fight."[10]

---

9   Thomas Augustus Le Mesurier, *The Feeding of Fighting Armies: Franco-German War of 1870–71*, 2 vols. (London: Harrison and Sons, 1904), vol. 1, 274. Ludwig Löhlein, *Campaign of 1870–1: The Operations of the Corps of General V. Werder* (Chatham: J. Gale, 1873).

10   Ibid., vol. 1, 273–4, 274–5.

The term "Prussian efficiency" merits emphasis with regard to supply, but all of this had to do primarily with railroads and their appreciation by the general staff. The officer of an Irish company with the French Army rightly noted that the Prussians had proper footwear for a winter campaign—long boots with two pairs of socks—while his men tramped about the snow with uniforms suitable to North Africa and wearing what amounted to slippers.[11] Compared to a unit in the US Civil War, a German regiment mustered in at about three times larger, and it reached the battlefield healthier and more intact, about six times bigger than its average American counterpart.

Rather than organize an infrastructure to supply the men, the old imperial French Army generally fell back on the antiquated practice of equipping and provisioning its expanded forces by having the officers present on site do so at an established per capita rate. That rate depended on a bureaucratically determined standard that never matched—or could match—the actual costs of provisions, particularly where large numbers of soldiers were concentrated and supplies were particularly short. One wonders how any but the most ritual-obsessed imperial bureaucrat could have actually believed that they could feed a force of any size moving through areas with varying populations, some drained of their foodstuffs, in the same way that you could provide for a small garrison in a secure area with flourishing agriculture. The lack of standardization had always been rife with corruption, and its use in the desperate conditions of 1870–1 made it particularly cynical.

The practice often forced officers to choose between not having enough to feed and equip their men and resorting to what the English called the "false muster." That is, the system itself gave rise to a tradition of pragmatically exaggerating the numbers one had to feed and of accepting the exaggeration at headquarters. This also jibed with the government's political desire to exaggerate the strength of their forces in the press. Such informal solutions had the additional advantage for the authorities of leaving many subordinates technically guilty of fraud. The English also spoke of this as "making dead men chew tobacco" by keeping them on the rolls to draw their rations. The option of such an

---

11   M. W. Kirwin, *La compagnie irlandaise: Reminiscences of the Franco-German War* (Montreal: Dawson, 1878) , 139.

arrogation of power would prove as useful to the new nominal republic as to the old monarchy.

All these armies faced a common set of new challenges. In the past, military operations always relied, to some extent, on what resources they could garner in the field. As armies grew larger, though—and as campaigns sometimes bogged, remaining in the same area for weeks or months—those local resources became increasingly scarce. This became a common problem not only for the armies directly engaged but for any officers of any nation expecting to fight a war at some point in the future.

As one focuses more closely on the realities of war between nations, it becomes increasingly clear that the dynamic of such conflicts tends to break down any national distinctiveness among the combatants. This runs through military organization, technology, and the management of logistic problems to the deep political contempt for their people, who had to be managed as thoroughly as other resource.

Even more paradoxically, this breakdown of national distinctiveness found its reflection in the diverse composition of forces, especially among the more cosmopolitan and imperial French. Their armies included subjects of Spain, the Italian states, Russia, and particularly Poles. The twenty-year old Horatio Herbert Kitchener was far from the only British participant. The son of a high-ranking British officer, he had received an education worthy of rank before heading off to France, where he caught pneumonia after regularly going aloft in a balloon. Enough Irish soldiers trained in the British Army turned up to fill entire units of the French Army, one officer of which left his reminiscence of a *compagnie irlandaise*. Philanthropy from across the channel, particularly among the Quakers, provided the hardest-hit communities with life-saving assistance.[12] War would no longer be simply a war between nations, if ever it actually had been.

At the start, though, nobody realized just how much aid it might take.

---

12   Byron Farwell, *Eminent Victorian Soldiers: Seekers of Glory*, 2nd edn (New York: Norton Paperback, 1985), 304; Kirwin, *La compagnie irlandaise*; and Lewis Appleton, *Reminiscences of a Visit to the Battle Fields of Sedan, Gravelotte, Spicheren, and Wörth, and the Bombarded Towns of Thionville, Metz, Bitche, Strasburg, etc.* (London: Simpkin, Marshall, & Co., 1872), 60–1.

Grand Strategies and Other Fantasies

Behind the military structures and practices, an experienced bureaucracy charted their plans. On July 20—the day after declaring war—Napoleon III announced that he would himself serve as the overall commander in chief. With the opening of hostilities, his minister of war, Edmond LeBoeuf—a veteran of North Africa who had commanded the French guns at Sebastapol—became Bonaparte's chief of staff, with General Barthélemy Lebrun taking his place as minister. Both were sixty-one, roughly the same age as all the principals commanding the armies.

In practical terms, Maréchal François Achille Bazaine—who had failed so miserably in Mexico—took charge of building and leading the new Armée du Rhin. He had joined the army as a private but found service in the Foreign Legion to his liking, wearing the uniform not only in Africa, Crimea, and Italy, but also in Spain's Carlist Wars, and in command of Napoleon III's debacle in Mexico, responsibility for which had been easily deflected onto the dead Emperor Maximilian.

The strategy of his government centered on replicating the conquests of the first Napoleon. It planned to rush forward three corps, organize them into an Armée du Rhin, and sweep across the border into the rich and industrializing Rhineland. In hindsight, one wonders whether they had railway maps. The very assets that made the Rhine desirable had already moved the Germans to build it a superb railroad network. Half a dozen essentially double-track lines rolled into the region, over which the military seized control. Three of these ran from Berlin and one each from Hamburg, Dresden, and Munich.[13]

The French had no similar complex tying Paris to Lorraine and Alsace, the territories adjacent to the Germans. Two major routes ran east from Paris in the general direction of the frontier. As elsewhere across the countryside, different companies jealously protected their assets and built rail lines that often lacked the second track. No direct routes went from Paris to the two cities essential for the projected troop concentrations—Metz with a population of over 50,000 on the Moselle river in Lorraine and Strasbourg with 86,000 on the Rhine in Alsace.

---

13   Geoffrey Wawro, *The Franco-Prussian War: The German Conquest of France in 1870–1871* (Cambridge: Cambridge University Press, 2003), 48–9, 74–5.

The major eastbound line from Paris went through Châlons-sur-Marne (presently Châlons-en-Champagne). A set of tracks veered northeast to the wrong border, going first to Sedan and then skirting the frontier of Belgium south before ending at Thionville on the Moselle near Luxembourg. The Fourth Corps took this route on July 23.

One officer who had lived for two years at Thionville, a small town of a little over 7,000 found the place "no longer recognizable." The community which had been "so dreary, quiet, boring even, had become the center of extraordinary activity. In every street there was a continual coming and going of soldiers, carriages and horses in the midst of an indescribably hubbub." Worse, he and his detachment could not find their regiment, an officer to whom they could report, or anyone who could tell them where to find such a person.[14] Thousands of men found themselves stranded, unfed and unsupplied, as they faced a hike of about thirty kilometers south to their starting point at Metz.

Another line ran more directly toward Metz from Châlons-sur-Marne, but it stopped at Verdun, the ancient Roman base later fortified by Vauban. There were plans to run tracks the further seventy to eighty exhausting kilometers east to Metz, but the only existing line from Verdun first veered down into Alsace. At Frouard, just short of Nancy, then a city of 53,000 people, a line chugged back north to Metz, while branches further along connected to Haguenau, Strasbourg and Belfort, albeit at the cost of additional shoe leather.

A simple route map indicated two serious problems. First, the easiest route for getting troops to the key points in both Alsace and Lorraine ran over the same rails, which would create constant snarls and delays. Second, Frouard, along with the bridge over the Moselle at Pont-à-Mousson, only about twenty kilometers distant, represented a decisively fatal vulnerability; its loss would effectively isolate the two points of French concentration both from each other and from Paris.

Despite all the plumage and the much-touted international reputation of France, the advantages hardly went to its imperial hierarchy. The Prussian Army could steam more than four times as many trains to the

---

14   Léonce Patry, *The Reality of War: A Memoir of the Franco-Prussian War and the Paris Commune (1870–1)*, trans. Douglas Fermer (London: Cassell & Co., 2001), 52–8, 68–9, originally *La Guerre telle qu'elle est (Campagne de 1870–71): Metz, armée du Nord, Commune* (Paris: Montgredien et Cie, 1897).

border than the French every day. The fact that the average train from Paris could get no more than a single unit to the front slowed the organization of an army corps where they needed it to three weeks, a task the Prussians could accomplish in less than a week.[15]

By the third week of July 1870, the late summer weather wilted what enthusiasm existed among the tens of thousands of French burdened by equipage and sweltering in their uniforms. Mostly peasants, they relied on their assigned superiors to know what they were doing, which did not prevent some of them from getting separated from the rest of their unit. Avoiding this fate was no guarantee of being fed or equipped. Most waged their first battle trying to manhandle weighty haversacks along the disturbingly quiet steel rails of the locomotives they expected to relieve them. So the realities of aching muscles, hunger, thirst, and heat burned off most of the misplaced enthusiasm for the glory of war.

Nevertheless, the military concentration at Metz had a good railroad running east through Saint-Avold to Forbach, a rural industrial community of nearly 5,500 people opposite German territory near Saarbrücken. As early as July 19, some French *chasseurs d'Afrique* came into initial contact with some Prussian uhlans along the border near there. Over these days, scouts and small patrols crossed back and forth over the border, periodically taking shots at each other, without much importance save to those maimed or killed or their families. By July 24, Bazaine had two corps of the Army of the Rhine near Saint-Avold and another, under General Charles Frossard, near Forbach.[16]

Napoleon III declared his wife Eugénie the regent in his absence on July 27, and left for the front the next day with their fourteen-year-old son, "Loulou," who had been baptized at Notre-Dame cathedral with Pope Pius IX and Queen Victoria as his godparents. He went on this picnic commissioned as a *sous-lieutenant*. They joined Loulou's mentor, Frossard, at the front.

Meanwhile, to cover the flank of this prospective invading force in Lorraine, another force deployed in Alsace under Marshal Patrice de MacMahon. He commanded several corps attempting to cover that part of the border. MacMahon, the Duke of Magenta, had attained his

15   Wawro, *The Franco-Prussian War*, 75–6.
16   August Niemann, *Der französische Feldzug 1870–1871* (Hildburghausen: Verlag des Bibliographischen Instituts, 1871), 56.

generalship for helping to crush the 1848 rebellion of the people of Paris, but he had also served in Africa, Crimea, and Italy before taking charge of the critical First Corps. Other old comrades and contemporaries, generals Auguste Alexandre Ducrot and Abel Douay, took the Second and Seventh Corps. The government broke precedent to bring troops from overseas into the country, particularly moving them from Algeria into a Third Corps at Strasbourg.

As the French pondered their own invasion plans, Moltke brought the most important lessons of the American Civil War to Europe. He and his staff responded quickly to the declaration of war by mobilizing and moving hundreds of thousands of armed men to the border, with all the materiel they needed. They organized the trains and arranged well-timed rendezvous points and schedules, and numbered cars to keep track of them, making particular assignments to move supplies and equipment to keep the troops as helpful as possible. They planned everything with clockwork precision.

The Prussians originally planned for four armies of about 100,000 each, but their very efficiency permitted real flexibility. They placed their troops where they could hold a strong defensive position, while also being capable of sweeping across Alsace, the easternmost bulge of France. As with the French, the size of each of the three German armies gathering along the border varied, depending on how many corps it had assigned. The First Army went to General Karl Friedrich von Steinmetz. It got two cavalry divisions and I, VII and VIII Armeekorps. To the border east of Steinmetz, Prince Friedrich Karl had command of the Second and the remnants of that projected Fourth Army with the III, IV, IX, X, and Saxon XII Armeekorps, Württemberg's Gardekorps, and two cavalry divisions. Crown Prince Friedrich Wilhelm—"Unser Fritz" to his troops—assembled the Third Army even farther east with the V and XI Armeekorps, with Bavarian, as well as more Saxon and Württemberg, troops.

Where the French planned an ultimately questionable invasion of the Rhineland, Moltke and his team formulated something of a master plan themselves. They held good defensive positions against which they expected the French to spend themselves quickly. After this, the Prussians would leave the First Army as the largely immobile hinge, while the Second and Third Armies would swing into France like a large gate, driving any possible opposition before them. Once it was able to seize Frouard and Pont-à-Mousson, the army of the German Confederation would face only episodic resistance.

That German hinge was to sit in the Saar basin, a fitting focus for a war over the emerging economic order.[17] Two rivers, the Sarre Rouge and Sarre Blanche, begin in France near Mont Donon, the highest peak in the Vosges, where the authorities had just placed an 1869 monument noting the sanctity of the place to the Gallo-Romans. The two converge into the Saar river near the hamlet of Lorquin. A Celtic hill fort on the Sonnenberg Hill testifies to the longevity of a community along the river, even before the Romans built their bridge there. A medieval castle rose at Saarbrücken, though baroque builders created a unique look, which eventually incorporated the market town of Saint Johann and a new industrial community called Malstatt or Burbach. The 1852 arrival of a rail line of the Palatine Ludwig Railway expanded production, giving rise to the Burbach ironworks in 1856.

Shortly after, the railroads and the canal network established ties to the same kinds of communities west of the border. Forbach had a history going back nearly a thousand years, and evolved into a small complex of villages. By 1851, nearly 5,000 lived there and in its several adjacent communities—Verrerie-Sophie, Schoeneck, and Stiring. The eastbound railroad reached the city in 1846, sparking the construction of a large steel mill at Stiring. To feed this complex, they located coal and began mining it at the Saint-Charles well of Petite-Rosselle, and the resulting increase in steel production in turn led to the opening of new shafts and escalating coal production. Railroad expansion continued as well, the rails reaching west to Saint-Avold by 1851, and east to Saarbrücken the next year.

By then, these municipalities had begun to bring gas into town, though this remained far beyond the reach of those who actually made the wealth of the district. Whether in a cluster of communities around Saarbrücken or around Forbach, most of the industrial workers came from somewhere else, with a sizeable minority from foreign countries.

Places like the Saar basin provided their own logic. Much of the vast amounts of raw material they produced would be used for processing and refinement by other communities, like the coal to fuel industrialization. Industry implied more industry. And the steam power

---

17   N. Bannenberg and H. Wagner, "History of the Iron, Steel and Mining Industry of the Saar-Lor-Lux region," : *Erzmetall* 55 (12) 678-87.

that fueled one would fuel others, and produced ever growing numbers of people who would know how to use it.

The Saar itself, watering its ancient and modern settlements, continued north into the Moselle river at Konz, near Trier. That ancient Roman community had been the birthplace of that Central European malcontent Karl Marx, who devoted his life to understanding the transformative nature of that matrix of changes that used to be called "the Industrial Revolution." Others had observed how the explosive demand for industrial labor coincided with the mechanic and chemical augmentation of agricultural production.

Marx, however, assigned a particular historic role to what he called the "proletariat." He believed them to be the natural antithesis of the new social relations shaped by the capitalist marketplace. Industrial societies, whether Forbach or Saarbrücken—Le Creusot or Essen— drew their workers from across much of the Western world into a community defined by work rather than associations of family or family lands. Atomized and relatively powerless, they seemed to be as much at the mercy of new aristocracies of wealth as had peasants to their feudal masters.

From London, Marx now apprehensively watched the fate of the peoples in the hands of modern nations. That brave new madness of Napoleon III had distilled the worst aspects of the French Revolution, while reducing its promise for the people. Astutuely, Bismarck would redefine nationalism as something of far greater importance than the mere people who constituted a nation.

It would be too much to expect the rulers of these nations to under-stand themselves as well as Marx did, but they never even seemed to draw the deeper lessons of the Napoleonic experience. The original Napoleon had utterly and ruthlessly subjugated the Germans of all the various states, who, with some justice, believed their aspirations for national unification had been frustrated by the French. As is often the case where cleverness passes for wisdom, Bismarck and his kindred spirits never realized how institutionalizing Napoleonic standards among their own countrymen might produce a similar effect on the French and their other neighboring states. It might have similar—or even worse—consequences.

In a more immediate sense, though, they began to learn that, in every modern war, the government's first conquest was going to have to be its own people. In Paris, the International brought antiwar demonstrators into the streets. Dumay and the local section of the IWA at the Schneider plant took solace in the fact that the patriarch of the industrial dynasty, Eugène Schneider, had crowds storming past his home in the capital chanting, "Death to the assassin of Creusot! Death to the exploiter of the workmen!" In short order, Schneider, the great beneficiary of imperial largesse, left the country.

Bismarck sought to build a nation on the bones of the Ratstatt patriots. Wilhelm Rüstow, the old Garibaldian advocate of a "people's militia" waging a people's war, remained to fight for German unification under Prussian auspices, as did Willich, the veteran communist who later hurried back from Ohio to do so. However, the Prussian authorities never saw themselves as desperate enough to welcome the politically questionable into their definition of German patriotism. Choosing to remain in Italy, another veteran of Baden, the historian Karl Hillebrand, warned against a Germany united under Prussian standards.[18]

The war almost moved the socialists back in Germany, where it hastened the drift of the ADAV and SDAP toward unity. In the Reichstag, Wilhelm Hasenclever of the former and August Bebel and Wilhelm Liebknecht of the latter saw the war as defensive and German national unity as desirable.[19] The Lassallean ADAV also believed that the logic of centralizing power would foster the advent of socialism.

In that conflict, of course, the authorities held all the cards, particularly within wider society. Berlin bakers rallied on July 28 after deciding two weeks earlier to have a strike vote. Citing patriotic motives, they now decided against any work stoppage. Bricklayers met at their hall on Brunnenstraße, suggesting that employers should impose a small deduction from wages to provide medical assistance to the troops. Local saddlers, who refused to let the war entirely sweep aside their concerns

---

18 Walter Kaufman, *Nietzsche: Philosopher, Psychologist, Antichrist* (Princeton: Princeton University Press, 1950, with revised edns in 1956, 1968, and 1974), 26, 179, 453–4.

19 On the manifesto of September 5, 1870, see Heinz Beike, *Die Deutsche Arbeiterbewegung und der Krieg von 1870/1871* (Berlin: Dietz Verlag, 1957), 101–7; and Werner Ettelt and Hans-Dieter Krause, *Der Kampf um eine marxistische Gewerkschaftspolitik in der deutschen Arbeiterbewegung: 1868 bis 1878* (Berlin: Verlag Tribüne, 1975), 231–2.

about wages and working conditions, had closer ties to Liebknecht and the SDAP.[20]

The emergence of new, more centralized, nation-states superseded the old utopian vision of a popular nationalism would define the nation and national identity. If the United Kingdom or France incorporated diverse populations within their borders, then Russia and Austria–Hungary enveloped even larger numbers of very distinct peoples and languages. Western civilization institutionalized the management what nationalism would and would not mean, a fact that would frustrate the national aspirations of many Europeans. As those governments began extending their power overseas, the contradiction deepened, laying the foundation for imperialist rivalries that would shape the next century.

In a remarkably short span of years within that long nineteenth century, the development of the state both coöpted and repudiated the old aspirational nationalism of Mazzini. In the process, the state translated into stark institutional terms the old revolutionary faith in an armed people willing to pay a high price in blood and treasure for a nation of their own. The health of the nation would rest with the state. That of the state turned on that of its military.

And the health of the army, the state, and the nation grew stronger through war.

---

20   Beike, *Die Deutsche Arbeiterbewegung und der Krieg*, 24–5, 26.

PART II
War for the Empire

4

The Guns of August:
Civilization Asserts Itself

On July 20, thirty Prussian horsemen pressed into service "a body of miners from the ironworks and collieries" found near Saarbrücken. The uhlans hoped to destroy a viaduct on a branch from Cocheren on the Metz–Forbach line skirting the frontier. The army needed "men experienced in the conducting of blasting operations, and ready to face danger for the sake of Germany." The miners required some quick "riding lessons" to keep up with the gallop to the bridge. Some French realized the threat in time to make an effort to drive them off, but the uhlans held them back "until artificers had completed the work." Once the job had been finished, the raiders made it back across the border "without a single casualty."[1] The identity and status of the workers after the action—whether they were volunteers and even their nationality—remain as obscure as if we were discussing an event in prehistory, because such, information would convey absolutely nothing of importance in modern war.

Any staff officer with a map could have seen the first stages of the war. The Germans, who had experience with a French invasion early in the century, realized that they needed to mobilize and deploy as much as they could to protect the Rhine, which their railroads tended to encourage. The French railroads, however, left no real alternative to concentrating their army in Lorraine, in preparation for a strike into the

---

1 Archibald Forbes, *My Experiences of the War between France and Germany*, 2 vols. (London: Hurst and Blackett, 1871), vol. 1, 28–9.

Rhineland while protecting Paris. It also permitted placing a secondary force into Alsace, the most vulnerable, easternmost tip of France. The rugged Vosges mountains separated these two positions and the July 20 Prussian raid aimed at severing the most accessible route connecting them. Coordinated by rail and telegraph, war broke out almost simultaneously in both Alsace and Lorraine.

War and the Transnational Realities of the National Ideal

The efforts of a modern state to distill a perfectly manageable perceived nationality remained incomplete in France and even an institutional state had thus far eluded the Germans. It had not yet superseded some serious internal language and ethnic differences. More deeply, Catholic France contained many Protestants and Lutheran Prussia commanded forces of Catholic, as well as Protestant, principalities. Jews contributed on both sides, and Émile Cahen later commemorated the battle with recollections of their diffusion across the world over thousands of years.[2] Moreover, while common experience of war, mobilization, and combat could deepen a national identity, it could also severely strain it.

The idea of race became part of the ideological rationalization behind the institutionalization of the European nation-state. The fiction of being part of a pseudo-scientifically described French "race" or German "race" could foster a deeper sense of unity. That said, the concept of race posed problems with new dimensions as European powers began to work their will in the rest of the world.[3]

Imperial France ruled vastly more disparate peoples than the Prussians. The troops of Napoleon III had fought in Algeria, Crimea, Italy, Indochina, Mexico, Tunisia and Madagascar, reflected in the presence of nearly 14,000 Muslims in their 1870–1 war against Prussia and its allies.[4] Most of these were concentrated primarily in several regiments of the *tirailleurs algériens*.

---

2 Émile Cahen, *Les morts de Wissembourg discours prononcé Lors du deusxieme anniversaire de la journée du 4 Août 1870*, 3rd edn (Verdun: Ch. Laurent, 1872), 9.

3 US Congress, *Dictionary of Races or Peoples* (Washington: Government Printing Office, 1911).

4 Victor Duruy, *Le 1er Régiment de tirailleurs algériens, histoire et campagnes, avec une préface par Ernest Lavisse* (Paris: Librairie Hachette, 1899), 165–98.

Though called Turcos, as one writer observed, "there is not a single Turk now in this corps, and perhaps none has ever served in it."[5] A prominent German traveler, Baron Heinrich von Maltzan, pointed out that the French raised these units in Algeria, theoretically among its 3 million natives, as opposed to the Foreign Legion. The former got more "liberal pay and allowance for board, each man receiving one franc daily. Now rations rather than an allowance." He encountered two Turcos—Mustapha and Hassan—with white skin, blond hair, and northern European features chattering to each other in Dutch. They had come to North Africa to join the Foreign Legion, but joined the Turcos instead. Some Germans also served among them. "Every European who becomes a Turco or Spahi (native trooper) must assume an Arabian name." Hence the rare Dutch, German, or French Mustapha marched among them.

Behind the common term, *turco* reflected the diverse population of Algeria. The Kulugis represented a mixed ethnicity, but claimed a common descent from the former imperial Janizaries and Arabian women. The word means "son of the one-eyed" and they enjoyed considerable status in Algeria. Reportedly, "only the most degraded among them" became *turcos*. They sported a "luxuriant growth of their beards, while the beard of the Arab is very scanty." Most of these recruits came from Great Kabylia and the province of Constantine and joined the army for the better food and drink, which included alcohol despite their Islamic identity. Heinrich von Maltzan observed "a great diversity of complexion among them," some "quite dark-brown, but who had no negro blood in their veins." In fact, members of this group "despise the blacks and will never marry a negress."

The German writer detected serious racial divisions. He saw mulattoes as "a most unwelcome addition," accepted reluctantly and viewed by the officers as "generally weak, in body as well as mind, and very difficult to govern—not so much on account of their licentiousness as their proverbial stupidity." The colonizing French had brought full-blooded sub-Saharan black Africans to Algiers as slaves, many of whom remained after the elimination of the institution in 1848. Their descendants, called Schuschân, described as "too indolent to work" and "born idlers," could be "found here and there, in the Turco regiments."

5   Maltzan, "The Turcos," 102. Edmond About, *Le Turco*, 2nd edn (Paris: Librairie de L. Hachette et Cie, 1867).

Despite an underlying commonality in official and quasi-official attitudes toward race, views among ordinary Europeans tended to run the gamut. One young Alsatian woman found the *Turcos* "all, without exception, splendid fellows, tall, slightly built with finely-made limbs." She realized that many of her neighbors "shiver at the very possibility of one Turco invading their dining-rooms, or taking them to dinner." Nevertheless, she became particularly interested in a "nut-brown sub-lieutenant" named Charlemagne.[6]

In contrast, the Germans had no empire.[7] With the exception of the most traveled of them, Germans tended to see the *Turcos* as a mystery, possibly barely human. When it became known that the French would send Africans to fight them, wealthy Germans offered rewards to any soldiers who would capture and return one, as though they were something of a zoo specimen. When the Prussian Army returned some among other French, Berliners got their first curious glimpse of the kind of world in which imperial France had functioned for years:

> They eyed the Turcos with especial greed, and the glances of the upright Berliners went first to their shoulders: There, according to an old wives' horror tale which no one could convince them was untrue, was the seat of bloodthirsty cats which, during close combat, leaped at the enemy's face and so prevented him from fighting.

Meanwhile, one of the royals sent a private courier to her man in the field "to ask him whether it was proper to send captive Negroes to Berlin." She fretted over interest in them as an "unworthy curiosity." The king suggested that seeing "that very cannon fodder drawn from foreign continents" permitted Germans to "see France without its halo." Also, police barricades would likely prevent "rude familiarity or its opposite, hostility."

The demands of war increasingly recast the importance of such identities. Napoleon III reached the front late in July 1870, finding only

---

6   *Lucie's Diary of the Siege of Strasbourg by a Young Lady of Alsace* (London: Smith, Elder & Co., 1871), 2–4.

7   Although Wilhelm J. C. E. Stieber's tales of his derring-do as a spy were entirely fictional, these observations about the impact of the war on the home front seem noteworthy, *The Chancellor's Spy: The Revelations of the Chief of Bismarck's Secret Service*, trans. Jan van Heurck (New York: Grove Press, 1979), 176, 179.

129,000 men in Lorraine and only 57,000 in Alsace. These numbers, fewer than expected, faced chronic shortages, largely due to disorganization. The railroads dropped the larger concentration into a miserably overcrowded cluster at Metz before parts of it began getting off toward the border.[8] Keeping them equipped, fed, and organized provided new challenges.

Both sides faced these logistical problems. "The men's boots were so wretchedly bad," recalled a French officer, "that the pebbles worked into them after the first kilometer had been passed over, and every halt was utilised in bandaging blistered feet, or stuffing wads of old garments into the gaping holes in the shoes." Their army did not even supply everybody with socks, while the Germans issued boots cut to take pant cuffs, which "almost effectually secured the feet from frost and pebbles." They faced "a war of boots, of clothing, of provisions, and of internal regimental economy."[9]

Already some soldiers openly scorned the abstraction of national honor and the beplumed officers who defined it. Some greeted the reactionary monarchist Marshal François Marcellin Certain de Canrobert—whose father had borne arms against the Revolution of eighty years earlier—with demands to go home, crying "À Paris!" *La Presse* mentioned this but, like other papers, would not dwell on any "discontent and irreverence" that would damage the war effort.[10]

As they had for centuries, the strong backs of the peasants bore the burden of war. The French soldier had a new regulation waterproof *havresac* a bit over a foot high, over fourteen inches wide and roughly four and a half inches deep, bulky with changes of clothes, the coat, tarpaulin, bedding, and tent with pegs. Infantrymen of all sorts also carried a cartridge pouch, bayonet, and drinking bottle, as well as a bag for a vest slung over shoulders well protected by padding. Where possible, the army used wagons or train cars to transport the weighty load, with soldiers keeping what they needed for cooking and eating and their cartridge cases and firearm.[11] A long march through the summer heat made even the relatively lightened load oppressively heavy, and whether

---

8 Henderson, *The Battle of Spicheren*, 37. See also Alfred Duquet, *Froeschwiller, Châlons, Sedan* (Paris: G. Charpentier, 1880), 3–20.

9 Kirwin, *La compagnie irlandaise*, 72, 139.

10 "La Garde Mobile à Chalons," *La Presse*, August 6, 1870, 1.

11 See "Französische Infanterie 1870/71," 2empire.de.

one ever retrieved the rest of what they needed depended on question-able logistical skills.

The largest troop concentrations of both sides centered around the Saar basin. Toward the close of July, General Charles Frossard pressed forward from Saint-Avold toward Forbach. Just across the border from Saarbrücken, a battalion of Prussian infantry waited, along with a regiment of mounted uhlans, horsemen who regularly ventured patrols across the border into France. Scouting parties provoked some shooting, but, "as regards aim, there was nothing to boast of on either side."[12]

The French staff realized that the Prussians had managed to amass a much larger force on the border than they had. They opted to confound the lines of communication among these different Prussian armies by seizing Saarbrücken on Tuesday, August 2. The emperor and his son came up by train to Forbach to observe 6,000 to 7,000 of Frossard's II Corps moving along multiple roads "about six abreast, with hardly a pretence at formation, but with a speed that was remarkable." Local lore later claimed that Frossard let the prince imperial, his former student, fire the first cannon into the town.

Archibald Forbes, an English reporter, left a good account of being on the receiving end of that fire. Civilians fled to get as far from the uniformed targets of the French guns as possible, while many of those targets hustled to cover as well. Many got to the train station in the adjoining village of Saint Johann. Soon, the imperial forces drove the Prussians from the town and mayor wisely posted notices for civilians to take no action against the French soldiers.[13]

None of the victors realized that their invasion of Germany had reached its high-water mark.

Alsatian Origins: Wissembourg

More significant developments took place to the east, in Alsace. Both sides seem to have remained strikingly unaware of the other's deployments. The massive Third Army of Prussian crown prince Friedrich Wilhelm lumbered forward. On July 24 or 25, Captain Ferdinand von Zeppelin and

---

12   Forbes, *My Experiences of the War*, vol. 1, 27.
13   Ibid., vol. 1, 67, 75.

a patrol of five uhlans scouted eight miles across the border to Niederbronn-les-Bains, between Bitche and Wissembourg. However, most of the German cavalry remained stranded behind the slow-moving infantry clogging the roads leading to the border.

Patrice de MacMahon deployed his corps to protect the strategic Strasbourg–Haguenau rail line back to Nancy with its links to Paris and Metz. Auguste-Alexandre Ducrot, veteran of French operations in Crimea, Algeria, and Italy, dispatched new troops sent from Paris by rail to Haguenau. General Abel Douay took a division to occupy Wissembourg.

All told, the French had only about 8,000 men with a dozen pieces of artillery to protect the pleasant little Alsatian border town of 6,000 souls. Wissembourg, or Weißenburg, had grown for a millennium around a Benedictine monastery tucked between two spurs of the Vosges. The Wolfsberg loomed to the north and the Geisberg to the south, with the Vogelsberg plateau on the western side. History also wedged it between two countries. The French Army relied heavily on the community to bake the bread essential for feeding the many more mouths it had placed on the border.[14]

Despite some reports of Prussian troops in wooded terrain within striking distance of Wissembourg, Douay had most of his available forces on the Geisberg to the south and the Vogelsberg to the west, with a couple of unfortunate companies down in the town itself.[15] The rains that came over the night of August 3–4 confirmed the mistaken belief that no enemy in their right mind would mount a serious move against them in such weather.

On Thursday morning, the first of what eventually became 60,000 Confederation troops with 144 guns went into action. They quickly got some of those guns onto the Wolfsberg and, by 8:30 a.m., fired the opening shots of the war's first big battle.[16] Their shells dropped onto

---

14   See also A. Rigaut, *Description et statistique agricole du canton de Wissembourg, typographie et aperçu historique de chaque commune, usages locaux qui y sont en vigueur* (Strasbourg; Typographie de Silbermann, 1860).

15   See also Adhemar De Chalus, *Guerre franco-allemande de 1870–1871: Wissembourg, Froeschwiller, retraite sur Châlons* (Besancon and Paris: Librarie Marion and Librarie Militaire Dumaine, 1882), 29–30.

16   Walter Schultze-Klosterselde, *Weissenburg, Wœrth, Sedan, Paris: Heiter und ernste Erinnerungen* (Leipzig: Th. Srieben's Verlag, 1889), 19–28; Duquet, *Froeschwiller, Châlons, Sedan*, 20–59. Also R. Gasselin, *L'artillerie allemande dans les combats de Wissembourg et de Wœrth* (Paris: Berger-Levrault & Cie, 1877); Helmuth von Moltke, *The Franco-German War of 1870–71* (New York: Harper Brothers, 1907), vol. 1, 16–19.

Wissembourg and over the nearby slopes. Their French targets slipped and slid into position with great difficulty because of the mud.

As the big guns directed their attention on the French troops on the high ground above the town, Bavarian infantry slogged through from the waterlogged vineyards to attack the small force of French soldiers who found themselves in the least enviable position of any troops in the battle, but they were among the first infantry of the two armies that clashed.

Foot soldiers in both armies carried firearms of approximately the same weight, a bit over ten pounds. The French *chassepot* used 86.4 grains of powder to push an eleven-millimeter lead bullet weighing 386 grains through a thirty-one-inch barrel, while the Prussian Dreyse used seventy-four grains of power to send a 15.4-millimeter bullet through a barrel of thirty-six inches. The larger charge for a smaller bullet gave the French an effective range of about 1,300 yards to the 650 for the Germans. The more durable and robust mechanism of the *chassepot* allowed the better-practiced and experienced of the French shooters to reach a significantly better rate of fire. The infantry encounters amidst the buildings and streets of Wissembourg did not immediately make apparent the innate superiority of the *chassepot*.

These technical and rather bureaucratic specifications framed immediate practical realities for those using them. French fire could pepper the soldiers of the Confederation hundreds of yards before they got within range of their own firearms. The buzz of these smaller shots surely terrified the newcomers to the battlefield, though the veterans knew that one often did not hear the *chassepot* before the projectile, so every metallic mosquito buzzing by them was one more that could not hurt them. A bullet to the forehead or heart usually just brought the victim crashing down into merciful oblivion. Someone hit in mid-torso tended to crumble with pain as if their entrails were being shredded. However, the shock of a hit through the lungs often numbed them until their next breath filled their mouth and nose with blood.[17]

The French also had their new secret weapon, their automatic gun, the *mitrailleuse*. Most new models had twenty-five rifled barrels, each of which fired what looked like an elongated shotgun shell that sent a bullet

---

17   Fermer, *Sedan 1870*, 147.

of 771.62 grains toward the enemy. Nevertheless, it fired seventy-five to 125 rounds a minute, and could reach 200 in maximum conditions. Its range ran to 3,700 yards, five times that of the German infantrymen. Moreover, the weight of the weapon meant that it had no recoil and did not need resighting after being fired. The army supplied it with over 43,000 shots or 7,200 rounds for each of the six guns, theoretically providing 1,440 loads or an hour and a half of continuous fire. In some models, the operator or *mitrailleur*, reloaded and fired by turning a crank, which led some to call it a coffee mill, a *moulin à café*. The army had a total of 200 of them.

The French Army treated them as *canon à balles*, an artillery piece that fired bullets. Rather than being scattered them among the infantry, the 750-pound machines were mounted on a carriage like a cannon, each weighing nearly a ton. The battery of six was assigned to each division, replacing a traditional battery of four cannons. Unlike the older artillery it replaced, the *mitrailleuse* had neither the range nor the power to hold its own in the artillery duels with the big new guns of Krupp. Had they been scattered among the infantry like later machine guns, they might have had a greater impact.

The psychological effect of this on the individual target must have been overwhelming. Soldiers in the field quickly learned to recognize its unique rapid thudding, lower and more distinct than the rattle of more modern machine guns. The bullet, which weighed roughly twice that of a *chassepot*, did much more damage, and the rapidity of the fire meant that one stood a good chance of being hit repeatedly. Under optimal circumstances, it could turn soldiers into a field of raw humanity. One who saw its aftereffects—and not the weapon itself—thought these "monsters" might make war into "nothing less than murdering men by machinery."[18]

Those Catholic Bavarians who thundered into Wissembourg in the interest of the Protestant Prussian monarchy faced no braver defenders of the Catholic French monarchy than the Muslims of Major Joseph Claude Liaud's *tirailleurs algériens*. Circular thinking fogged the responses of many Europeans. Their "betters" on both sides acknowledged the heroism and determination of the *Turcos*, but ascribed it to "the savage fury of wild beasts." The terrified Germans

---

18 Appleton, *Reminiscences of a Visit to the Battle Fields*, 67.

frankly acknowledged that they tended to give no quarter to the *Turcos*, who lost 500 at Wissembourg.[19] That, in turn, made the *Turcos* fight all the more desperately.

"The employment of such savages in a European war is a disgrace to that nation," wrote Maltzan. "But it is a still greater shame that, instead of regulating the wild instincts of the Turcos, they inflame them by giving to these ignorant hirelings the most horrible descriptions of their enemies."[20] In other words, the Bavarians gave them no quarter because they faced alleged beasts inflamed by French accounts that they would likely get no quarter from the Bavarians.

Defeat did nothing to ease their treatment, even for those Africans taken prisoner. Germans stared at them like "zoo animals," and felt their "poodle hair." Or they "gesticulated at them, barked gibberish, or offered them cigars or flasks in hopes of hearing what sort of noises might come out of them." Some of their white French fellow prisoners pilfered the rations meant for their African comrades, or "angrily refused to be transported with this 'jungle rabble,' as they called them." The *turcos* responded with "their habitual indifference at all these people who push themselves to study them more closely," but rose quickly to salute the officer.[21]

In the end, the greater numbers of the German Confederation flowing into the town overwhelmed the French. They lost nearly 1,600 dead and wounded, while the French left 1,300 of their own and another thousand taken prisoner. Among the dead was General Douay, cut down when a German shell struck the caisson of a *mitrailleuse* battery.[22]

Despite Wissembourg, MacMahon still hoped to block the Prussian

---

19   The French description in Maltzan, "The Turcos," 102. See also Victor Duruy, *Le 1er Régiment de tirailleurs algériens*, 168. See also Adhemar De Chalus, *Wissembourg Foeschwiller: Retraite sur Châlons* (Besançon and Paris: Librarie Marion and Librarie Militaire Dumaine, 1882), 46–48.

20   Maltzan, "The Turcos," 103.

21   La France moderne, *De Wissembourg à Ingolstadt (1870–1871): Souvenirs d'un capitaine prisonnier de guerre en Bavière* (Paris: Librairie de Firmin-Didot et Cie, 1891), 58. Leopold von Winning, *Erinnerungen eines preussischen Leutnants aus den Kriegsjahren 1866 u. 1870/71* (Heidelberg: C. Winter, 1911), 92.

22   L. Baudoin, *Le combat de Wissembourg: Récit des opérations tactiques de la journée du 4 août 1870* (Paris: Librairie Militaire de L. Baudoin et Cie, 1889), 15–16. Further, General Ducrot, *Guerre des frontières: Wissembourg. Réponse du général Ducrot à l'état-major allemand*, 2nd edn (Paris: E. Dentu, 1873).

advance into Alsace. He guided the defeated veterans trickling southwest from Wissembourg and Lauterbourg onto the ridge around Frœschwiller northwest of Haguenau into a line extending beyond it. The French center around Elsasshausen overlooked Wœrth on the Sauter river. Their right ran through Niederwald and Morsbronn, with advanced positions at Gunstett and as far as Spachbach. He got 37,000 men with 101 guns into that line, and expected more.

The French command realized the scale of what they faced as the German Third Army—badly bruised but triumphant—reorganized and shifted south toward Haguenau. The French planned a withdrawal to even more defensible heights of the Vosges, perhaps northwest to the citadel of Bitche, where MacMahon had left some of his troops.[23]

At noon on Friday, August 5, Prussian cavalry stumbled into French soldiers near Wœrth with their main force on the heights beyond. That evening, the Bavarians skirmished with the French forces before the woods near Frœschwiller. The 2me Tirailleurs Algériens stubbornly held their ground, checking the Germans until nightfall, forcing its withdrawal.[24] This ended talk among the French commanders about abandoning any hopes of getting to another field.

The violent storm that swept the area frustrated the plans of the Prussian Crown prince. Genuinely moved by the aftermath of the battle at Wissembourg, he had fantasized about a brief and decisive battle that would quickly end the war. The weather bogged efforts to bring the rest of his army to bear in the field, but he already had roughly 80,000 men with 300 guns and vastly outnumbered the French.[25]

Around 5 a.m. the next morning, French cavalrymen approached the Sauer at Wœrth to water their horses and Prussian rifles opened on

23 Lieutenant-Colonel de Cugnac, *Les prodromes de Froeschwiller, ou 40 heures de stratégie de Mac-Mahon*, 2nd edn (Paris and Nancy: Librairie Militaire Berger-Levrault, 1911), 50.

24 Werstein, *The Franco-Prussian War*, 100–2; Henderson, *Wærth*, 36. Alfred Duquet, *Guerre de 1870–1871: Froeschwiller 1 juin–6 aout* (Paris: Bibliotheque-Charpentier, 1909), 312.

25 On Wœrth see Moltke, *The Franco-German War of 1870–71*, vol. 1, 20–5, as well as George F. R. Henderson, *The Battle of Wærth August 6th, 1870* (Camberley: A. Bradford, 1911); Ducrot, *Guerre des frontières*; Duquet, *Froeschwiller, Châlons, Sedan*, 60–132; Schultze-Klosterselde, *Weissenburg, Wærth, Sedan, Paris*, 29–48; *La journée du 6 août 1870, par un Lorrain. Froeschwiller. Forbach. (Mars 1887.)* (Paris: Dentu & Cie, 1887), 3–20.

them from the opposite bank. The sounds of gunfire began waking tens
of thousands of men. Soon after, their big guns chimed in, dragging
even the heaviest sleepers to their feet.

At Frœschwiller, Marshal MacMahon pulled himself up and got into
the field. Aiming at the spire of the church there, a Bavarian division of
the German V Korps came under fire of the French 7th Brigade, which
included what was left of the 1re Tirailleurs Algériens, badly mangled at
Wissembourg. Once again, the *turcos* proved fiercely stubborn and held
the French position until a fresh brigade came up to sustain them.[26]
Around 10 a.m., their stubbornness had stabilized the French line
enough to prepare a counterattack through the woods.

From 9:30 to 10:15 a.m., the more numerous and superior German
guns dominated the artillery duel that raged over the high ground at the
center of the line. At this point, fresh German troops crossed the Sauer
into Wœrth. They found that, to their left, those of their comrades who
had already crossed the river had made gains against the French right
around Gunstett and Spachbach. However, starting around 11 a.m., the
3me Zouaves and 3me Tirailleurs Algériens slowed the Prussian
advance. With more men and a better position than their countrymen
had had at Wissembourg, they prevented the complete collapse of the
French center. Nevertheless, as the troops on either side fell back, the
Turcos found their ammunition depleted and fell back to avoid
encirclement.[27] The Turcos left thirty officers and 850 men—roughly
half the regiment—behind them, and the Zouaves dropped forty-five of
their sixty officers and 1,775 of their 2,200 men.

One observer later described the experience of the Turcos. They had
been "ordered to take a battery at the point of the bayonet." They charged,
only to fall into a deep ditch the enemy had dug a few yards before their
guns. "All hope was now lost, and endeavoring to extricate themselves
and retreat, the Prussians poured a volley into their backs." The French

---

26   See also, on the Turcos there, Émile Delmas, *De Froeschwiller à Paris: Notes
prises sur les champs de bataille* (Paris: Alphonse Lemerre, 1871).

27   On the third and its ammunition issue, see De Chalus, *Wissembourg Foeschwiller*,
112, 114; Louis de Narcy, *Journal d'un officier de turcos 1870* (Paris: Bernard Giovanangeli,
2004), 88–9, 93–4. Also Lt. L. Darier-Chatelain, *Historique du 3e Régiment de tirailleurs
algériens, histoire et campagnes, avec une préface par Ernest Lavisse* (Constantine:
Georges Heim, 1888), See also A. Touchemalin, *Guide du touriste sur le champ de bataille
de Froeschwiller, avec cartes, notice historique, vues d'ensemble et croquis dessinés d'après
nature* (Strasbourg: Edouard Fietta, n.d.), 8, 21–2. Delmas, *De Froeschwiller à Paris*.

officers had difficulty understanding what had happened because the regiment generally spoke Arabic. A wounded Turco later scandalized a comrade in the French ambulance. "The barbarous nature of these men showed itself occasionally by such remarks as these: 'I killed four of them,' 'I cut his throat,' and they would roll their bloodshot eyes fiercely and ask how soon they would be well enough to fight again."[28]

The battle lines teetered into the afternoon. A renewed German advance threatened Spachbach and Gunstett, until a French counterattack stopped them. These reinforced Germans drove them back near the Niederwald. Most dramatically, though, General Alexandre-Ernest Michel led a brigade of his horsemen, light glinting from their sabers, breastplates, and plumed helmets, in a desperate, colorful sweep from Reichshoffen toward Elsasshausen and Morsbroon before they were cut to pieces. In the end, only fifty officers and men out of 1,100 returned.[29] Yet the sacrifice slowed the advance enough to permit the retreating infantry to fall back in some order.

Nevertheless, the collapse of the French right quickly threatened to take the center with it. The Prussians seemed to be throwing an endless supply of fresh reserves into the fight. The battled came to a rapid end when the Germans got artillery onto the ridge of Elsasshausen beyond Wœrth. French efforts to mount another counterattack found themselves swamped by their own solders fleeing the front. The Germans had gained everything south of the Frœschwiller–Wœrth road.[30] Their assault on what remained of the French center coincided with a renewed Bavarian advance northeast of Frœschwiller. Shooting sputtered on into the dusk, as the last of MacMahon's army slipped off into the night.

Two factors secured victory for the German Confederation. Certainly, its numbers overwhelmed the superiority of the French *chassepot* and the unrealized potential of the *mitrailleuse*. In the course of the day, the Prussians had managed to pit 71,000 rifles and 4,250 sabers against the 32,000 rifles and 4,850 sabers of the French. Most dramatically, the superb artillery rolling out of the works at Essen—the

---

28   For this and the following paragraph, see George Halstead Boyland, *Six Months under the Red Cross, with the French Army* (Cincinnati, OH: Robert Clarke, 1873), 23.

29   Henderson, *Wœrth*, 23, 28; De Chalus, *Guerre francoallemande de 1870–1871*, 115–17; and Gustave Toudouze, *Les cuirassiers de Reichshoffen*, 2nd edn (Paris: E. Dentu, 1873), 12–13.

30   Werstein, *The Franco-Prussian War*, 102–11.

product of a highly skilled and well-organized radical workforce—made that victory decisive. Some 9,270 Germans fell on the field, killed and wounded, and 1,370 had gone missing. The French suffered 8,000 killed and wounded and lost another 12,000 missing, mostly captured. That is, the Germans lost around 14 percent and the French 41 percent of their forces. "I do not like war, gentlemen," sputtered the Crown prince to a pair of French journalists. "If I should reign I would never make it."[31]

Physical casualties tended to reflect the depletion of morale. Thirteen French regiments had lost over half their men. Those suicidal cavalry charges brought the casualties of the Thirteenth Hussars to over 87 percent. Also, the three regiments of *turcos* lost 3,588 out of 5,040—over 71 percent.[32] Those who went into battle with the greatest elan had the most fighting spirit to lose.

Notwithstanding their victory, the Prussians had been too battered to get enough cavalry forward to pursue this success. The French slipped away into the darkness, but their forces lost much of their organization before leaving the field. The first of the retreating men reached Lunéville, near Nancy, the next day, August 7. From there, MacMahon's forces began clambering aboard some of the last trains to Metz or to Châlons.[33]

Lorraine: Spicheren and the Course of War

While the fighting created these lopsided outcomes in Alsace, French positions to the west along the border of Lorraine had crumbled as well.[34] Helmuth von Moltke had planned to swing the three great German armies into Alsace and Lorraine like a huge gate. The First

---

31   Henri Bonnal, *Frœschwiller* (Paris: Chapelot, 1899); Hermann Kunz, *Schlacht von Wörth* (Berlin: Luckhardt, 1891); René Tournès, *De Gunstett au Niederwald* (Paris: H. Charles-Lavauzelle, 1907).

32   Henderson, *Wœrth*, 41.

33   On MacMahon's withdrawal, see De Chalus, *Wissembourg Foeschwiller*, 161–92; Duquet, *Froeschwiller, Châlons, Sedan*, 132–43.

34   For developments in Lorraine, see Dick De Lornay, *Français & Allemands: Histoire anecdotique de la guerre de 1870–1871*, vol. 5, *L'investissement de Metz* (Garnier frères: Paris, 1891); Georg von Widdern, *Kritische Tage. I. Teil* (Berlin: Eisenschmidt, 1897); Philipp Elliot-Wright, *Gravelotte-St-Privat 1870* (London: Osprey Publishing, 1993).

Army of old General Karl von Steinmetz was to be designated as the essentially stationary hinge of this operation, while Prince Friedrich Karl's Second Army crossed the border to the east, and the Third, under Crown Prince Friedrich Wilhelm, crossed further over, through Alsace. However, that irritating French presence at Saarbrücken goaded Steinmetz, who remembered the occupations under Napoleon in his youth.

On the same day as Wissembourg, Steinmetz moved his army from the Rhine though the lower Moselle and knocked the French back from Saarbrücken.[35] The French scurrying back across the border carried with them whatever reality remained of Napoleon III's dreams of an easy invasion of Germany.

With much of Marshal François Achille Bazaine's aspirationally named Armée du Rhin spreading back toward Metz, General Frossard rallied his retreating force at the frontier. On the night of August 5, they lit watchfires on the heights overlooking the town, even as they regrouped on the border, and hoped to by time for the rest of the French Army to come forward.

Early the next morning—the same day as Wœrth—Steinmetz completely disregarded the plans and decided to press his advantage by crossing into France from Saarbrücken. In the face of this, Frossard, the old artillerist, formed his 27,000 men with ninety guns along the very defensible heights between Spicheren and Forbach. Thinking he faced only a retreating rearguard, the Germans launched a direct assault by two brigades.[36]

Thanks to the *chassepot*, Frossard's outnumbered men held fast against the Prussian assault, even as more arrived and moved against their flanks. As the day wore on, some elements of the German Second Army managed to get through the jammed roads to join the battle.[37] Yet, by 1 p.m., the French had stopped the Prussians cold,

---

35 For developments in Lorraine, see De Lornay, *Français & Allemands*; Widdern, *Kritische Tage*; Elliot-Wright, *Gravelotte-St-Privat 1870*.

36 M. Weil, *La bataille de Spicheren envisagée au point de vue stratégique*, trans. M. Weil (Paris: Ch. Tanera, 1872); and *La Journée du 6 août 1870*; but also George F. R. Henderson, *The Battle of Spicheren*; and Lieutenant-Colonel Maistre, *Spicheren (6 Août 1870)*, with preface by M. le General H. Langlois (Paris and Nancy: Berger-Levrault, 1908).

37 Moltke, *The Franco-German War of 1870–71*, vol. 1, 25–34.

while the artillery from the Krupp works once more thwarted any hopes for a French counterattack. Another Prussian attempt in late afternoon ended by being driven back down the slopes, some almost to the border.[38]

Beyond the neat margins of military reports, civilians struggled with the advent of war. As leaden pests buzzed nearby, individually or in swarms, women gathered their children and rushed them into the woods to find the shaded comfort in its lower, more sheltered hollows. Those men not swept up by the armies felt the pinch of lost wages, but tended to remain with their families to provide what feeble protection and help they could. Moreover, their employers and managers hesitated to send men beneath the earth to retrieve what could no longer be predictably moved. The insanities of war descended from the board rooms in the tallest buildings of Paris and Berlin to the depths of the deepest mineshafts in the Saar.

Near the end of the day, more Germans untangled themselves from the traffic jam of the roads and entered the battle. The skillful working of the artillery and well-practiced infantry movements gained the heights and turned the French flank. Meanwhile, rumors that the Prussians had gotten cavalry behind them spread along the French line. By the time reinforcements had come up, they found themselves overwhelmed by their fleeing comrades.[39] Steinmetz had lost about a tenth of the 37,000 he managed to bring into the fight, while Frossard, though largely on the defensive, had lost more, about 4,100.

When darkness fell, Frossard managed to slip away toward the Moselle. Meanwhile, at Saint-Avold, Napoleon III received word that most of two German armies now stood between Bazaine's army and the frontier. Moreover, the Prussians were closing in on that town. The emperor then exercised his overall command by ordering Bazaine's entire army to fall back to Châlons, in hopes that it could combine there with the forces being driven from Alsace and Lorraine.

In the course of their unexpectedly rapid retreat, the armies of Bazaine and MacMahon left thousands of their comrades engulfed and besieged by the general rapid advance of the Prussians. On August 8, the

---

38   Lieutenant-Colonel Hucher, *Troisième conférence d'histoire: 1870. Spicheren* (Paris: Charles-Lavauzelle & Cie, 1921), 30–9, 54–60.
39   Werstein, *The Franco-Prussian War*, 98–100.

Germans bottled several thousand French soldiers into the old citadel at Bitche. The next day, the advance reached Phalsbourg to the northwest of Strasbourg.[40]

On August 9, two days after the emperor had ordered the withdrawal, Frossard's retreating troops reached Lemud and collapsed for the night. The next day, French troops skirmished with Prussians at Grostenquin, south of Saint-Avold. Within hours, hussars encountered Germans at Boulay (Boulay-Moselle) to the north of Saint-Avold.

The last of the reinforcements on their way to Bazaine encountered the vanguard of the relentless German advance through Alsace. Canrobert's corps reached Frouard near Nancy from Châlons on August 12. When they tried to continue north to Metz, they encountered Prussians at Pont-à-Mousson. The French infantry chased them off, however, and pushed through to the city. While they might have counted themselves lucky, a large Confederation force returned shortly after and closed that crucial rail link to Metz. As to the reinforcements from Châlons, some of Canrobert's cavalry, artillery, and service units who had to turn back to Châlons might well have counted themselves more fortunate than those who got through.

The same day Canrobert and his infantry reached Metz, Bazaine tried to organize his massive army for a desperate and chaotic hike back east along the single road to Verdun. It would later be said that the general had been clearly out of his depth, but systemic problems with the military ensured him of plenty of company in this. The lethargic Napoleon III claimed sickness, likely complicated by an entirely appropriate bout of depression. Interestingly, Bazaine and the high command realized that Canrobert had seniority and offered to place him in charge of the entire army as soon as he got there. For his part, though, Canrobert had enough experience and sense to see the problems in their frightening totality, and turned down the offer, preferring the role of Bazaine's obedient subordinate.

Meanwhile, the human refuse from these disasters began to make itself a factor, at both Châlons and Metz. In the first engagements of the war, the French forces in Alsace had "lost without a fight a portion of its equipment, and almost all its baggage." The Africans among

---

40   Bitche held out from August 8, 1870, to March 26, 1871; Phalsbourg from August 9 to December 12, 1870.

them—"veterans covered with renown"—had stubbornly contested the Germans at Wœrth, but the effect of the Prussian artillery that had driven them from the field left them "with dissatisfied and mutinous feelings." One observer understated the issue with the army, noting simply that "its solidity was not such as might have been desired." Generals complained about their superiors and their underlings, and the emperor grumbled that he had been "deceived as to the capacity of the War Office for sending him reinforcements."[41] The decision of Napoleon III to concentrated the retreating forces from Alsace with those from Lorraine at Châlons seemed reasonable, but, on another level, it threatened to consolidate problems.

Developments at the front had an immediate political impact at home. Mass protest rallies took place in Paris, with radical calls for the arming of the people, a *levée en masse*. On August 7, the problem of public confidence forced a major cabinet reshuffle. The new government also authorized the raising of two new corps at Châlons and Paris, respectively under generals Louis Trochu and Joseph Vinoy.

Two days later, as the news percolated through the capital, crowds gathered in protest. There Paul Déroulède encountered "about two or three thousand protesters" in the Place de la Concorde clamoring for the government to arm the people. Déroulède, who called these civilians "mutineers," advised them "to go ask for weapons where they would be given, that is, at recruiting office." Less than amused, the crowd seized him with the intention of tossing him into the Seine.[42]

Europe had not hosted a prolonged war among major powers for nearly sixty years, and the character of the Napoleonic campaigns had spread the carnage and damage over a larger area. In part, civil and military officials on both sides presented themselves as practical gentlemen, men who advocated the only kind of peace possible in this world. They said they believed that the only means to such a desirable end required suffering and inflicting suffering with the *chassepot* and the Dreyse on others who had nothing to do with their grievances, real or pretended.

41   Edmund Ollier, *Cassell's History of the War between France and Germany 1870–1871*, 2 vols. (London, Paris, and New York: Cassell, Petter, and Galpin, 1871), vol. 1, 17.

42   Paul Déroulède, *1870, feuilles de route: Des bois de Verrières à la forteresse de Breslau* (Paris: Librairie Felix Juven, 1907), 55.

In mass societies, this translated the brutalities of the past into the modern, civilized imperatives of militarism. Equally regrettably, the first enemy against which war had to be waged was the people of one's own nation who failed to follow this logic. Paradoxically, as elites waged increasingly desperate war against each other, they naturally strove to enlist people from beyond the nation into their conflict, even that part of it waged against their own countrymen.

The scale of modern war though tended mightily to concentrate the mind. The casualties at Wœrth or Spicheren bear comparison to those of Shiloh, the great battle eight years before in the Civil War in the United States, but it had taken the Americans a year to reach that level of intensity, while it had taken the Franco-Prussian conflict only a few days. The violence in America had become so intense that it actually transformed the war goals of the Union. Of course, the crowned and shoulder-strapped could not face the fact that the course they chose ran a similar risk. Better to blame it on agitators, as did Marshal LeBoeuf, who claimed that, before going into action, he had identified "sixty agents of the Socialist International in the army."[43]

La Boeuf's men were restive owing not to the questionable influence of dubious radicals but because of what faced them down the road. What the officers ordered assured a proliferation of malcontents in uniform.

---

43   Quoted in Wawro, *The Franco-Prussian War*, 90.

5

This High Road to Verdun: Turning Points in Lorraine

The peasants along the Vionville road, hoping to avoid the midday heat, started work early on Tuesday, August 16. The presence of the French Army over the previous few weeks had introduced unavoidable and unwanted changes in seasonal habits. They had surely heard about the clashes with the Prussians farther east, and rumors winged reports of very unfavorable outcomes for the army, but rumor remained no more than that. Early that morning, heads popped up in the fields, as two regiments of cavalry thundered west along the road. Those with a good view saw that the horsemen were escorting a carriage, and those with the best view might have even spied the imperial personages of the Emperor Napoleon III and his son, the fourteen-year-old prince imperial. Not a good sign in itself and, later, other troops turned up along the road wearing those characteristic and intimidating spiked helmets. Not long after, a visitor wrote that "this high road to Verdun has indeed become famous, for along it Napoleon and his body-guard had passed, narrowly escaping capture from the ever-wakeful Uhlan."[1]

Nothing in those early days threatened to break the run of German triumphs. In short order, the massive Armée du Rhin had fallen back

1   Quintin Barry, *Franco-Prussian War 1870–1871. Volume 1: The Campaign of Sedan. Helmuth von Moltke and the Overthrow of the Second Empire* (Warwick UK: Helion and Company, 2011); Appleton, *Reminiscences of a Visit to the Battle Fields*, 66.

into Lorraine and found itself fighting desperately for its very survival. A battle larger than Waterloo followed, with participants moving with fixed bayonets over shell-torn open ground against entrenched troops defended by machine guns. Being bogged down and surrounded at Metz, they would await their rescue by a new Armée de Châlons. The massive numbers of the dead, injured and displaced persons created an unanticipated immediate crisis for the wider society.

Borny-Colombey to Mars-la-Tour

The weekend of August 13–14 deluged the French high command with terrible news. Prussian patrols turned up north of Metz, around Thionville, and the Germans had taken Frouard and Pont-à-Mousson, cutting the rail link back to Paris. The speed of the Prussian movements had already isolated French garrisons at Bitche and Phalsbourg. On Sunday, they cut the telegraph links through Nancy, and demanded a ransom from the city. Some 13,000 Germans continued west from Nancy, pinning a French force of about 2,400 in Toul. Meanwhile, General August von Werder's 40,000 troops from Baden and Württemberg backed 17,000 French into well-fortified Strasbourg, an old city of 86,000 people. The Germans began a bombardment of the city a week later, even after the Bishop of Strasbourg and the local government offered to pay 100,000 francs for every day without shelling.

In Lorraine, Marshal Bazaine and his officers faced an endless and inglorious problem trying to manage the unmanageably massive numbers crowding not only onto the main route to Verdun, but also on the adjacent back roads and village lanes. Tens of thousands churned up roads that would ordinarily been bearing no more than dozens of individuals, horses and vehicles. It took immense amounts of time and effort to cover even relatively short distances.

On Sunday, part of General Karl von Steinmetz's army encountered the French just southeast of Metz, at Borny-Colombey. Despite orders to avoid attacking precipitously, Steinmetz did just that, throwing nearly 68,000 men against what he thought was a small rearguard resistance. In fact, the bulk of Bazaine's army engaged the Germans and exacted a heavy toll on them. Bazaine himself gained a reputation as "the Lion of Borny" for rushing nearly 84,000 into action. Thousands fell on both sides, accomplishing seemingly little.[2] However, it delayed Bazaine's effort to get his forces on the road to Verdun for a critical twelve hours.

A closer look at the French Army reveals a growing discontent with Bazaine and his circle. As thousands of Prussians moved on his position, the captain of a company without orders to join a general French withdrawal ordered his men to pull back. His superior rode up, insisting that they remain, but the captain said, "I do not want to go kill one hundred and fifty men against five thousand Prussians. Such a foolishness is not my duty." Turning to his men, he said they should not bleed "without France or anyone profiting by your blood. You are given an absurd mission," adding, "I will not drive you like a flock of sheep, to the slaughterhouse."[3]

The duties of engineer and staff officer Captain Louis Nathaniel Rossel did not require his service at the front, but he regularly fell in to fight with *francs-tireurs*. Tall, lean, and robust, the bespectacled bohemian retained great affection for the arts as well as science, and gained some prestige for an essay on the construction of railroad bridges. He also had his own connections at Metz, through Jean Macé, the local promoter of public education. He spoke a sober, choppy, caustic language, though he was capable of poetic and spiritual digressions. His biographer described him as a man of talent who wound up in the army, though "no career was less suited to his nature." Military hype aside, his experience at Borny began his "disaffection with the clique."[4]

Nor was Rossel alone. That Sunday, Napoleon III attended Mass at the ancient cathedral of Metz. The sort of crowds that used to turn up to cheer him had shrunk with the prospects of victory. Going to war had left him weaker and exhausted. He leaned on the arm of one of his

2   Moltke, *The Franco-German War of 1870–71*, vol. 1, 40–7; Georges Hardoin, *Français et Allemands: histoire anecdotique de la guerre de 1870–1871. L'investissement de Metz, la journée des Dupes, Servigny, Noisseville, Flanville, Nouilly, Coincy, Blocus de Metz, Peltre, Mercy-le-Haut, Ladonchamps, la capitulation* (Paris: Garnier frères, 1891); Widdern, *Kritische Tage. I. Teil. Die Initiative und die gegenseitige Unterstuetzung in der deutschen Heeres- und Truppenfuerung*, vol. 1, *Die I. Armee bei Colombey-Nouilly am 13. u. 14. August 1870* (Berlin: R. Eisenschmidt, 1897).

3   Félicien Champsaur, *Metz en 1870* (Paris: Mignot, 1916), 103–4.

4   E. Gerspach, *Le colonel Rossel, sa vie et ses travaux, son rôle pendant la guerre et la Commune, son procès: Études sur la Commune* (Paris: E. Dentu, Librairie-Éditeur, 1873), 9, 10, 11, 41, 4; William P. Fetridge, *The Rise and Fall of the Paris Commune in 1871* (New York: Harper & Brothers, 1871), 2041.

generals. At one point, a boy shouted "Vive l'Empereur!" but one of the brass waved him to silence.[5]

The next day brought reports that Prussian patrols had begun turning up farther west, at places like Longeville-lès-Metz and Mars-la-Tour, threatening the road between Bazaine's army and Verdun. So it was that, early in the morning of Tuesday, August 16, the Emperor Napoleon III and his son dashed through an area more contested than they had realized. Perhaps to show himself his uncle's nephew, as the emperor bade farewell to Bazaine and his staff, he suggested that they get the army on the road to Verdun as quickly as possible. Then the royals headed off in that direction themselves with an escort of heavy cavalry.

Prussian patrols had already tentatively probed the road. The First Hanoverian Dragoons happened upon the head of Bazaine's column on its way west from Metz, hoping to reach a crossing of the Meuse and possibly converge with reinforcements coming up from their well-fortified base at Verdun. Helmuth von Moltke pressed Prince Friedrich Karl to send the 30,000 men immediately available to turn the column near Vionville, east of Mars-la-Tour. As both sides rushed reinforcements to the battle, the peasants at work along the road scurried off to their homes or sought whatever cover they could find.

Eventually, though, fully 80,000 soldiers of the German Confederation went into action around Mars-la-Tour against 127,000, the bulk of Bazaine's army. By early afternoon, the Prussians had become desperate enough to send 800 horsemen to silence the guns. They angled through a slight depression on the field until they were a mere kilometer from their target, after which they stormed into view, breaking the French lines and scattering the infantry, preventing the French horsemen from mounting a counterattack. Although the "Death Ride" would be often described as the last successful cavalry charge in Europe, it left half the participants as casualties, including Herbert von Bismarck, the chancellor's son. Its apparent success also had the unfortunate effect of encouraging the repetition of such romantic ventures long after the technology had doomed them. Reported German losses ran to 15,780, while the French ran to 17,007. These totaled nearly 32,787. The Germans had lost

---

5   See the account of a newspaperman in *L'Armée du Rhin et le blocus de Metz 1870 par un collaborateur du journal L'Avenir* (Luxembourg, J. Joris, 187?), 59.

roughly a fifth of their entire force, "a proportion unequalled in modern European warfare."[6]

Soldiers at Mars-la-Tour fought so desperately because they could actually see the stakes in front of them. Germans understood that victory there would likely bottle up the largest French army in the field and the French knew that German success in cutting Bazaine's army off from Paris would virtually doom their entire war effort. In its aftermath, skirmishing took place elsewhere, as at Rezonville en Moselle, only a few miles west of the village of Gravelotte.

That said—and despite the hype of the high command about itself—the fighting left the French forces drained and deeply demoralized. Paul Déroulède complained that soldiers tended to "outrage at random and without reason any officer superior met in isolation. Mutinies followed mutinies." In the end, he grumbled, the beleaguered officers found it "necessary to have recourse to the deplorable system of collective punishment, which restored order, but provoked general discontent."[7] A war crime if imposed on the enemy or on civilians, the practice of "collective punishment" on one's own soldiery reflects the desperation of the French authorities about their control over the army.

Fortunately for the emperor and his entourage, they had left most of these numbers behind them, though they had likely been within earshot of the guns of Mars-la-Tour. Around 1 p.m., they reached Verdun, and there boarded the next train to Châlons on Wednesday morning.

Gravelotte-Saint Privat

As the sun rose on Thursday, August 18, over 300,000 soldiers groped their way to cover in the fields north of the Moselle river just west of Metz. Operating on their own terrain, the French clambered onto wonderful ground of their own choosing. With the exception of the far right, on the northern end of the line, where the troops had lost track of their tools, the French had dug a series of rifle pits and trenches, extending from the woods along the Moselle north to the area around Saint

---

6   Moltke, *The Franco-German War of 1870–71*, vol. 1, 47–66; Werstein, *The Franco-Prussian War*, 147–9. Also see Forbes, *My Experiences of the War*, vol. 1, 142–3.

7   Déroulède, *1870*, 71, 82–3.

Privat. The French positions generally ran south along the crest of the Rozérieulles plateau to Amanvillers, continuing to Saint-Hubert. Farther south, their position became more formidable physically, as the slopes became steeper, more rugged, and wooded.[8]

The Prussians moved toward them blindly from the west.[9] Their cavalry was not rested enough for scouting, and Prince Friedrich Karl's Second Army angled northeast from Mars-la-Tour to intercept the rear of the presumably French line of retreat. Since the French had not taken that course, the prince's route wound up in an angular approach across a well-positioned French Army. By mid-morning, the French III Corps reported a large German force moving across its front. Around 10 a.m., the Second Army saw French tents on the Amanvillers ridge.

The advance overran some forward positions, one in the church at Gravelotte. Locals recalled that the defenders had "converted it into a small fortress." When they refused to surrender, the Germans wiped them out on the spot, leaving the floor of the building "crowded with dying men, the slain lying scattered in heaps waiting to be carted away."[10]

Ahead of them, General Paul de Ladmirault's IV Corps, running from Jerusalem Farm south through Amanvillers and abutting III Corps to the south, waited with as much confidence as ludicrous red trousers allowed. However, their trenches and rifle pits had dropped those lovely scarlet targets below the line of sight, and their comrades in the artillery wheeled cumbersome *mitrailleuses* into place for use against any who might move across the open slopes before them.

By 10:30, Moltke realized the Germans faced an entrenched position, but assumed that the French force at Amanvillers represented the northern flank of Bazaine's army rather than its strongly fortified center. The IX Korps prepared a frontal assault, with the X and III Korps moving up

---

8 For a concise view of the battlefield, see *Bataille de Rezonville (Gravelotte), 16 août 1870. Campagne de Metz: récit de la bataille, explication du panorama, reproduction totale du panorama développé, portraits de MM. Detaille et de Neuville* (Paris: [Société du] Panorama national [portraits par Henri Thiriat], 1887); and Elliot-Wright, *Gravelotte-St-Privat 1870*.

9 In addition to the sources cited elsewhere, on this battle see H. Bonnal, *L'esprit de la guerre moderne: Le manœuvre de Saint-Privat 18 juillet–18 aout 1870*, 2 vols. (Paris: Librairie R. chapelot et Ce., 1906), vol. 2, 263–348 until 4:30 in the evening, and 349–466 for after 4:30 p.m.; and Lacroix, *Les étapes d'un évadé: Souvenirs d'un ancien combattant de Gravelotte (Lacroix)* (Bourges: Tardy-Pigelet, 1907).

10 Appleton, *Reminiscences of a Visit to the Battle Fields*, 65–6.

as a reserve, while the Imperial Guard and XII Korps swung north to find the actual French flank. There, Canrobert's VI Corps held the gentler slopes around Saint Privat and Sainte-Marie-aux-Chênes, along with Roncourt south to the farm buildings of Jerusalem.

Around 11:45 a.m., Prince Friedrich Karl realized that he needed to reposition the IX Korps, but the wheels were already in motion. Within minutes, the attack began. The Prussians had moved nine batteries into a forward position, inadvertently under the direct fire of the French artillery. For an hour, shot and shell ripped at the Hessian gunners. When the Germans tried to withdraw the guns, around 1 p.m., French infantry rushed them and captured two of the guns, and only a desperate countercharge saved the remaining guns at a cost of 400 men.

Meanwhile, the Prussian infantry advanced over the open ground and up the slope toward the well-prepared French works protected by artillery. Long before the Germans got to where their Dreyse would be of any use to them, shells began crashing among them. Then they faced the *mitrailleuses*, which—unusually and largely by accident—found themselves in a position to support the French infantry. Those who still managed to move forward came into range of the *chassepot*—still long before they could shoot back: by early afternoon, the Prussians had got more guns into position, as the fighting brought all combatants to the edge of their destruction and dangled them helplessly there for hours.

To the south of this slaughter—on the German right—Moltke placed Steinmetz's First Army, to challenge and hold the French along the Mance Ravine near the Moselle, while the battle unfolded up the line over more favorable terrain. Around 1 p.m., he again cautioned Steinmetz not to open serious hostilities. Moreover, opposite them, they faced the same troops they had dislodged at Spicheren, General Charles Frossard's II Corps whose line extended from Saint-Hubert to Point-du-Jour over the Moselle.

Starting around 2 p.m.—and once more despite his orders—Steinmetz advanced toward the farm of Saint-Hubert. From their well-dug rifle pits, slightly below the ridge on the eastern slope of the Mance Ravine, the French stopped the Prussians in less than half an hour. By 3 p.m., though, the Prussians had perched 150 guns on the western brink of the ravine, blasting the forward defenders at Saint-Hubert back to the main line. Under the cover of those guns, the German onslaught rushed into the ruins of the farm. Steinmetz gleefully reported taking the heights, though they actually had no more than a precarious toehold where they remained pinned and pummeled by two French corps. More realistically, he had jammed a foot in the door which the French would pound mercilessly through the day.

At 4 p.m., ammunition shortages slowed the French barrage, and the old general sent the VII Korps forward to break the stalemate. After it, too, quickly bogged down, he sent the First Cavalry Division of his I Korps. It galloped down from just north of Gravelotte, thundering across the narrow causeway over the ravine in columns of four in hopes of deploying on the Rozérieulles plateau. They tried to provide cover to move four Prussian batteries there, but two of them got shot to pieces before they could unlimber, and only one of them was able to contribute what fire it could from the treeline. The other found some shelter among the troops pinned at Saint-Hubert, with only one of its cannons remaining in action as night fell.

At this point, Steinmetz convinced the king to throw the last of the remaining reserves of the army—elements of the VII Korps and VIII Korps—to expand the major breach he claimed to have made in the French line. At the king's side, Moltke knew better, but said nothing. Just after 6 p.m., they crossed over, rallying some of the remnants of the previously shattered units and moving up the eastern slope and through the woods into the open, where they were shredded. By 6:30 p.m., thousands of the surviving men and horses were scrambling back up the western slope, French shells crashing among them. Those remaining on the field clung to what cover they could find along the floor of the Mance Ravine. At 7 p.m., Steinmetz send the first of the newly arriving II Korps into the same place, suffering 1,300 casualties in a matter of minutes. To make matters worse, in the gloom of twilight, the unnerved defenders of Saint-Hubert exchanged friendly fire with other German units until they finally broke and abandoned their tenuous hold for the safety of the ravine. The one as-yet-unbloodied division managed to stabilize the line around 8 p.m.

Meanwhile, on the northern end of the line, the battle took a different course. Around 2 p.m., the Guards and the XII Korps found themselves at the foot of a long slope leading up to Saint Privat, allowing the latter to sweep around to the northeast, probing for the end of the French line near Sainte-Marie-aux-Chênes, a little village to the northwest occupied by 1,500 or so people. Around 3 p.m.—after nearly an hour of cannonading—the Prussians moved on Sainte-Marie-aux-Chênes, though the superior range of the *chassepot* frustrated the attackers until the French could withdraw in good order around 3:30 p.m.

Just before 5 p.m., Imperial Guards advanced against Ladmirault's IV Corps, losing nearly 2,500 Germans in about forty minutes. Their goal had been to hold those units in position, while Prince Augustus of Württemberg moved 18,000 men up an open slope for a mile against 8,000 French defenders of Saint Privat, where Canrobert had over sixty pieces of artillery in a very strong position behind the walls of the village and nearby farms. The Imperial Guards moved into position for the main assault, still carrying packs and equipment. Worse, Prince Augustus sent them in piecemeal. Before they covered half the distance, the *chassepot* cut to pieces the two Prussian batteries moved forward to support the infantry. The survivors found themselves pinned in a small depression in the field about 800 yards from the French line, under fire of the *chassepots* but short of the 700-yard range of their own Dreyse.

When Canrobert's troops had gotten to Saint Privat earlier in the day, they found that they did not have their entrenching tools. Although part of them had positions behind the thick walls of Saint Privat, they had taken a severe battering by around 5:15 p.m. In another hour, some of Prussian survivors still pinned in the field managed to get within 700 yards of the French, using the bodies of their fallen comrades for cover.

Just before 6:30 p.m., Prince Friedrich Karl managed to coordinate the efforts of the Guard, the XII Korps and the X Korps. Some of those Germans who had earlier been pinned in the field had crawled to within 600 yards of the distracted French defenders of the Jerusalem Farm. The prince also ordered an artillery concentration at Saint Privat to prevent the French from completely rolling back his men.

By this point, the rest of the Royal Saxons of the XII Korps had finished their march around the north and found the actual right flank of the French at Roncourt north of Saint Privat. Around 7 p.m., the hard-pressed French there gave way, falling back in good order to the Bois de Jaumount. However, the appearance of the Saxons just north of the burning ruins of Saint Privat inspired the Guards Brigade to rush remaining defenders there and around the farm at Jerusalem. Canrobert's force had been under fire for half an hour from artillery and infantry from several sides. Now, with the Saxon and Württemberg bayonets coming for them, they found themselves with neither fresh ammunition nor the reinforcements they had been requesting from the army's reserve.

General Charles-Denis Sauter Bourbaki, in charge of the reserves, failed to send any relief to Canrobert's exhausted men. The son of a Greek officer killed in that country's struggle for independence, he had graduated from the prestigious École spéciale militaire de Saint-Cyr and became a well-connected figure in the imperial military, enjoying an overblown and unmerited reputation after coming back from Italy. Only around 8 p.m., when Canrobert's line broke, did some of Bourbaki's men moved forward to cover their retreat. Over the next two hours, darkness stifled the battle.

In the immediate aftermath of the battle, the French, who had held most of their positions, pulled back into Metz. Few of the victors left in possession of the field had the energy for celebrating. "The wearied and powder-grimed Germans threw themselves down on the field," wrote one journalist, "and slept among the dead who littered it." Even from the heights of the social pyramid, King Wilhelm muttered as he looked out over the field, "War is a foul thing."[11]

The battle engaged over 300,000 soldiers with 1,252 guns along an eight-mile front. The reported 188,332 Germans with 732 heavy cannons advanced on 112,800 French with 520 guns. Between the French *chassepots* and Krupp's artillery, the casualties for the single day's battle left both sides literally decimated. From just before noon until nightfall, the fighting cost the Prussians 5,238 dead, 14,430 wounded, and 493 missing to total 20,161, while the French lost 1,146 dead, 6,709 wounded, and 4,420 captured or missing to reach 12,275 casualties overall, or nearly 11 percent for the Germans and over 12 percent for the French. Some units left half or more of their number behind them. On the northern end of the line, near Saint Privat, the Guards had lost 8,000 out of 18,000 men, one battalion suffering losses of almost 62 percent. Their French opposite numbers lost over half of their defenders of the village. Moreover, Gravelotte actually represented a continuation of the fighting two days earlier at nearby Mars-le-Tours, which totaled 65,223 casualties.

Nevertheless, from this point, Bazaine's aspirationally named Armée du Rhin not only would fail to get that far east, but would never get as far west as Verdun. In its aftermath, the Prussians sealed off the city,

---

11   Forbes, *My Experiences of the War*, vol. 1, 191.

leaving the French there to wait for a relief column. Every hour brought more Germans into position between the French Army and Paris. Not without reason, the Prussians would later sing the "Siegesmarsch von Metz" which uses parts of "Die Wacht am Rhein."[12]

From a soldier's perspective, though, the experience along the Mance Ravine to the south of the line raised the question whether anybody could do much of anything against well-placed troops with long-range rifles and modern artillery. So, too, what happened on the northern end of the battle posed equally persuasive arguments about whether one could resist the onslaught of troops with such weapons at their disposal. Either way, it seemed clear who would be the primary loser.

The Course of the Army of Châlons

After Gravelotte, the fate of France would hang on a hastily organized Armée de Châlons. When Napoleon III arrived, fresh from Verdun, he readily overlooked the disastrous record of Patrice de MacMahon in Alsace to give him command of the new army. The planners believed that, once gathered, organized, and supplied, MacMahon's force of more than 120,000 men would rush east through Verdun and slash its way through the Prussian encirclement of Metz.

The core of this new army remained problematic. When he had passed through on his way to the front, Marshal Canrobert had, as was the custom, asked the Gardes mobiles at Châlons if they had any complaints. Breaking with custom, many actually began taunting him, one body raising the chant "Back to Paris!" Canrobert berated them as being unworthy of the name of Frenchmen, and reminded them that they were under orders. One source reported that he had two of the noisiest offenders shot out of hand, under the authority of a drumhead court-martial. An officer specified that the men behaved so badly "under the pretext of political grudges," implying they were less than fond of the imperial authority.[13]

The railroad had quickly brought up from the capital thousands of

---

12   For a triumphalist German account, see Carl Bleibreu, *Gravelotte: Die Kaempfe um Metz* (Stuttgart: Verlag von Carl Krabbe, 1898),

13   Ollier, *Cassell's History of the War*, vol. 1, 40; Déroulède, *1870*, 71, 82–3.

unenthusiastic new recruits, who had their own objections to the military project. *Le petit journal* described them as "the most mutinous of the volunteers." An American journalist agreed that the noisiest of the malcontents as Parisians.[14] Creating a viable army of such recruits would have challenged the most inspiring generalship and even an officer corps deeply associated with and trusted by the soldiery.

What assembled at Châlons had few such officers and no such generals. In fact, MacMahon's new Armée de Châlons would be fully "new" only in the most bureaucratic sense. One observer thought it "very much superior in number" to the Prussians, but wanting in morale and courage.[15] In many cases, though, this problem did not reflect the nervousness of newcomers to the battlefield, because their solid experience of how recklessly the army and their officers squandered their own lives and health.

Many, however, were not new recruits but soldiers who had already tasted defeat in Alsace. Of the 38,500 men who had been with MacMahon in Alsace, only 16,000 had straggled back into Châlons, with more trickling in, all to be added to this "new" army of rescue.[16] Then, too, the army scooped up an indeterminate number of escapees from the trapped army at Metz.

Success required a workable plan of action. Knowing the state of these forces, MacMahon wanted to fall back to a defensive position behind the walls of Paris. However, those more familiar with the political situation in the capital warned that the appearance of a defeated army could invite revolt. In the end, they agreed to leave the XIII Corps to cover Paris while taking the rest to the relief of Bazaine's army.

Napoleon III, MacMahon, and the other decision makers supposed that the siege of Metz had so strained the German forces that the French would be able to move east with little initial opposition. Moltke made an unsuccessful effort to take Verdun on August 24, and did not find it worth the cost of another. The French strategists knew that their best chance meant moving as quickly and unrelentingly as possible.

On August 25, the French only made it only about halfway from

14   Mile Gaboriau, "Route de Berlin: Les Volontaires de 92," *Le petit journal*, September 4, 1870, 2; Werstein, *The Franco-Prussian War*, 166–7.

15   Ollier, *Cassell's History of the War*, vol. 1, 88.

16   Duquet, *Froeschwiller, Châlons, Sedan*, 164–90.

Châlons to Verdun before encountering Germans at Sivry-sur-Ante and Passavant (Passavant-en-Argonne).[17] Rather than pushing forward, though, MacMahon decided to outflank the Germans by moving north. The Prussians were quite content to pursue them and, two days later, attacked the French at Buzancy, and, after another two days, at the nearby Bois-des-Dames.

On Tuesday, August 30, the Prussian pursuit struck French troops north of Buzancy and Bois-des-Dames. As the fighting continued, more of the Confederation Army filed off the roads from the south into battle lines around the village of Beaumont (Beaumont-en-Argonne). In the end, the French withdrew ten kilometers north, to Mouzon, a crossing of the Meuse. Sweeping up the local garrisons, MacMahon's retreat had gathered a force of nearly 140,000.

Nevertheless, the French command had disastrously wedged itself between the Meuse and the Belgian border. The newly organized German Fourth Army crossed the Meuse to block any French attempt to turn back toward Metz, while Crown Prince Friedrich Wilhelm's Third Army moved quickly up the west side of the river, to prevent a French recrossing.[18] Meanwhile, elements of the neutral Belgian Army formed just over the border, ready to disarm and take into custody any combatants that strayed into their country.

By August 31, the Fourth Army plundered Raucourt (Raucourt-et-Flaba), building campfires with the furniture, as the noncombatants huddled in terror. An advance company of Bavarian Jaeger crossed into adjacent Bazeilles. It hurried through nerve-wracking fire to cover about sixty meters over the railway viaduct above the river before continuing into the quiet weaving village of 2,048 souls only a few miles south of Sedan. Realizing that the loss of Bazeilles would also close off a major crossing of the Meuse and any immediate prospect of withdrawing from Sedan, the French sent *troupes de marine* to clear out the Bavarians, who retreated after losing 142 men, including their commander. As the survivors retreated, German engineers placed pontoon bridges alongside the viaduct in preparation for their return.

West of Sedan, King Wilhelm himself urged the XI Korps north over

---

17   For these movements, see particularly ibid.
18   Schultze-Klosterselde, *Weissenburg, Wœrth, Sedan, Paris*, 59–67.

the loop in the Meuse river to cut the rail link from Sedan to Mézières. They siezed the existing bridge and added pontoons. Moltke chortled, "Now we have them in a mousetrap." A Württemberg division took the next crossing west near Flize, where they clashed with elements of General Joseph Vinoy's corps, operating independently of MacMahon.

German commanders fretting about a possible linkup between MacMahon at Sedan and Vinoy's forces deprived many of their men of well-earned sleep. Starting around 3 a.m., Moltke and his staff roused their groggy troops and goaded them across the river. Most had gotten into position by 7 a.m. on Thursday, September 1, but would have little time to make up for their lost sleep. Even as they were crossing, shooting resumed to their southeast, as the Bavarians reentered Bazeilles in the predawn hours.[19]

At sunrise on Thursday, the rattle of firearms became more insistent and the thunder of artillery began to roll over the hills toward them with dreary regularity. For the gentlemen officers—French, German, or Belgian—sipping their morning coffee, what was taking place over those hills had to do with national institutions or dynastic concerns. Yet the failure to look beyond dynastic considerations to the experience of the people rendered tenuous their grasp of what would happen at Sedan.

The Human Harvest

The burden of war always falls heaviest on those with no power to avoid it. A story from the war in Lorraine romanticizes the tragedy. Before the war, a German student stayed in a village to learn French and fell in love with a maid. When war broke out, he went home and returned a lieutenant with the Prussian Army. She had organized military resistance and, as "the Maid of Alsace," tormented the occupation troops. His troops captured her and he dutifully signed the order authorizing her execution as a *franc-tireur*. "On seeing her lover, just before her execution," went

---

19   In addition to previously cited general histories, see N. Hardoin, *Français et allemands. Histoire anecdotique de la guerre de 1870–1871. Niederbronn — Wissembourg — Froeschwiller — Châlons — Reims — Buzancy — Beaumont — Mouzon — Bazeilles — Sedan* (Garnier frères, 1888). Pierre Milza, *Napoléon III* (Pierre Milza, Perrin edn, 2004); W. J. Lowe, *The Nest in the Altar or Reminiscences of the Franco-Prussian War of 1870*, (London: Chapter Two, 1999).

the story, "she discovered herself to him when it was too late to save her life." Just as the firing squad leveled its weapons, he rushed to her side "and the lovers lay on the ground in the last embrace of death."[20]

Modern war produced unanticipated numbers of dead, wounded, and captive. The German Confederation took unprecedented numbers of prisoners. One observed

> the famous *chasseurs d'Afrique* sitting in melancholy postures in their saddles, the dark-skinned Zouaves, Turcos and Zephyrs, chattering like parrots. They were troops from distant regions of the world whose small figures, with their torn stockings and bare feet, made them seem alien to civilization; they looked as if, instead of being trained soldiers, they belonged in an exotic "foreigner show."[21]

The course of the war left the Prussians many more of those prisoners than they knew how to handle, and they came in such numbers as to frankly make the fear of revolt greater than concerns about clean water or hygiene. Most immediately, they would throw together the most minimal shelters using planks to provide some protection from the rain in courtyards under the mouths of cannons that "left no illusions to our men on the means available to repress any mutiny." The Prussian high command removed the French prisoners by the thousands to camps across the German states, but always feared the possibility of mass revolt, as had been rumored at Carthaus in October, and there were later rumors of a Christmas Eve conspiracy among the French prisoners at Cologne, Koblenz, and Mainz.[22]

The most immediate impact remained on the field of battle, and most of the villages and farmland through which the war had passed showed the scars of the fighting for years. In places such as Beaumont, severe

---

20 Le Mesurier, *Feeding of Fighting Armies*, vol. 1, 266–7.

21 Stieber, *The Chancellor's Spy*, 176. Each officer got to take one servant with them. Ibid., 178.

22 La France moderne, *De Wissembourg à Ingolstadt (1870–1871)*. Alferd Quesnay de Beaurepaire, *Souvenirs d'un capitaine prisonnier de guerre en Bavière* (Paris: Librairie de Firmin-Didot et Cie, 1891), 183; Ollier, *Cassell's History of the War*, vol. 1, 423; H. Allnutt, *Historical Diary of the War between France and Germany, 1870–1* (London: Estates Gazette Office, 1872), 248. See also Yoann Cipolla-Ballati, "Les captifs oubliés de 1870–1871: Expériences et mémoires des soldats français en Allemagne," MA thesis, Université de Bourgogne, 2016–17.

fighting settled for hours over the town. At Gravelotte and Saint Privat, few of those who lived around such intense fighting had cellars to shelter themselves from the heavy fire and the shelling. Even worse, the positions around Metz stalled for weeks over the city and the villages and hamlets of the surrounding countryside.

Communities that numbered in the hundreds or the dozens suddenly had several hundred thousand more mouths to feed, and an avaricious demand for human and animal labor, voluntary or not. They also had to clear miles of equipment and baggage. A reporter traveled over it for five miles without being able to find usable water for his horse, which was then stolen. "Within a space of about six miles in length by four in depth there was not a space so large as Piccadilly Circus that did not bear some token that one or more men had fallen upon it." It took three days to retrieve what wounded they could and would help, and a week to bury those they could not.[23]

The armies took, lost and retook one chateau, leaving the wounded of both armies lying around about it. French shelling set fire to the surrounding houses in the evening after the battle. Many perished as the flames spread, leaving their charred remains in the ruins. The Prussians used the chateau as a hospital, but lost three-quarters of the 800 placed there.[24]

Where the battle raged around Gravelotte, it "suffered comparatively little from the fury of fray, for though infantry and cavalry frequently sought the protection of its walls, they quickly emerged with their bayonets fixed or their swords drawn upon the enemy, but only to perish, alas! in their desperate attempt."[25] In an otherwise deserted house, an English journalist

> found a room which was tenanted only by two sorely wounded men and an hospital attendant. All the other houses were packed full of wounded, and one was in luck in getting the use of a chair, and of the

---

23   Forbes, *My Experiences of the War*, vol. 1, 207, 216; Werstein, *The Franco-Prussian War*, 102–11. For a fictional depiction, see Charles Deslys, *Le blessé de Gravelotte: Suivi d'autres nouvelles*, 2nd edn (Paris: Librairie Blériot, 1900).

24   Appleton, *Reminiscences of a Visit to the Battle Fields*, 64–5.

25   In addition to Forbes, *My Experiences of the War*, see, for the following account of conditions west of Metz, Appleton, *Reminiscences of a Visit to the Battle Fields*, 65, 60, 61, 62–3, 83.

common frying-pan in which to cook a piece of bacon bought from a market tender.

Around bitterly contested Saint Privat, Lewis Appleton, something of an early battlefield tourist, found that in "every available spot, lie the slain French soldiers, but very few wooden crosses are to be seen 'in memoriam,' except where officers lie together." Little children followed him to offer "a great variety of relics of the strife." The women had treated the wounded indiscriminately. A middle-aged woman living in the ruins of a cottage offered him "some needle-guns and chassepots" as souvenirs, but he hoped not to add to his baggage, "left her a mite and bade her adieu."

The war left each field around Amanvillers "an unfenced cemetery, full of graves." Eight months after the battle, Appleton met the mother, widow, and sister of a young Saxon, roaming about with a group of gravediggers looking for the body. Near Vernéville, they unearthed half a dozen sites, including a mass grave with two dozen bodies, stacked eight in a row. He saw the "gory and ghastly" faces of the first row of eight, but those below them, though buried for eight months, "appeared as if asleep, their faces unmarred, and tranquil in death, as though they had not gone." He stood, "a stranger amongst strangers from a far off land, watching the silent dead—if perchance their loved and lost one was with that heap of slain—once the beautiful and strong of their race, now the marred and mutilated, laid low by 'the curse of war.'"

Appleton also encountered a heart-wrenching scene. "a crowd of miserably-clad and half-famished children surrounded me, and burst out in a united but plaintive chorus," pleading for coins. He turned his horse over to their care and continued on. In the half hour he spent in the village, he "only saw one man, and he was on crutches." The half dozen women he met "looked stupefied" and told "a tale of suffering and woe that I venture to say, for a village population, has few parallels." He realized that "they have lost all—their sons and husbands, their bread-winners, their furniture; and, above all, their homes are destroyed."

Witnesses to these tragedies came from far afield. The soldiers of 1870–1 theoretically waged war under the new convention agreements of the International Society at Geneva. Clara Barton, the plebeian-born heroine of the American Civil War, had taken its lessons to Europe and helped promote and implement the standard of humane conduct there. The Germans seemed to understand the idea well, but the imperial

French had no awareness of it. According to the surgeon-in-chief of the French ambulances of Metz, they remained so ignorant of it that none of them ever even used the flag of the Red Cross to protect themselves in the conduct of their work.[26]

In Paris, English philanthropy combined with the regrettably recent American experience of battlefield medicine to give rise to an Anglo-American ambulance. Dr. Thomas W. Evans, the American dentist to the royal family—a pioneer in the use of nitrous oxide and amalgam fillings—had the connections and the resources to make it happen. He recruited its two surgeons, eight aides, a chemist, twenty-three stretcher bearers, teamsters, two squad captains, a bookkeeper, seventeen female nurses, a director of linen, a superintendent of the kitchen, and a superintendent of grounds (with an assistant).[27]

Although unacknowledged in Evans's quasi-official history of the ambulance, Hélène Bernois became a key figure in the project. We know what little we do about her because she spent part of one summer morning talking about her past with a young Yale student, a surgeon's son stranded by the war. Her mother had been a Louisiana mulatto taken to France and then back to slavery in America, and her father, "a bold, reckless, unprincipled ruffian," had been a seaman regularly smuggling goods along the Mexican coast for sale in Louisiana. Hélène and her mother became one of those items, sold for $1,800 to a prosperous gentleman, Felix James Francis Percy. While "still almost a child," she married a young Englishman, for whom her beauty "overbalanced so completely the common prejudices of blood and color." In the course of this, she gained her freedom, and had at least two children, before he abandoned her and "sailed to Europe, taking one child with him, and leaving a boy behind with the mother. She took the son to Paris, where a divorce would not be recognized, and he would remain legitimate.[28]

---

26 Mario, "Garibaldi in France," 609 f.

27 Dr. Thomas W. Evans, *History of the American Ambulance Established in Paris during the Siege of 1870–71* (London: Low, Low and Searle, 1873). See also Ralph Keeler, "With the American Ambulance Corps at Paris," *Lippincott's Magazine of Popular Literature and Science*, 12 (July 1873), 84–94; and Greg Seltzer, "The American Ambulance in Paris, 1870–1871," *Madison Historical Review*, 6 (2009), 1–21.

28 Louis Judson Swinburne, *Paris Sketches* (Albany: Joel Munsell, 1875), 96–7, 99–100. Louisiana records identify her owner as being from a large family with numerous slaves, including a fifteen-year-old girl showing up in the 1860 slave schedules. The Percy household was determined by a process of elimination using census records.

The attractive young black woman proved a resilient and resourceful dynamo. She "taught herself to write a fair hand and to play passably on the piano." She sometimes worked as "an emissary of the Emperor and a seamstress of the Princess Mathilde." Naturally social and entertaining, she functioned in a thoroughly bohemian milieu, with "politicians, third-rate artists, and newspaper reporters." Every afternoon, she and her little boy walked in the Bois de Boulogne, where she was recalled as speaking with those associated with the court, the archbishop, generals, artists and journalists. Most of the journalists visiting the ambulance at the front knew her.[29] Behind the scenes, she performed the day-to-day management of the funds, supplies, and resources necessary to keep the ambulance working.

One of the more thoughtful Germans had charge of a makeshift little hospital in a boxcar. Despite his Swiss citizenship, Friedrich Nietzsche had left a professorship teaching at Basel to volunteer for the Prussian Army. His military service had ended three years before after being thrown from a horse, but he returned to serve as a medical orderly. His reactionary and anti-Semitic sister, Frau Förster-Nietzsche, later said that the war had offered Nietzsche an epiphany about the importance of the will as he watched emaciated Prussian soldiers moving against the French.[30]

In truth, Nietzsche's war experience imploded the star of his genius into a black hole of despair from which he seems never to have really escaped. The fighting before Metz landed him in charge of half a dozen severely wounded men sharing a boxcar. In addition to their wounds, all of them suffered from dysentery and diphtheria. For three days and nights, he single-handedly treated them, having been left on his own by his superiors. Before relief came, Nietzsche himself succumbed to both diseases and never fully recovered from the physical and psychological drain of the war. Nietzsche returned to Basel to write his *Birth of Tragedy* and became a close friend of Paul Rée, a wounded Jewish veteran of the war.[31] After years of warnings against the weaknesses of compassion and empathy, the traumatized combat veteran ended his career by throwing his arms around the neck of a horse being beaten in the street and wept out his reason.

---

29   Swinburne, *Paris Sketches*, 100–1, 102–3.

30   Wather Kaufman, *Nietzsche: Philosopher, Psychologist, Antichrist* (Princeton: Princeton University Press, 1974), 26, 179.

31   Ibid., 26, 48.

Humanity and genius hardly served him better than any of that first generation that experienced mass industrial warfare.

The nineteenth century could well have screamed in anguish with Nietzsche that it had killed God, but its lords and masters actually knew better. In the summer of 1870, the Krupp works had begun to explode the old Napoleonic world in the most literal sense. Over the roughly six months of the Franco-Prussian War, the German Confederation fired 362,662 rounds. The intensity of its battles stood between Gettysburg, which can be measured in tens of thousands of shells, and Verdun, in which the numbers run to tens of millions. In a qualitative sense, though, the American war still relied heavily on smoothbore cannons, often with solid shot, though they also used exploding projectiles detonated by chemical fuses, a process the French took into the war with Prussia. However, the new Krupp guns used percussion shells at twice the rate of the most common French guns and had three times the accuracy.[32]

Most strikingly, even as the proportion of explosive power on the battlefield tended increasingly to be artillery rather than small arms, ordnance began accounting for a growing proportion of casualties, making their threat on the field loom ever larger and more overwhelming. The secularized religion of nationalism and national markets had manufactured its own gods, capable of an artificial bolt of lightning that seemingly came down on its targets from nowhere to blast mere mortals to pieces, leaving nothing behind but a faint reddish spray that dissipated almost immediately, to be followed by the fading memories of a real human being.

"What I relate," wrote Nietzsche, "is the history of the next two centuries . . . For some time now our whole European culture has been moving as toward a catastrophe."[33] Thus spoke the sickly philosopher in the boxcar.

---

32 William Barclay Parsons, *The American Engineers in France* (New York and London: D. Appleton and Company, 1920), 264; Mark Hughes, *The New Civil War Handbook: Facts and Photos for Readers of All Ages* (El Dorado Hills, CA: Savas Beatie, 2009).

33 Friedrich Nietzsche, *The Will to Power*, trans. Walter Kaufmann and R. J. Hollingdale (New York: Vintage Books, 1968), 4.

6

Blood and Irony:
Paris, Metz, and the Salvation of the War

For the friends of order, war and its dislocations threatened the hegemony of the established institutions that had guided their countries into the disaster. Perhaps with an eye to the Fenians, Britain's *Penny Illustrated Paper* warned France of the "parasites who are so destructive of all healthy national life; these bombastic memorialists, who mouth and rant till Europe is fain to stop its ears so that it cannot listen even to the voice of reason and humanity." It blamed opportunistic lawyers and would-be politicians for magnifying the influence of the "professional agitator" and those workers "fancying they have attained political knowledge by a perusal of two or three eleventh-rate books." The article particularly warned of "leagues, societies, and congresses."[1]

This kind of radicalism loomed larger as military prospects continued to fade. The tide of war and conquest that raised Paris to the pinnacle of Western civilization now lapped at the gates of the capital itself. Events had stranded the largest remaining army of France withered, by desertion as well as atrophy, in the largest city in Lorraine. Meanwhile, the former imperial functionaries now officiating over the republic exercised a remarkably inconsistent management of the nation's defense. Over the rest of France that remained in French hands, confidence in the ability of the authorities to defend the country tended to disintegrate.

---

1 "Serpents in the Tree of Knowledge," *Penny Illustrated Paper*, October 29, 1870, 274. "Apes in the Tree of Liberty," *Penny Illustrated Paper*, October 29, 1870, 274.

Sedan

The battle of Sedan began with a resumption of the fighting in Bazeilles, though most of the Bavarian Korps moved around the town in a broad flanking maneuver to the northeast, striking French positions around the park of Monvillers Château.[2] The Royal Saxons of the Fourth Army bypassed them to reach farther to the north, encountering the French by 6 a.m around the village of La Moncelle.

Painfully aware of the vulnerability of his position, MacMahon rode out toward Bazeilles, until shrapnel from a Prussian shell knocked him out of commission. He passed command to General Auguste-Alexandre Ducrot, who decided to concentrate the army to the north on the plateau at Calvaire d'Illy adjacent to the Belgian border to avoid being backed into the aged fortifications of Sedan. However, two other generals actually had seniority—Emmanuel de Wimpffen and Félix Charles Douay, the old Bonapartist whose brother Abel had been killed at Wissembourg (another had died at Solferino). "What we need is not a retreat but a victory!" Wimpffen told Ducrot, who replied that he would be lucky to manage a retreat by the day's end.[3] When someone suggested consulting Napoleon III, Ducrot snarled, "Fuck the Emperor. He's the one who got us into this mess."

In Bazeilles, the *troupes de marine* and other French soldiers fought the Bavarians street by barricaded street and house by house, with the help of organized *francs-tireurs* and armed civilians. Most famously, Arsène Lambert, with a small group of marksmen, occupied the Auberge Bourgerie, the last house on the road climbing out of the town to the north. Rifling the cartridge pouches of eighteen of their fallen comrades, they fought until they ran completely out of ammunition before

---

2   On Sedan, see Ernest Picard, *1870 Sedan* (Paris: Librairie Plon, 1912); George Hooper, *The Campaign of Sedan* (London, New York, and Toronto: Hodder and Stoughton, 1914); and Fermer, *Sedan 1870*; but see also Duquet, *Froeschwiller, Châlons, Sedan*, 350–75, 376–402; Schultze-Klosterselde, *Weissenburg, Wœrth, Sedan, Paris*, 68–84.

3   For Wimpffen's self-justification, see his *Sedan* (Paris: Librairie Internationale, 1871). For a more laudatory description of the emperor in the field, see Roger Allou, *La campagne de 1870: Récit des événements militaires depuis la déclaration de guerre jusqu'à la capitulation de Paris. Wœrth, Sedan, Metz, Paris. Traduit du "Times"* (Paris: Garnier Freres, Libraires, 1871), 120.

surrendering around 11 a.m.[4] They emerged with a white flag, and surrendered.

Other prisoners fared differently, particularly those taken out of uniform. The Bavarians executed dozens of civilians. Most tended to be men of military age, but they also shot some women and children, and accorded none of them the nicety of a trial. That said, though, the Germans elsewhere captured and kept civilians who had fired on them at Neuf Breisach.[5]

Once through the ruins of Bazailles, the Bavarians relentlessly drove the French, the Germans pushing on to the heights of La Moncelle at the edge of Belgium. In the process, they swept away Captain Paul Déroulède's company of the Third Zouaves, which tried to cover the withdrawal of a battery near the town. About half of them wound up in German hands or in Belgium, including Paul Déroulède, who chose to stay to assist his badly wounded brother. German batteries hit 200 men from Louis de Narcy's 1re Tirailleurs algériens, one shell blowing to bits two of his sergeants and his lieutenant, that "civilized and intelligent negro" Salem ben Guibi, a hero of Mexico.[6]

Meanwhile, west of Sedan, Crown Prince Friedrich Wilhelm of Prussia got 52,000 Prussians with 249 guns across the Meuse, between Mézières and Sedan, by 7 a.m. Leaving some Württemberg troops to guard against any action by General Joseph Vinoy, the Prussians turned east toward Sedan. Over the next two hours, they pushed to the northwest, driving Douay's VII Corps from Saint-Menges, and getting their own guns onto a ridge east of Floing. In response to Douay's reports, Wimpffen sent a maddening reassurance that the army coming for him was probably just a diversion. By late morning, though, Douay and his staff heard the sounds of battle behind them, from La Chappelle and the Givonne northeast of Sedan. Just after noon, infantry of German Third

---

4   Dick de Lonlay, *Français et Allemands: Histoire anecdotique de la guerre de 1870–1871*. Niederbronn, Wissembourg, Froeschwiller, Châlons, Reims, Buzancy, Beaumont, Mouzon, Bazailles, Sedan (Paris: Garnier frères, 1881), 524–31. Alphonse de Neuville painted the defense a few years later, and it became a museum, La maison de la dernière cartouche.

5   Ollier, *Cassell's History of the War*, vol. 1, 423. See also Mark R. Stoneman, "The Bavarian Army and French Civilians in the War of 1870–1871: A Cultural Interpretation," *War in History*, 8(3) (2001) 271–93.

6   Déroulède, *1870*, 181–5, 187 ff., 238–9; and Narcy, *Journal d'un officier de turcos*, 180–1.

Army made contact with squadron of hussars from the Fourth Army near Calvaire d'Illy.

With the noose closing around the French Army, Ducrot had had enough. He quipped crudely, "Nous sommes dans un pot de chambre, et nous y serons emmerdés."[7] He resurrected the plan to get what remained of his corps onto the plateau at Illy, which required a brief disengagement with an enemy that was not cooperating. The French commanders decided to send General Jean Auguste Margueritte with 1,800 horsemen to shatter the Prussian line, turn their flank to the right, and silence the enemy batteries. Margueritte doubted the wisdom of the enterprise before saluting and getting his men into position. Then a bullet tore through his cheek, nearly severed his tongue and broke his jaw before throwing him off his horse. To reassure the ranks, staff members remounted him and led him forward, though one wonders if seeing their commander weaving in the saddle and bleeding profusely from his face might have had an effect different than that desired.

Command fell to the Gaston Alexandre-Auguste de Galliffet, promoted partly based on a reputation for ruthlessness in Mexico. His first charge faced volleys of lead at fifty meters and veered back toward their lines, though some slashed their way along the Prussian infantry, temporarily knocking one battery out of commission, and a few even rode into Floing. In the course of these attacks, one Prussian commander actually ordered his men hold their fire, reasoning that the French were already beaten, and some of the French cavalrymen riding behind Galliffet raised their sabers in salute to their foes. On the other hand, as they moved obliquely across the front of the French line, some of their comrades mistook them for Prussians and opened fire on them.[8] Of the 2,408 horsemen who started the day, only 1,327 answered the roll call the next morning.

By some accounts, at one point, Galliffet rode to his superiors, arguing vehemently for permission to lead another charge. His disheartened superior told him that surviving the battle might be of better service to the country. Paris would later have reason to ponder that.

---

7 Barthelémy-Edmond Palat, *Histoire de la guerre de 1870–1871. Sedan* (Paris: Berger-Levrault & cie, 1907), 499.

8 "De Gallifet's Last Charge at Sedan," *New Zealand Herald*, 43 (April 25, 1906), Supplement, 2. Also André Gillois, *Galliffet le fusilleur de la Commune* (Paris, France-Empire, 1985).

By then, the Prussians had hundreds of guns in position, and lobbed what would become 33,134 rounds into the few square kilometers into which the shattered French huddled. Krupp's brilliantly accurate cannons took out the French guns and even successfully hit their caissons. Formations of their human targets, who had been fighting since the morning without food, essentially disintegrated. Men and horses stampeded toward apparent safety behind the great stone walls of the overcrowded old fortress of Sedan. Soldiers fleeing from the east ran into their comrades running from the west.[9]

Negotiations proved short. When French generals warned that they could attempt a breakout or hole up in the fort, Helmuth von Moltke acknowledged that some Zouaves, *turcos*, and regulars might persist, along with a "bold and fearless" cavalry. However, the Confederation had taken more than 2,000 prisoners with functional arms and estimated that the French retained only 65,000 effectives, roughly half of what they had had a few days before. These had no more than two days of food left, and little ammunition.[10]

Few armies ever attained so complete an immediate victory as did the Prussians at Sedan. It had cost the Germans roughly 9,000 casualties out of 250,000 men, but they inflicted over 17,000 killed and wounded on the French, who lost an additional 21,000 captured, before their general surrender, which placed another 103,000 in the hands of the German Confederation, for a total loss of 139,000 men, a thousand wagons, and 419 guns.[11]

The toll might have been higher had not thousands of the French soldiers not drawn perfectly rational conclusions about the situation before their superiors and slipped out of the trap. In the end, about 3,000 French cavalry escaped into Belgium, and 8,000 to 10,000 managed to reach Vinoy's old position to the west, at Mézières.

In a practical sense, the French soldiers themselves had taken leadership of their own destiny. Their erstwhile commanders described

---

9   Ollier, *Cassell's History of the War*, vol. 1, 89.

10   Gaspard-Marie-Stanislas-Xavier Aragonnes d'Orcet, *Froeschwiller, Sedan et la Commune racontés par un témoin: Lettres et souvenirs du général Vte Aragonnès d'Orcet/ publiés avec une notice biographique et des notes par L. Le Peletier d'Aunay* (Paris: Librairie academique Perrin et Cte, 1910), 134–6.

11   Docteur Henri Conneau, *Ami le plus fidèle, confident le plus intime de l'Empereur Napoléon III* (Biarritz: Bernard, Hervé, 2008).

them as "a defeated horde, mad with grief, stung with shame, distrustful of its officers and of itself, relaxed in discipline, and apprehensive of the future." Wrote one observer,

> a soldiery exasperated by defeat, after bloody but impotent struggles, is no less terrible in its excesses than an army drunk with triumph after it has burst into a vanquished city. Rage, and mortification, and fear, perform in the one instance what the insolence of victory and the lust of revenge accomplish in the other.

Enlisted men at Sedan openly mocked and upbraided their officers, and every shell thrown in their direction spread doubt about the command. By nightfall, the officers had lost all control and "hell had broken loose in Sedan."[12]

The battle probably should have marked the end of the war. In a month of fighting, what had been the greatest military power in Europe had lost battle after battle and then its government. The German Confederation had devastated and forced the reorganization of one large French army, besieged another, and now forced the surrender of a third. The casualties of the major initial fighting in early August had topped 30,000, while those of mid-August would reach nearly double that number. Those at the start of September more than doubled the losses of mid-August to reach 150,000.

Sedan changed the balance of power for generations. France had lost not only an army but an empire. Bismarck himself thought Napoleon III must have "slipped off to Paris," and the emperor could have easily made it into Belgium. He also declined to participate in Wimpffen's scheme to lead a breakout by 5,000 to 6,000 men. Instead, to his credit, he remained to share the fate of his army, and to get the best terms he could for their surrender. On September 3, the victors sent him into a short gentlemanly captivity at Schloss Wilhelmshöhe, near Kassel.

The Germans won more at Sedan than they realized. Just as the old Napoleonic triumphs beyond the Rhine had returned to France in the form of a vast Prussian-led invasion, the Germans cultivated the kind of imperial hubris and arrogance that would bring down upon them a similar scourge in future decades. One of the officers on the receiving

---

12   Ollier, *Cassell's History of the War*, vol. 1, 94; Allou, *La Campagne de 1870*, 120.

end of those French cavalry charges, Major Alfred Graf von Schlieffen, would go on to a brilliant career as a staff officer, codifying the invasion of 1870 into a plan that enshrined the German faith in a swift and easy subjugation of France. Elsewhere, on that field, the twenty-two-year-old adjutant Paul von Hindenburg saw the same mirage.

Some of them would live to reap, with their children and grandchildren, the dragon's teeth sewn at Sedan.

Of Victories and Defeats

Sedan left the old republican faith in a national community mortally wounded. The German Confederation demanded a peace that included not only large financial reparations but the cession of Alsace and Lorraine, though the masses of people there remained even more closely attached to France than those French not living in the borderland. Friedrich Engels rightly called the demand an "arbitrary act," performed as "revenge against the French Revolution." Karl Marx quipped that the people of France gained from their defeat by getting a republic, while "the Germans would become what the French have been."[13]

Back home, as the Prussians illuminated the Brandenburg Gate, Wilhelm Hasenclever and other followers of Ferdinand Lassalle in the ADAV wanted peace. Hasenclever—a military veteran himself—had supported a defensive war to thwart a French invasion, and even Bismarck's desire to unify Germany. Sedan had settled the national problem and the prospect of territorial acquisitions threatening to shape an imperial future for Germany, to the detriment of the old republican aspirations.[14]

Within the Reichstag, this position allied Hasenclever with the most radical of his colleagues, such as Wilhelm Liebknecht and August Bebel.

---

13 Frederick Engels, "The Role of Force in History," *MECW*, vol. 26, 494; G. C. Mins., *DFI*, 4 (September 6, 1870) 58.

14 Carl Wilhelm Tölcke, *Zweck, Mittel und Organisation des Allgemeinen deutschen Arbeiter-Vereins: Ein Leitfaden für die Agitatoren, Bevollmächtigten und Mitglieder des Vereins* (Berlin: C. Ihring, im Selbstverlage des Vereins, 1873), 77. See also Arno Herzig, *Der Allgemeine Deutsche Arbeiter-Verein in der deutschen Sozialdemokratie: Dargest. an d. Biographie d. Funktionärs Carl Wilhelm Tölcke (1817–1893)* (Berlin: Colloquium Verlag, 1979), 238–40.

They refused to vote further funding for the war, and called for the fraternization of the German with the French workers. This common response marked a critical phase in the history of socialism in Germany, moving the ADAV toward a regroupment of the Marxists and quasi-Marxists of the IWA. The authorities of the Prussian-dominated Confederation denounced such Germans as "fatherless" and "cowards."

In Hasenclever's case, the authorities could do more than call him names. Later in the year, they called him up for service in the Landswehr with orders sending him to France. A Scottish paper that described him as "one of the five Socialist Democrats who in the Reichstag opposed the further prosecution of the war and the annexation of Alsace and Lorraine." He would now "have to take part in a contest which he disapproves." The *Sozial-Demokrat* predicted hopefully that things would change after the peace settlement.[15]

The German demand for reparations and territorial concessions denied France any opportunity to accept defeat gracefully. With the loss of the emperor and the absence of any clear successor, politicians in the remaining imperial National Assembly launched their new *gouvernement de la défense nationale*, and acceded to the wishes of Léon Gambetta and others to declare themselves a new Third Republic. They did this, with neither an election nor a mandate, and the Bonapartist apologists for the *coup d'état* of December 2, 1851, sometimes spoke of this as the *coup d'état* of September 4, 1870.

The body of the new republic retained much of its institutionally imperial soul. Bonapartist and Orleanist officials still clung to power in the Church and the army, as well as mayors, prefects, and other functionaries. Many saw "the republic" as no more than a popular label for the temporary absence of a suitably imperial successor. The cleverer among them scrambled to thwart a republican project by joining it and bending it to their own purposes. Many genuine republicans remained skeptical, like Jesse White Mario, who scoffed at the mere declaration of a republic, and the Paris radicals held rowdy demonstrations at the Hôtel de Ville, venting their rage in the symbolic trashing of imperial

15 *Glasgow Herald*, December 31, 1870, 5. Miriam Raggam, *Walter Hasenclever: Leben und Werk*, eds. Ludger Heid, Klaus-Dieter Vinschen, Elisabeth Heid (Bonn: Dietz, 1973); Raggam, *Wilhelm Hasenclever: Reden und Schriften*, ed. Ludger Heid, Klaus-Dieter Vinschen, Elisabeth Heid (Bonn: Dietz, 1989).

insignia.[16] The legitimacy of this new republic grew less from the consent of the governed than the hope of military success.

Nevertheless, on September 6, Gambetta's new government defiantly rejected German demands and pledged itself to drive the enemy troops out of France. Such a goal would require policies with their own dynamic. It would rely heavily on the Garde nationale and tightened exemptions from service in the Garde nationale mobile. This would be essential in Paris where the arrival of the Prussians would implode the local economy and leave most of the city's workforce dependent on their military pay.

Beyond, the *francs tireurs* became even more vital to supplement the various reserve and garrison troops uninvolved in the earlier fiascos. Already, small groups of irregulars operating behind the lines in Alsace and Lorraine mercilessly harassed the Prussian efforts to keep supplied and reinforced, requiring the deployment of ever-growing numbers of the Germans to defend these routes. The occupation forces warned that they would treat them as bushwhackers, and regularly executed those who fell into their hands.[17] This hardly ended the trouble.

Although adopted from purely military necessity, it naturally fueled the old faith in the *levée en masse*, the logistical application of the republican faith in a self-governing active citizenship. The German *Achtundvierziger*—a veteran of 1848—Wilhelm Rüstow had long urged a "people's militia" in the waging of people's war. A veteran of Garibaldi's 1860 campaign, he offered to fight for German unification ten years later, but the authorities of Prussia never became as desperate enough to bring back the exiled critics to fight for the fatherland.

The Prussians at Sedan seemed to be in no hurry. They took a few days to bury bodies and process prisoners. They revisited Verdun, which they had failed to take on August 24, and invested the town on September 7, though the French held out there well into November.[18]

However slowly, the Germans coiled themselves around Paris. On September 15, Moltke ordered the official investment of the city, with Prince Albert's army swinging around the north of Paris. If the French

---

16   Mario, "Garibaldi in France," 455–6, 458.
17   See also Stoneman, "The Bavarian Army and French Civilians."
18   Barry, *Franco-Prussian War* , vol. 2, 93–5.

needed to hold on in the hope that the Prussians might make some serious miscalculation, the Prussians had to keep the French forces elsewhere in the country from breaking the siege.

General Louis Trochu had beat the Prussians to Paris with a core of regulars that had escaped capture at Sedan, though he never fully shook rumors that he had actually used his position as an officer to get a parole, which he then violated. French authorities put him in charge of defending the city, and had some reason for confidence in their strategy to hold the city long enough for the Germans to make some mistake.[19] Taking a major city of 2 million posed an unprecedented set of problems.

Worse, in the aftermath of Napoleon's final defeat, the city had built an impressive new system of walls and forts upon deep foundations based in often outdated experiences and untested assumptions. In 1841, Marie Joseph Louis Adolphe Thiers authorized new walls, running thirty-three or thirty-four kilometers—some twenty miles—around the city. These included ninety-four bastions, five crossing points for rivers or canals and eight for railways, seventeen *portes*, and twenty-three lesser *barrières*, as well as eight posterns, secondary and often concealed gates. The army divided the wall into nine *secteurs*, six on the right bank of the Seine to the north and three on the left bank to the south. Alongside the walls ran both the Rue Militaire, and a *chemin de fer de petite ceinture*, a belt railway.[20]

Beyond these walls, the built or rebuilt forts rose within the *secteurs*. Fort de L'Est and Fort Briche stood east and north of the city, where the walls met the twisting Seine at St. Denis. Continuing clockwise, stood Forts Aubervillier, Romainville, Noisy, Rosny, and Nogent on the Marne, with Fort Charenton beyond the Marne, and Fort Vincennese, where the Seine loops north back into the city. Other forts covered the southern approaches to *secteurs* seven, eight, and nine of the wall: Ivry, Bicêtre, Montrouge, and Vanves. As the Seine flowed to the southwest from the

---

19   Robert Tombs, *The Paris Commune, 1871* (Milton Park UK: Taylor and Francis, 1999), 14. At Ingolstadt, twenty officers who were liberated at Sedan on parole voluntarily gave themselves up to captivity in order to avoid importunities to break their engagement and reenter the army. Ollier, *Cassell's History of the War*, vol. 1, 423.

20   "Tableau de correspondances en secteurs militaires et chefferies," in Guy le Hallé, *Histoire des Fortifications de Paris et leur extension en Île-de-France* (Lyon: Horvath, 1995), 189–90, and the breakdown at 191–223.

city, it passed Fort Issy.[21] Fort Mont-Valérien loomed over the western approaches to the Seine and *secteurs* five and six. A few kilometers down the river to the north, it flowed under the eighteenth-century stone bridge at Neuilly with another kilometer to Courbevoie, and—further along—back to Saint-Ouen and Saint-Denis.

They estimated that they had access to half a million raw recruits, mostly the city's 450,000 wage earners, its 140,000 master artisans and shopkeepers—most of whom would be later be called white-collar workers—and 100,000 other servants of various sorts. Many of these nearly 700,000 civilians—those with the wherewithal, or with rural relatives—left the city. Trochu had the authority to organize 384,000 Parisians into 254 neighborhood battalions of the National Guard, some of which became increasingly skeletal.[22] Although the range of artillery had doubled since the construction of these fortifications, the city's position was strong.

The city's defenders did little to stop or slow the Prussian encirclement of Paris. The received wisdom among French commanders seemed to be that Moltke would storm the city's defenses, squandering his numerical and logistical advantages. However, they had no reliable backup plan should he not do so.

On September 17, a small force ventured beyond the Bois de Vincennes and across the Marne just above where it flows into the Seine. Hoping to reach a supply depot near Villeneuve, they skirmished with a party of Germans at Mont-Mesley. The following day, Vinoy, who had also avoided the Prussian trap at Sedan, probed German positions southeast of the city around Villeneuve-Saint-Georges. Within the next forty-eight hours the Prussians cut communications with Orleans, took Versailles, and cut off Paris from the rest of the country. At the end of the month, Vinoy could make only a half-hearted stab at the Prussians at Chevilly, southwest of the city.[23]

The siege inspired innovations of all sorts, as when what was left of the government in the city flew away. On October 7, Gambetta clambered aboard a balloon, the *Armand-Barbès*, named for the lieutenant of the

---

21   Hallé, *Histoire des fortifications de Paris*, 228–30, 231–3.

22   David G. Chandler, *Atlas of Military Strategy* (New York: Free Press, 1980).

23   "War Notes," *Morning Post*, September 18, 1870, 2; "The War between France and Prussia," *Aberdeen Journal*, September 21, 1870, 2. Also *Bury and Norwich Post*, September 26, 1870, 2.

revolutionary Auguste Blanqui, to organize resistance beyond. A second balloon quickly followed, with two passengers, one of them an arms dealer from New York, in flight both over the Prussians and from creditors.

Seven years earlier, the veteran Jewish republican Pierre-Jules Hetzel had published a first book by Jules Verne, *Five Weeks in a Balloon*. A veteran of the 1848 revolution, Hetzel had experienced a self-imposed exile before returning to Paris and launching a periodical for specialists to reach a vastly wider audience. Verne earned further success, including the Legion of Honor, though he had remained admirably unmoved by the drumbeat for war. "I don't that much want to give the Prussians a good hiding . . . Let's not be stupid or boastful and admit that the Prussians are as strong as the French, now that everyone's fighting with long-range weapons."[24] The power structure appreciated a visionary's insights into ballooning without having to acknowledge his views on war.

Sixty-six known balloon flights departed from the city during the siege. One of them established a distance record by coming down in Norway. They carried information out into the rest of the world, and the French also used them out of Tours and later Poitiers. They also photographically reduced letters to save weight. This was despite the Prussian use of the first antiaircraft gun, their innovative and highly specialized *Ballonabwehrkanone*.

A city of grand appetites, Paris had already begun to suffer, as a prolonged siege dropped the city's economy into free fall, and Parisians abandoned the closed workshops. This left the pittance earned from the Garde nationale something of a social safety net for much of the population. Conversely, the military authorities had even less respect for the working-class civilians of Paris than for those in the ranks. The people of the city grew increasingly hungry and more restive under the martial rule of a government they trusted less. On October 5, radical demonstrations took place at the Hôtel de Ville.[25]

Then, too, the infrastructure strained to endure the travails of the siege. The actress Sarah Bernhardt took charge of bringing cots into the Odéon theatre and converting it into a hospital for the wounded. She

---

24   William Butcher, *Jules Verne: The Definitive Biography* (New York: Thunder's Mouth Press, 2006), 210–12, 213, 214.

25   "The War," *Oxford Journal*, October 15, 1870, 7.

personally assisted surgeons with operations and worked as a nurse. By the end of the siege, Bernhardt's makeshift hospital had cared for over 150 wounded soldiers, including a young Ferdinand Foch.

A short walk away, Hélène Bernois labored relentlessly to sustain the Anglo-American ambulance. Her coworkers realized that the polyglot black woman from New Orleans swam in "the undercurrent of that great hidden life of Paris, about which we know so little." After Sedan, the ambulance replaced its mess chief, and Bernois took charge of that function." She recruited a Pole named Jasienski and an Italian named Rienzi to scavenge the city not only for beef, but also for coffee, sugar, chocolate, and wine. By the end, this Louisiana ball of energy seems to have managed the base and taken charge of one of the wards, even staying up all night to stay with a single dying young soldier.[26]

Hunger, the burden of war, and periodic news from its almost always depressing course would not be the only plague. Prussian field commanders and the Crown prince balked at shelling Paris, pointing out that firing on civilians violated the rules of civilized warfare and could turn world opinion against them, to no certain outcome. However, US General Phillip H. Sheridan, present as a neutral observer, had scorched the Shenandoah valley six years earlier, and argued that harsh measures against civilians would shorten the war. Bismarck agreed.

The Crisis of Legitimacy

By this point, the last great imperial army, had passed nearly a month in and around the old medieval walls of Metz in an unsuccessful effort to break out of the siege. They well knew that every day they remained cut off, the food supply shrank and the rate of sickness would grow. At the close of the month, the French threw everything into a desperate attempt at a breakout to the east. About ten kilometers beyond the walls of the old city, they captured and held the high ground near Noisseville. On the next day, the Prussians concentrated what they needed to batter the Armée du Rhin back into the city with a loss of roughly 3,000 to each

---

26   Swinburne, *Paris Sketches*, 102–3, 87–8, 90–1, 93–6, and 100, 101; and Evans, *History of the American Ambulance*, 25.

side. On October 7, they launched a large and desperate sortie. They reached no farther than Bellevue, several kilometers east of Metz. The Prussians drove them back into the city, and always seemed to have access to reinforcements.[27]

The fighting had demolished much of the countryside ringing Metz. One who rode around the besieged city wrote, "Gaunt and grim stood its houses, burnt to the shell, the graves lying all around, the holds in the fields where the shells had burst, the breastworks behind which had stood the German foreposts." In the city itself, the siege disrupted life, as everyone struggled to adjust to a depletion of their necessities. Local newspapers began to appear in red ink and heralded what would quickly become increasingly desperate food shortages.[28]

Metz itself had so large a population that, as was said of Paris, the bourgeoisie and the workers had their own gods.[29] The old city remained walled and well defended, but civilians naturally tended to look at the tens of thousands of uniformed men consuming their limited resources less as an army and more like a horde of very broke tourists. Moreover, after Sedan and the declaration of a republic, these civilians felt no less the burden of an imperial army.

The soldiers themselves shared this discontent. As at Sedan, some of them refused to obey the commands of their superiors, and the threat of open mutiny became less avoidable. In general, they "forcibly made their way into the shops and houses, and ransacked them from cellar to garret, carrying off what they found in the shape of provisions, but in most cases offering to pay for what they carried off."[30]

The discontent extended to the officers as well as the men. A contemporary French observer noted that he found "no man willing to give up the prerogatives of his position … I say the culinary prerogatives!" Marshal Bazaine, he pointed out, that sworn that he would shoot any soldier speaking of surrender and defeat, after which he himself became just such a soldier "without being shot!"[31]

27 Particularly because the later controversies around Bazaine generated an extensive literature about the siege of Metz.
28 Forbes, *My Experiences of the War*, vol. 1, 381, 413, 425.
29 Moltke, *The Franco-German War of 1870–71*, vol. 1, 217–21.
30 Ollier, *Cassell's History of the War*, vol. 1, 321
31 *L'Armée du rhin et le blocus de Metz 1870*, 80.

Metz republicans rightly suspected Bazaine and kindred patriots of the old army of trying to reach a secret agreement between the monarchists and the Prussian crown. Indeed, a businessman named Édouard Regnie found recruits of all sorts for his plan to place Napoleon's heir apparent on a restored throne established on the bones of the republic. The monarch had sent his son and designated successor as a courier from Sedan into Belgium, where he had heard of the defeat. Dazed, he soon learned of his father's internment and made his way to England. He arrived there on September 6, and his parents eventually joined him.[32] The only realistic monarchist solution would turn on finding a way to get him onto the throne of a restored empire. Such a conspiracy may seem far-fetched but something like that had transpired only twenty years before.

Regnier hurried to Sedan to secure Prussian cooperation and gained a pass through the lines to consult with Bazaine and his staff in besieged Metz. Prominent in the plot was General Bourbaki, who had held the Imperial Guard in reserve at Mars-La-Tour and Gravelotte, contributing to the army's being bottled at Metz. At this point, he left the beleaguered army and passed through Prussian lines into Belgium, after which he went to England to confer with former Empress Eugénie, while Regnier headed to Florence.[33]

Many of the lesser officers with less treasonable aspirations found common ground with the republican middle class. Captain Louis Rossel and others seem to have heard rumors about the Bazaine–Regnier–Bourbaki plot and Prussian cooperation with it. He approached General Nicolas Anne Théodule Changarnier, the nearly eighty-year-old veteran with the highest rank among the critics, and asked him to take command. Changarnier advised Rossel not to pursue the plan. On the night of October 6, the determined captain dressed himself as a peasant and set

32   Ellen Barlee, *Life of Napoleon, Prince Imperial of France*, (London : Griffith and Farran, 1880); Maurice d'Irisson Hérisson, *Le prince impérial*, (Paris: P. Ollendorff, 1890); and, André Martinet, *Le prince impérial*, (Paris: Chailley, 1895). See also, on contemporary republican awareness of this scheme, Élie Sorin, *Auteur du texte: Alsace et Lorraine: Strasbourg, Metz, Belfort, 1870–1871* (Paris: Au bureau de L'Eclipse, 1871), 81 and generally 22–65.

33   David Ascoli, *A Day of Battle: Mars-La-Tour, 16 August 1870* (London: Harrap, 1987), 53, 165–6, 254, 281, 282; John-Allen Price, *The War That Changed the World: The Forgotten War That Set the Stage for the Global Conflicts of the 20th Century and Beyond* (Kingston, Canada: Legacy Books Press, 2009), 258–60.

off into a night of torrential rain, but German outposts stopped him.³⁴ Rossel returned the army with the realization that the only solutions he could find would be in Metz.

Increasingly, though, the people of the cities did not need a siege to think about grasping for power on their own. In particular, the country's largest secondary cities, Lyon and Marseille, shared the kind of social tensions appropriate to a city of between 300,000 and 325,000 residents and had republican movements of fluctuating strength.³⁵ The defeats of French arms invariably weakened confidence in the ruling institutions. In particular they challenged prevailing ideological assumptions about the value of so centralized a state, and the imperial practices of national defense. Increasingly they doubted the readiness, willingness, and abilities of the national authorities to look out for their protection.

Matters took an ominous turn at Marseille. Belonging to a distinctly Mediterranean world, the community had its own radical traditions with an active range of opponents to Napoleon III, many of them associated with the Freemasons. Republicans and the local followers of Auguste Blanqui shared membership in a lodge of "Select Friends" that inspired other reform organizations. A number of republican newspapers, though monitored by the police, secured a serious readership. Gambetta himself had emerged from this milieu before it sent him to the National Assembly as the deputy of the Bouches-du-Rhône. Others included the lawyer Gaston Crémieux, the newspaperman Gustave Naquet, and Henri-François-Alphonse Esquiros and Adolphe Carcassonne. Crémieux, one of the founders of La Réforme lodge at Marseille, had helped bring Gambetta into the lodge only two years earlier. Esquiros had become a master in the lodge a year before.³⁶

34 Gerspach, *Le Colonel Rossel*, 43, 44–5, 292–4.

35 Timothy B. Smith, "Public Assistance and Labor Supply in Nineteenth-Century Lyon," *Journal of Modern History*, 68 (March 1996), 20, 22. "The War in Europe," *New York Tribune*, November 1, 1870, 1; "Latest Intelligence," *London Examiner*, October 15, 1870, 5; "The Provinces and the War," *Leeds Mercury*, October 15, 1870, 5; *Leeds Mercury*, October 15, 1870, 12; "The War," *Nashville Union and American*, October 11, 1870, 1, October 15, 1870, 1.

36 Jacobus Petrus van der Linden, *Alphonse Esquiros: De la bohème romantique à la république sociale* (Heerlen and Paris: Winants and Nizet, 1948); and Anthony Zielonka, ed., *Alphonse Esquiros, 1812–1876. Choix de lettres* (Paris and Geneva: Champion and Slatkine, 1990). Also useful is *Les francs-maçons dans l'enseignement* (Paris: Bureaux de l'Association anti-maçonnique de France, 1911); Sudhir Hazareesingh,

Early German victories inspired the call at Marseille that the government arm the people. On August 8, Prefect Leveret flatly refused, and Crémieux, Naquet, and Maurice Rouvier led a mass protest of 40,000. Thereafter, one of the radical factions actually captured the city hall and established a revolutionary committee. The central authorities moved against them, arresting fourteen of the ringleaders, sentencing them to prison terms on August 27, but the republicans swept the elections, despite their division into three rival slates.[37]

With Sedan and the national declaration of a republic, the movement at Marseille secured the release of their revolutionary leaders. With Gambetta's support, they began installing republican officials on September 7. Prefect Alexandre Labadié generally accommodated republican expectations, but sparked a crisis when he tried to exercise the old imperial control over the hiring of schoolteachers. Crémieux, Carcassonne, and two others launched a new Committee of Public Safety with the support of the local Civic Guard.[38]

Gambetta and his officials, however, viewed any regional or local initiatives in the southeast as a possible threat to the integrity of a central French government. After all, the empire had only recently acquired Savoy, with its large Italian population, and the subsequent unification of Italy could create a dynamic that would draw the region out from under a defeated France. Indeed, as republicans in the provinces chafed at deferring to the central government, an American observer thought that "the darkest and most desperate enterprise known in history was afoot—the attempt to transform France and the world into a system of 'communes,' erected upon the ruins of all national governments."[39]

"Republicanism, War and Democracy: The *Ligue du Midi* in France's War against Prussia, 1870–71," *French History*, 17 (March 2003), 65; Louis M. Greenberg, *Sisters of Liberty: Marseille, Lyon, Paris, and the Reaction to a Centralized State, 1868–1871* (Cambridge, MA, Harvard University Press, 1971), 178–80.

37   William Hamilton Sewell Jr., *Structure and Mobility: The Men and Women of Marseille, 1820–1870* (Cambridge: Cambridge University Press, 1985), 147; Greenberg, *Sisters of Liberty*, 172–3.

38   Greenberg, *Sisters of Liberty*, 174–5, 178–9. Antoine Olivesi, *La Commune de 1871 à Marseille et ses origins* (Paris: M. Rivière, 1950).

39   Train, *My Life in Many States and in Foreign Lands*, 301. There was later suspicion that Cluseret had been involved in a conspiracy to separate Savoy. May 21, in *Procès-verbaux de la Commune de 1871*, ed. Georges Bourgin and Gabriel Henroit (Paris: Lahure, 1945), vol. 2, 501.

Revolt also simmered at Lyon. Sprung from his prison cell, Louis Andrieux, the lawyer who had conducted the short-lived weekly *Le Travail*, became the key leader of the effort to defend the city in the wake of Sedan. On the morning of September 4, backed by a large crowd, the revolutionaries simply strolled into the Hôtel de Ville and took charge. Without any word from Paris, they proclaimed a republic from the balcony. One member of the IWA helped declare the new commune and half a dozen had seats on the local Committee of Public Safety. Even after news arrived that the authorities at Paris had declared a republic, the revolutionary government at Lyon continued to use the red flag in lieu of the tricolor and put three members of the IWA on its ten-member delegation to negotiate with Gambetta's new government.[40]

Two days after the revolt, on September 6, the prefect appointed by Gambetta's new government reached Lyon, expecting to exercise the kind of power imperial officials had enjoyed. After some intermittent talks, representatives sent to Paris returned with the authorization for Andrieux to restore order in Lyon, and the IWA sent in Gustave P. Cluseret to take charge of the city's defense. On his return to France, he had proclaimed himself a socialist, and slipped through the fingers of the government, which had ordered him arrested on sight. The hostile press put "general" in quotes when mentioning Cluseret and shrieked about "his frantic and fantastic demonstration at Lyons, under the 'Red' flag of the Socialist Democracy."[41]

Tensions escalated until September 17, when the insurgents made a direct bid for power. When the army sent troops against them, the soldiers mutinied and some even helped to arm the radicals. Elsewhere, units of the National Guard seized caches of weapons, as their officers retreated to the barracks, leaving the Committee of Public Safety in charge. A revolutionary network of workers' associations and citizens' militias began to take form, loosely knit together by the plebian

---

40   G. C. Mins., *DFI*, 4 (September 13, 1870) 60–1; Greenberg, *Sisters of Liberty*, 173; Joseph-Philippe-Toussaint Bourdon Bordone, *Garibaldi et l'Armée des Vosges: Récit officiel de la campague* (Paris: Lacroix, Verboeckhoven & Cie, 1871), 3 vols. consecutively paginated, vol. 1, 109–10. See also Maurice Moissonnier, *La Premiére Internationale et la Commune à Lyon (1865–1871). Spontanéisme—Complots et "luttes réelles"* (Paris: Éditions Sociales, 1972), 255.

41   Bordone, *Garibaldi et l'Armée des Vosges*, vol. 1, 14, 109 and note; "Le Général Cluseret," *La Mascarade*, September 25, 1870, 3; and quote on the flag from the, *New York Tribune*, October 19, 1870, 4.

republican Légion garibaldienne. At this point, Mikhail Bakunin, newly arrived from Switzerland, urged the IWA to take action on its own, inspiring a rising in adjacent Guillotière, just cross the Rhône.[42]

Although Cluseret's designated role was military rather than political, he mistrusted Bakunin's judgment, and tried to maintain the unity of the movement. As Bakunin pushed the IWA into ever more aggressive actions, Cluseret increasingly doubted that it would be able to fill the vacuum of power itself.[43] Throughout these days, Cluseret kept in touch with the International through its representatives at Saint-Étienne and Mâcon.

On September 26, the insurgents issued a red poster calling the people to arms. They declared the old "administrative and governmental machinery of the state" abolished and a mass meeting of 6,000 people in the hall of the Rotunda, the Brotteaux, authorized a new government. "The disastrous situation in which the Country finds itself; the impotence of official powers and the indifference of the privileged classes have brought the French nation to the brink of the abyss. If the revolutionary organized people do not hasten to act, their future is lost, the revolution is lost, all is lost."[44] It replaced the payment of taxes and mortgages with "contributions" from "the wealthy classes in proportion to the needs of the salvation of France." "The justice of the people" would replace all criminal and civil courts. They declared that Lyon, "the second city of France," would look to its own defense and called the people to arms. The remaining authorities moved to arrest Bakunin and Cluseret, but the crowd successfully disarmed ten companies of National Guard and seized the Hôtel de Ville.

Cluseret struggled to provide military clout to match the political claims. On September 28, "a huge crowd of workers who protested a decrease of wages" proclaimed Cluseret "commander of the local defense forces." However, he had a real sense of both the military strength of the government forces and the ruthlessness of the authorities. As with the

---

42   Cesare Aroldi, *L'ultimo dei vecchi garibaldini* (Viadana: Editrice Castello, 1973), 122–3. The Légion garibaldienne survived long enough to cheer Garibaldi himself when he visited in mid-October. "L'Armée des Vosges: Comité Central Organisateur," *Le petit journal*, October 18, 1870, 3.

43   For Cluseret's activities at Lyon, see Braka, *L'honneur perdu du Général Cluseret*, 109–17; and *Procès-verbaux de la Commune de 1871*, vol. 2, 488 n.489.

44   Moissonnier, *La Premiére Internationale et la Commune à Lyon*, 208.

Fenians, Cluseret had no control over a movement ready to follow Bakunin into self-isolation and defeat.

As the local insurgent leadership followed Bakunin into issuing decrees rather than organizing a defensive force, Cluseret was unable to contest the troops who stormed the Hôtel de Ville and drove out the erstwhile revolutionary government. Bakunin later blamed the failure of the movement entirely on Cluseret's "cowardice," but the movement might well have had a better grasp of political and military realities than Bakunin. Cluseret later said that, even in hindsight, he could not see a better course than that he had taken.[45]

Meanwhile, as Paris began to tighten its belt, it joined a series of French communities still holding out hopefully at Verdun, Montmédy, Phalsbourg, Bitche, and north of Metz near the border with Luxembourg at Thionville. The dawn of September 23 opened a bombardment at Toul, the fortified town south of Metz, near Nancy, and, by 3 p.m., 2,433 shells had brought its surrender. Five days later, Strasbourg finally opened its gates to the Prussians. They had periodically bombarded the city for more than a month, even when the Bishop of Strasbourg and the civilian authorities begged for a ceasefire and offered 100,000 francs for every day the enemy would refrain from shelling the city. On September 11, a Swiss delegation showed up to evacuate "several hundred old men, women, and children." They brought reliable news that no French relief column could be expected. On September 19, civilians urged Uhrich to capitulate, and a Prussian assault carried one of the key forts. On September 27, the French opened negotiations and surrendered the next day. Only the shortage of German shells minimized damage to the irreplaceable holdings of the museum and the library.[46] Clara Barton, backed by German women, prepared to bring the International Red Cross into the relief efforts.

The nature of the war politicized its conduct. Differences existed in the national government over how to handle the situation at Lyon. In

---

45   May 21 in *Procès-verbaux de la Commune de 1871*, vol. 2, 504; G. C. Mins., *DFI*, 4 (Oct. 11, 1870), 67–73; "A Red Republic at Lyons," *Darlington Northern Echo*, November 3, 1870, 3; "War Notes," *Lloyd's Weekly Newspaper*, November 13, 1870.

46   Rachel Chrastil, *The Siege of Strasbourg* (Cambridge, MA: Harvard University Press, 2014). Also M. de Malaric, *Le siège de Strasbourg pendant la campagne de 1870* (Paris: Librairie du Moniteur Universel, 1871), 121–3.

early October, when his colleagues sustained the prefect at Lyon after the civilian arrest of an unpopular general, Admiral Fourichon resigned, leaving the portfolio to be taken up by Gambetta after his arrival. The admiral ascribed all of this republican nonsense to the mutinous character of the troops, especially the *francs-tireurs*. In fact, just down the street from the temporary officers of the government at Tours, one of these units that had not been paid for a month imposed a siege of their own on their officers in a hotel.[47]

With the declaration of a new republic on September 4, popular initiatives and organizations strove to mold what that republic would mean.

---

47   Ollier, *Cassell's History of the War*, vol. 1, 358.

PART III

War for the Republic

7

The Specter Haunting Europe: The Emergence of the People and the *Levée en masse*

The crises in the autumn of 1870 amplified serious radical voices in France. Even under military rule in beleaguered Metz, elements of the Garde nationale went into open revolt, with civilians—particularly the long-repressed local republicans—taking action of their own. At one point, a local republican editor brandishing a pistol and mounted on a white horse led locals through the town, shouting for the blood of Marshal Bazaine. "The mob, composed in a large proportion of civilians, laid hold of an officer of the Imperial Guard," recalled one observer, "and holding pistols at his head, forced him to carry in the front the Republican flag." When some of these imperial officials warned about the German threat, street urchins drowned them out by chanting "Vive la République!"[1] The course of the war rather suddenly left officers accountable to their soldiers, the military to civilians, and even at times command to the people.

Sedan had left an essentially notional republic in the hands of mostly former imperial officials. Without Alsace, Lorraine and large swaths of their country—and with Paris surrounded—they struggled to develop and sustain a defensive strategy. Pressed by military necessity, much of the southern front, left largely to its own devices, organized its own Ligue du Midi, particularly anchored by the country's major secondary cities, Lyon and Marseille. There, the legendary revolutionary leader and long-time enemy of the French Empire, Giuseppe Garibaldi, arrived

---

1   Forbes, *My Experiences of the War*, vol. 1, 423.

from Italy to help defend the new republic. The remaining imperial army at Metz even underwent a crisis of legitimacy that offered a microcosm of that in the nation generally. With further reversals, the people of those desperate communities in the south and their representatives explored an increasingly radical version of republicanism.

The Ligue du Midi and the Armée des Vosges

News of the declaration of a republic posed the possibility of reconstructing French society. Radicals in Paris had mixed feelings as they sensed the war that they had opposed rolling toward their doorsteps. They addressed the German people, reminding them that, as "the man who had declared war against Germany was in their hands it was now the duty of the German armies to retire." However, they joined in the city's defense.

Like the trade union bodies and serious republican groups, the IWA in Paris concluded that "the present Government was not theirs but they must support the Republic." They participated in organizing committees of vigilance in each neighborhood. These, in turn, established a Republican Central Committee of the Twenty Arrondissements. The followers of Blanqui, among others, discussed the possibility of making a bid for power themselves.

The prospect also moved the International, but it wanted to coordinate what it did with a world congress, representing similarly minded organizations and individuals of other lands. On September 9, Karl Marx, in the second address of the IWA's General Council on the subject, warned Parisian comrades that "they must not allow themselves to be swayed by the national remembrances of 1792 ... They have not to recapitulate the past, but to build up the future." Marx suggested that they "calmly and resolutely improve the opportunities of republican liberty, for the work of their own class organization." Conversely, he warned, "any attempt at upsetting the new government in the present crisis, when the enemy is almost knocking at the doors of Paris, would be a desperate folly." Marx especially wanted to dissuade his audience from undermining the feeble new republic.[2] Some

---

2   G. C. Mins., *DFI*, 4 (September 6, 1870), 56. Also G. C. Mins., *DFI*, 4 (September 9, 13, 1870 Special Meeting), 59, 60.

radicals from outside France were already entering the country in hopes of sustaining that new government.

That government, in turn, pinned its hopes on a new concentration of forces in the Loire valley and the city of Orleans. It concluded, in the wake of Sedan, that it could do nothing immediately to rescue the dying imperial army at Metz, without first relieving Paris. The concentration in the Loire aimed at that.

Even after the fall of Strasbourg, the French military maintained few garrisons in Alsace. Despite the Prussian sweep through the area, there remained holdouts around Colmar. Local forces at Neuf Brisach, opposite Breisach on the Rhine, stubbornly defended the old fortifications along the Rhine well into November. On October 24, some 2,400 men with 120 guns at Sélestat (Schelestadt) near Colmar surrendered.[3]

Most famously, Colonel Pierre Philippe Denfert-Rochereau worked furiously with a force of 17,000 to strengthen the fortifications of Belfort, a modest little town of barely over 8,000 souls in preparation for the arrival of General August von Werder's westbound Prussians. Denfert's success in mobilizing the community's drive to survive produced a stubborn defiance that made Belfort a very tough nut to crack. In the end, it became one of the few French triumphs of the war, a site where French resistance actually outlasted the war.[4]

Nevertheless, after besieging Belfort, German forces continued on into Franche-Comté and Burgundy, moving against Besançon and Dijon, strategic cities of 45,000 to 50,000. On October 25, Prussian forces had already gotten far enough west to cut communications between Belfort and Langres, roughly eighty kilometers or fifty miles north-northeast of Dijon.

More broadly, the Germans now moved into the rich valleys of the Saône and Rhône rivers, including the country's major secondary cities of

3 For developments in the region, see Adolphe Joanne, *Géographie, historie, statistique et archéologie des 89 départements de la France: Côte-d'Or* (Paris: Hachette, 1869); L. Gaudelette, *Histoire de la guerre en Bourgogne* (Paris: H. Lecène & H. Oudin, 1887); and *La Bourgogne pendant la guerre et l'occupation Allemande 1870–1871: D'après la Gazette officielle de Carlsruhe*, trans. Dr. Louis Marchant (Dijon: s.n., 1875); "Les Prussiens dans la Haute-Saone," *Le petit journal*, October 27, 1870, 1.

4 Élie Sorin, *Alsace et Lorraine: Strasbourg, Metz, Belfort, 1870–1871* (Paris: Au bureau de L'Eclipse, 1871), 89–106; and B. Von Tiedemann, *The Siege Operations in the Campaign against France, 1870–71*, trans. Major Tyler (London: Superindence of Her Majesty's Stationery Office, 1877).

Lyon and Marseille. The looming military threat and the failure of the central government's defense inspired movements for local self-defense, which implicitly posed the question of local self-government. Already, on September 18, Marseille and Lyon became the anchors for a new Ligue du Midi, which united four dozen local communities over sixteen departments across the south of France to cooperate in their defense. "We are determined to make any sacrifice," declared one participant, "and if we stand alone, we will appeal to the revolution, the implacable and inexorable revolution, the revolution with all its hatred, anger, and patriotic fury."[5]

Still, even as common defense concerns united local republicans and socialists, they began to fall out over the character of the government they hoped to save. When matters became sufficiently difficult at Marseille, Gaston Crémieux withdrew from his temporary duties as a prefect, and León Gambetta appointed his friend and brother Mason, the merchant Louis-Antoine Delpech. Delpech had long been critical of the empire, though he had been in the army until 1856 and had served as sub-prefect in Aix-en-Provence, before taking that post in the department of Bouches-du-Rhône.[6]

On October 8—in the midst of all this political turmoil—the sixty-three-year-old Garibaldi landed at Marseille. Dissatisfied that Italian unification had not yet included the Papal States, he had attempted to inspire another armed march on Rome. Its encounter with a joint Papal and French force at Mentana on November 3, 1867, left Garibaldi himself badly wounded. After a brief imprisonment, he accepted a kind of house arrest at his home on the island of Caprera.[7]

In the fall of 1870, the living legend limped stiffly from his latest in a lifetime of wounds borne in the service of the universal republic. After having fought imperial France for years, he now showed up

5 Hazareesingh, "Republicanism, War and Democracy," 63; "La guerre de partisans," Le petit journal, October 18, 1870, 2–3.

6 See J. Joly, Dictionnaire des parlementaires français: Notices biographiques sur les ministres, députés et sénateurs francais de 1889 à 1940 (Paris: Presses universitaires de France, 1966).

7 For Garibaldi's image in America, see Dennis Berthold, American Risorgimento: Herman Melville and the Cultural Politics of Italy (Columbus: Ohio State University Press, 2009), 192–5, 196. Notes Marx to Engels, 29 August 1868, and Engels to Pasquale Martignetti, 25 July 1892, MECW, 43: 91–2; and, 49: 483. See also Karl Marx, The Fourth Annual Report of the General Council of the International Working Men's Association, MECW, vol. 21, 12–17.

hoping to defend France's new government. The local republicans of Marseille gave him a hero's welcome. The mayor spoke, and the general replied,

This is the second time I have come to Marseille. The first time, I had been condemned to death by my country's oppressors and you generously gave me asylum. Now I have come to repay my debt to France, to cooperate in freeing her territory from the Prussian hordes and in raising once again the glorious banner of the Republic.[8]

The national government-in-exile, then at Tours, grappled with how to deal with Garibaldi's presence, particularly in a city as volatile as Marseille. They could not conceive of victory without the military establishment and the Church, both of which saw the appearance of the old revolutionary as something that "would strengthen the Socialists." "He's really coming," moaned one official, "as though we hadn't enough troubles already!"[9] In the end, though, they assigned him to raise an Armée des Vosges at Dole, on the Doubs river on the fringe of the Jura.

To be on the safe side, though, Gambetta sent along the thirty-six-year-old sculptor Frédéric Auguste Bartholdi, a republican of long standing. Although he had his large workshops in Paris, the outbreak of war brought him back to his native Colmar, to look after his mother and the local Garde nationale in that community. Gambetta also made soldier – scholar Luigi Frapolli, Garibaldi's chief of staff, charged with raising, paying, and supplying the recruits.[10]

In fact, Garibaldi had no more immediate interest in fostering social revolution than did the International, at least not at the expense of the war effort. Delpech at Marseille shared this perspective so completely that he resigned as prefect to join Garibaldi at the front. His replacement,

8   "Garibaldi à Tours," *Le petit journal*, October 11, 1870, 2; "Lettres de Tours," *Le petit journal*, October 12, 1870, 2; "Garibaldi and His Army," *New York Tribune*, November 25, 1870, 1; "With Garibaldi" (from the *Daily News*), *Birmingham Daily Post*, November 8, 14, 1870, 6.

9   Andrea Viotti, *Garibaldi: The Revolutionary and His Men* (Poole: Blandford Press, 1979) 456, 175, 176; "The Protestants of Alsace," *Pall Mall Gazette*, November 2, 1870, 10.

10   Robert Belot and Daniel Bermond, *Bartholdi* (Paris: Perrin, 2004), 152–4. Luigi Polo Friz, "Frapolli, Lodovico," in *Dizionario Biografico degli Italiani*, vol. 50, 1998 treccani.it/enciclopedia/lodovico-frapolli_(Dizionario-Biografico), p 129.

Alphonse Esquiros, the leader of the radical Club of the Alhambra, had similarly outstanding republican credentials, and also spent much of his effort raising troops, especially foreign volunteers.[11]

Nevertheless, building a new army at Dole proved terribly difficult. Without a centralized force to see after supplying and paying the troops, Frapolli, Gambetta's brother Masons, had to put together a committee back at Lyon to negotiate its way through the political factions and teams of profiteers. He seemed to be much more successful at those negotiations than in actually getting the army what it needed, so Garibaldi replaced him Joseph-Philippe-Toussaint Bordone, a French veteran of his 1860 campaign in Sicily.[12] The central government never appreciated Garibaldi's show of independence in this regard.

A hard-nosed realist, the newspaperman Edward H. Vizetelly predicted a bleak future for Garibaldi's project. With Prussian advances against both Besançon to the east and Dijon to the north, even the most hardened veterans with Garibaldi would now face "the iron battalions of the Germans" rather than the Neapolitans, and they functioned under a government with, at best, an indifferent desire to cooperate with them. The real shortage of horses, especially after Wœrth, nobbled any attempt to scout and locate enemy forces. They also lacked any functioning artillery to meet the exceptionally well-armed Prussians. As to the general's prospects, Vizetelly thought that "the best his friends can hope for him is a series of drawn skirmishes and wearing disappointments."[13]

11   Greenberg, *Sisters of Liberty*, 178–9, 179–80, 174–5, 68–9, 74, 177–8; Hazareesingh, "Republicanism, War and Democracy," *French History*, 17 (2003), 63; and Quentin Deluermoz's treatment of Garibaldi and his contribution to the war in his *Commune(s), 1870–1871: Une traversée des mondes au XIXe siècle* (Paris: Seuil, 2020), 30–4, 36–8, 40–1.

12   October 14, 15, 18, 19, 25, 1870, "Procès-verbaux des séances du Comité organisateur de l'Armée des Vosges a Lyon," Armée des Vosges Papers, LG, (Series L covers the war of 1870-1871, Paris Commune, and G specifies the Armée des Vosges); Aroldi, *L'ultimo dei vecchi garibaldini*, 125; Mario, "Garibaldi in France," 461; Bordone, *Garibaldi et l'Armée des Vosges*, vol. 2, 179 n., 166, 180 n.; Foule, Mâcon to GG at Autun, November 21, 1870, LG3; "Latest Military Operations," *New York Tribune*, October 14, 1870, 1. Frapolli's operation was "got up, they say, by some Socialists, and annoyed the General extremely." J. T. Bent, *The Life of Giuseppe Garibaldi* (London: Longmans, Green, 1882), 285.

13   "With Garibaldi" (from the *Daily News*), *Birmingham Daily Post*, November 14, 1870, 6; "Garibaldi and His Army," 1; "Garibaldi" (from the *Daily News*), *Pall Mall Gazette*, November 10, 1870, 11.

General Albert Cambriels, wounded at Sedan, commanded the largest French force in the area. When a rumored Prussian force threatened Cambriels at Besançon, he commanded a reported 35,000 men, but wanted Garibaldi's partly unorganized and barely armed little force at Dole to threaten the right flank of the enemy. When Garibaldi replied that his men lacked arms, Cambriels replied, "I have scarcely sufficient myself. Do what you can with such means as you have." Garibaldi sent north those men he could arm. When Cambriels realized that the Prussians had not moved, he stopped Garibaldi's detachment, which had gone about thirty kilometers north of Dole.[14]

Some hope flickered when the Ministry of War replaced Cambriels with General Michel. He met directly with Garibaldi and not only agreed to share intelligence and consult, but also sent the Armée des Vosges what was its first artillery.

Yet many of the French authorities continued to resent the presence of foreign volunteers and their responses. At one point, Garibaldi boarded his Genoese carbineers and some of the *francs tireurs* of Oran and steamed north to look for Germans. Local officials near Auxonne warned him that the rail and the telegraph lines had been broken by the Prussians. After the general noted that the enemy was nowhere near, the official claimed to know nothing certain about what had happened. When further pressed, he admitted that the *mobiles* in retreat had destroyed the lines fearing Prussian pursuit. When the general grumbled about such panicked conduct, the indignant official looked disdainfully at the Italians and North Africans behind him and snarled, "Where are the French?" To this, Garibaldi replied, "To what nation do you belong?"[15]

This sort of exchange prodded a sore spot.

The arrival of Garibaldi—with his sons—heralded the active involvement of Italian republicans in the war. Some lived in France, particularly in Savoy, a largely Italian area recently acquired by France as part of the price for permitting Italian unification. Many wound up as French *mobiles*.[16] Most of Garibaldi's highest-ranking officers had been

---

14   "Garibaldi and His Army," 1; Gambetta to Cambriels, October 13, 1870, in Bordone, *Garibaldi et l'Armée des Vosges*, vol. 1, 128–9.

15   Mario, "Garibaldi in France," 464; two pieces under the title "With Garibaldi," 6; "Garibaldi and His Army," 1.

16   Frederic Sassone, *La Savoie armée pendant la Guerre franco-allemande 1870– 1871* (Chambéry: Vonne, Conte-grand et Cie, 1874), 11–12.

among the legendary "Thousand" that had taken to the field in Sicily a decade before, and they tended to expect the already battered and demoralized French to rally as had the enthusiastic and hopeful Sicilians in 1860.

The Mediterranean generally provided the bulk of the volunteers. Antonio Orense, the son of José María Orense, a veteran Spanish republican, arrived at the head of his own command. The Basque nationalist Léon Hiriart brought a battalion of his countrymen. Units also came from across North Africa, particularly the provinces of Oran and Alger, with French, Spanish, and South German populations, as well as Arabs. From the far end came the Guérilla française d'Orient, commanded by a Greek resident of Constantinople who had fought for France in Mexico. A native of Havana who had traveled much of the world led the Chasseurs égyptiens.[17]

Poles contributed heavily. General Count Józef Hauke-Bosak, a veteran of the 1863 rising, took charge of the first brigade of Garibaldi's army. Broceslas Wolowski, who signed his name "Spartacus," led a circle at Lyon raising a *légion polonaise*.[18] A small squadron of *lancier polonais* turned up in Garibaldi's army, but administrative and logistical issues stalled the sending of a larger Polish force.

Designated for field command was Jaroslaw Dombrowski (also known as Zadlo-Dombrowski or Zadlo-Dabrowski), the son of an old Polish noble family, trained as a Russian officer. His brother had been a prime mover among the Poles in the International Association in London. Serving in the Russian Army, Zadlo-Dombrowski had become a leader of the secret "Officer Committee of the First Army," cooperating with the revolutionary movement for "Land and Liberty," Zemlya i Volya. Dombrowski, who chose to escape to France in 1865,

---

17   A. Martinien, *Corps auxiliaires créés pedant la guerre 1870–1871. Ie partie: Garde nationale mobilisée* (Paris, 1896), 27; Alexandre Waille Marial, *Les Algériens en France. Étapes d'un franc-tireur oranais* (Paris: Challamel aîné, 1873), 5, 147 ff.; Sassone, *La Savoie armée pendant la guerre franco-allemande*, 153–5. See also Luigi Pennazzi, *L'Armée des Vosges et ses détracteurs* (Lyon: imprimerie Association typographique, 1871).

18   Ladislas Wolowski, *Campagne de 1870–71: Corps Franc des Vosges (Armée de l'Est) souvenirs suivis de dépêches, décrets, etc.* (Paris: A. Laorte, éditeur, 1871). On Zadlo-Dombrowski, Wrobiewski and the Poles at Lyon, see also Deluermoz, *Commune(s)*, 43–4. See also Mark Brown, "The Comité Franco-Polonais and the French Reaction to the Polish Uprising of November 1830," *English Historical Review*, 93 (1978), 774–93.

became increasingly immersed in the world of revolutionary secret societies.[19]

Germans provided hundreds for the force Garibaldi led against the Prussians. The Garibaldian *francs tireurs* of Mont Blanc consisted largely of Swiss and German recruits, and Hanoverians in Switzerland reportedly organized a force. Recruiters operating out of the Hôtel Louvre et Paix at Marseille informed Garibaldi and his staff that 400 German volunteers eager to fight the Prussians would soon join them. They likely reached the front as part of one of the larger units sent from the city.[20]

Moreover, the early references to distinct companies of English and Americans likely disappeared because the army folded them into other units. For this reason, the names of those combined units often disguised their actual composition. Captain Damone's Chasseurs du Havre, for example, included natives of England, Ireland, Poland, Switzerland, Belgium, Denmark, and Italy.[21]

More scandalous than the republican foreigners to the regular army was that an indeterminate number of the "men" of Garibaldi's army were actually female. The land of Joan of Arc certainly had a tradition of the woman warrior, which even the most monarchist and religious authorities accepted. A pious Polish Catholic, Antoinette Lix, assumed an officer's rank and battled for emperor and the Virgin Mother.[22]

19   Gambetta to Garibaldi and nearly three dozen items on the Légion polonais in LG4; Jerzy Zdrada, *Jaroslaw Dabrowski, 1836–1871* (Kraców: Wydawnictwo Literackie, 1973); Bronislaw Wolowski, *Dombrowski et Versailles* (Geneva: Carey, 1871); "L'Armée de Garibaldi," *Guignol illustré*, December 4–11, 1870, 5.

20   M. Marc-Monnier, "La Suisse pendant la guerre de 1870: Nos émigrés de Strasbourg et nos soldats de l'armée de l'est," *Revue des deux mondes*, 2nd series, 93 (May 1871), 36; telegram of Capitaine Foule, Mâcon, to Garibaldi, Autun, November 21, 27, 1870, and Bordone to Foule, Hôtel Louvre et Paix, Marseille, December 21, 1870, LG3.

21   Robert Molis, *Les francs-tireurs et les Garibaldi 1870–1871: Soldats de la république en Bourgogne*, preface by Jean-François Bazin (Paris: S.A.R.L. Éditions Tirésias, 1995), 270–2, 274–6; Michel Cordillot, *La sociale en Amerique: Dictionnaire biographique du mouvement social francophone aux Etats-Unis, 1848–1922* (Dictionnaire biographique du mouvement ouvrier international) (Paris: Les Éditions de l'Atelier, 2002), 258–9, with 413–16 of the presence of F. Tuefferd with the F. Latour group from New York.

22   Le Mesurier, *Feeding of Fighting Armies*, vol. 1, 259; and Françoise d'Eaubonne, *L'amazone sombre: Vie d'Antoinette Lix (1837* [sic]*–1909)* (Paris: Encre, 1983). See also Joseph Turquan, *Les femmes de France pendant l'invasion, 1870–1871* (Paris: Librairie militaire Berger-Levrault, 1893), 25–6, 28, 45, and, on Paris, 124–5.

On the other hand, Garibaldi's army provided numerous examples of radical women under arms. The Prussian-born Donna Wilhelminna Puccinelli had married a former French officer in Algeria, recruited Spanish volunteers for the Army of the Vosges and fought alongside them. Another woman wore the insignia of the International on her arm and her hat. Another, "whose tight-fitting costume displayed her figure to advantage, took care that her uniform carried more lace," but her orders "were obeyed with alacrity." The wife of a former postal official at Oran won her commission direct from Garibaldi because of her performance in battle. One tiny company of his *francs tireurs* had "no fewer than eighteen amazons."[23]

Governments across the continent took notice of Garibaldi's army. It captured and tried a succession of Prussian spies, but they were hardly alone. The French authorities kept close tabs on them as well. The Italian government paid his son-in-law, Colonel Stefano Canzio, to keep it informed of anything that might work to their detriment. Laurence Oliphant, who did clandestine work for the British Foreign Office, also turned up as a reporter, though he made no bones about his scorn for the "Red Prince," who had carried "the Red Flag of Lyons to the Lillies of the Franche Comté."[24]

Yet the Armée des Vosges slowly assumed the more credible and effective appearance.

23   Le Mesurier, *Feeding of Fighting Armies*, vol. 1, 258; Garibaldi, *Souvenirs de la campagne de France*, 23; Julien Sée, *Journal d'un habitant de Colmar pendant la guerre* (Paris: Berger-Leveault et Cie, Libraires-Éditeurs, 1884), 116; "Affaire Jeanning, femme Jeanning et Leroux, lieutenant a la 2me Co. des francs tiereurs du Vaucluse," LG6. Michel Cordillot and Jean-Pierre Bonnet dans Michel Cordillot, *La Commune de Paris 1871. L'événement, les acteurs, les lieux* (Ivry-sur-Seine: Les Éditions de l'Atelier, janvier 2021); and Le Maitron, *Dictionnaire Biographique. Mouvement Ouvrier, Mouvement Social* at maitron.fr/spip.php?article69087.
24   On Canzio, see Viotti, *Garibaldi*, 176 ff.; Margaret Oliphant W. Oliphant, *Memoir of the life of Laurence Oliphant and of Alice Oliphant, His Wife*, 3rd edn, 2 vols. (Edinburgh and London: William Blackwood and Sons, 1891), vol. 2, 127–8; "A strange, a brilliant, yet in some respects a disappointing career." "Laurence Oliphant," *Methodist Magazine*, 34 (September 1892), 247. Oliphant to Russell, October 22, 1870, from Darmstadt, on his way to Metz, Ampthill Papers, FO 918.78, National Archives at Kew.

Metz

In contrast to the development of Giuseppe Garibaldi's forces, the last large imperial French army found itself less and less able to function like an army. Metz went overnight from a city used to feeding about 50,000 from open countryside to having over 200,000 hungry mouths with very limited access to the fields beyond. The reports on numbers are often inconsistent, partly because the situation changed over time, and it is quite likely that Bazaine and his staff would have been hard pressed at any point to give precise numbers. The army started shedding numbers from the first step on the march to the front, and thousands fell in the battles of August, along with many more quietly slipping off to safety. On the other hand, Bazaine conscripted thousands more from the local population. They had a clearer notion about 11,000 cavalry and 280 guns.

Necessities dwindled. The coal, usually well supplied from the mines on the border, disappeared quickly, a loss felt more acutely as the autumn wore on. Butter and chickens became scarce, and the lack of fresh produce soon wore on their health. Just past the middle of October, they got a final piece of bread and had received rations only in horseflesh. Those in advance outposts had already taken to scavenging for themselves, grabbing tomatoes forgotten in the field or even gnawing grasses or roots. Dysentery and bronchitis broke out, and the Germans captured deserters suffering from scurvy. By the end, a threatened gas shortage resulted in extinguishing lamps at seven o'clock, though the local supply of candles remained plentiful.[25]

Conditions inspired political responses. "Mutiny, desertion, and starvation are very formidable enemies within a fortress under any circumstances," declared one paper, "but when that fort is surrounded by two hundred thousand enemies the genius of Hope itself might succumb." With the news of Sedan and the collapse of the empire, things took an overtly political turn, as the city and the ranks of the army began expressing what had been a latent republican sentiment.

---

25 Forbes, *My Experiences of the War*, vol. 1, 423–4; General Devaureix, *Souvenirs et observations sur la campagne de 1870 (Armée du Rhin)* (Paris: Henri Charles-Lavauzelle, 1909), 408; and "A Mutiny Expected at Metz," in "The War," *Leeds Times*, October 15, 1870, 2.

Martial law, now a political as well as a military necessity, placed the city under something of a reign of terror. One day they arrested seventy-eight people for spying, of whom they shot eight for the sake of prudence.[26]

It became possible for the officers to live something of a life apart from the soldiery. Those who could, crowded into the rooms of the city's hotel. Individually, they also tended to have "more of the readies" to purchase better fare for themselves. Their ability to discuss things in the absence of the ranks also tapped a seething discontent.

Captain Louis Rossel had abandoned his earlier plan to escape and reach Gambetta with warnings of Bazaine's treachery. Trapped in Metz, he embarked upon a public campaign for the officers to replace their command. Although news of this reached the highest levels of the army, officers held open meetings to discuss it, but the sheer inertia of military tradition blocked any action. By October 12, generals and colonels told a large meeting of officers that Bazaine's course led "straight to a surrender to the enemy." They believed they could still break the Prussian hold on the city should they put their forces into motion quickly, before hunger further weakened the army. Bazaine caught wind of it and brought Rossel in for questioning. According to the captain's account, they discussed the situation of the army, though he could not recall the details. In the end, the marshal sent him away, giving only advice to stop his propaganda.[27]

"Great disaffection prevails in the army, and a mutiny seems to be impending," summarized one report. "Some of the men refuse to join in the sorties on account of the risk, and it is difficult to force them to perform outpost duty." The generals had the ringleaders of such resistance shot. They feared that such persistent discontent among the *mobiles* spread to the rest of the army. An officer newly appointed to a regiment tolerated its "state of mutiny" for three days, after which he entered the barracks and threatened an old soldier influential with the other soldiers. After hearing his statement of their collective grievances,

---

26   *Cork Examiner*, October 27, 1870, 2; "A Mutiny Expected at Metz," in "The War," *Leeds Times*, October 15, 1870, 2; Forbes, *My Experiences of the War*, vol. 1, 420–2.

27   Gerspach, *Le Colonel Rossel*, 45, 297, 311–12. Léonce Patry, *The Reality of War: A Memoir of the Franco-Prussian War*, trans. Douglas Fermer (London: Wellington House, 2001), 152–3; originally *La guerre telle qu'elle est (1870–71). Metz, Armée du Nord, Commune* (Paris: Montgredien, 1897).

the officer took "a pistol from his pocket, blew out the mutineer's brains."[28] Nobody seems to have kept count of the numbers so dispatched.

Enlisted men had other options. The end loomed ever more tangible as October progressed. Over the final four weeks of the siege, soldiers forced their way into the shops and houses. They ransacked them from cellar to garret, searching for any provisions they could take. In most cases, they offered payment, but such deeds speak to the growing desperation and a shrinking confidence that the officers would see them right.[29]

Desertion always seemed a plausible alternative. Well into mid-October, individual soldiers could come and go through the city gates as they pleased. One group looked out over the open fields near the city and speculated as to whether they could get away. "Lots had been drawn who should make the first attempt, and if the experiment succeeded, the others were to desert likewise." "Men were deserting whenever the chance offered."[30]

In the last ten days, the high command closed the gates of the city, probably to get control over the movements of the men. Then, on October 20, the bread rations ended and the army began consuming their horses, at a rate of roughly a thousand per day. While the numbers of horses at their disposal, like those of the men, remain uncertain, the most optimistic estimates left them no more than a few weeks.

On October 27, Bazaine and the staff finally decided to surrender his army. That morning, they parceled out the very last of the bread, about fifty grams each with a small handful of flour. This probably made any official announcement of their pending surrender superfluous. Within hours, local republican crowds began confronting high-ranking officers.[31]

About 200 officers met on October 28 in the headquarters of the engineering staff to discuss their options. Rossel favored the idea of

---

28   "A Mutiny Expected at Metz," 2; "A French Colonel Worthy of His Epaulettes," in "The War: The Capitulation of Metz," *Leeds Times*, October 29, 1870, 8; Ollier, *Cassell's History of the War*, vol. 1, 40.

29   Ollier, *Cassell's History of the War*, vol. 1, 321

30   Forbes, *My Experiences of the War*, vol. 1, 375, 376; "A Mutiny Expected at Metz," 2.

31   Devaureix, *Souvenirs et observations sur la campagne de 1870*, 414; Forbes, *My Experiences of the War*, vol. 1, 423.

assembling as many soldiers as possible to break through the Prussian lines in a night attack. Where others hesitated to take responsibility, Rossel offered to do so and volunteered to take the Mazelle gate. One suggested that those present take up arms themselves, adding "We will pierce the lines or we will be killed!" Others proposed barricading themselves in Fort Saint-Quentin, and defending it to the last. Still others suggested blowing up the magazine in the arsenal and burning the flags rather than surrendering them. The idea of shooting Bazaine was rejected, preferring to leave him "to the justice of the country." In the end, most wanted "big epaulettes" to lead them, but the higher-ranking officers reported that they had met with brigade commander Justin Clinchant, but he dismissed all plans for further resistance as useless.[32] Significantly, within hours of the meeting, Clinchant pesonally abandoned his men and slipped out of the city.

An English journalist reported a garbled version of this breakout plan, attributing it to Bazaine and his most loyal officers, who allegedly talked of gathering some 25,000 volunteers to fight their way out. The officer returned to his hotel, made out his will and gave it to his friend. The next morning, though, he retrieved the will, explaining that the commanders "could not get a man to follow them."[33]

In the end, the French soldiers shuffled through the gates of the city into bivouacs where the Germans supplied them with food, as they did the civilians of the city. They were permitted to remain largely unsupervised until the victors sent the prisoners east through camps at Saarbrücken and Trier guarded by the Landswehr. Bazaine went to a gentleman's detention at Kassel.[34]

Radical Insurgency in the South

Within hours of the fall of Metz, the Prussian forces that had bypassed Belfort and gone through Franche-Comté turned up in Burgundy and closed on Dijon. The several thousand local *mobiles* gave as well

---

32   Gerspach, *Le Colonel Rossel*, 47, 48, 49, 50, 51, 314–15.
33   Forbes, *My Experiences of the War*, vol. 1, 452–2.
34   Moltke, *The Franco-German War of 1870–71*. vol. 1, 221–2; Forbes, *My Experiences of the War*, vol. 1, 419.

as they got in the preliminary skirmishing, but the serious push began on October 28. Two days later, the German's drove Dr. Jean Lavelle's men out of the city, despite their good arms and a battery with two *mitrailleuse*. Armed with the *chassepots* denied Garibaldi's army, the *mobiles* were said to have thrown down their valuable rifles and fled. The victors levied what amounted to $100,000 from the city as security, and demanded provisions for 80,000 men. The natural tendency of the defeated to exaggerate the size of the forces they faced helped protect the Prussians there from a successful counterattack. Worse, without enough mounts for scouting by the French to the south, rumors spread that the Prussians would continue in that direction. Thousands of German cavalry reportedly concentrated around Mirabeau.[35]

In the process of taking Dijon, the Prussians isolated a mixed force to the north at Langres. The day after the city fell, the government warned commanders of "mutinies" among the *mobiles* of the Haute-Marne. It advised officers to be "severe to these young soldiers" after warning them "for the last time."[36]

About a week later, the Ministry of War redeployed the tiny Armée des Vosges to Autun from Dole, which had become very vulnerable. This relocated them about fifty miles to the west of Dijon, and just south of the pass through the Morvan astride the Massif Central. The government's main focus remained west in the Loire valley, particularly around Orleans. The logistically reasonable shift, inadvertently perhaps, drew Garibaldi's force closer to the strategic center of the line of French defenses running across central France.

Autun also placed the general and his international forces just up the road from Le Creusot and its section of the International. Jean-Baptiste Dumay and a delegation of a hundred workers met with the general and his staff. Despite the exemption of workers in the vital industrial works from military service, some 6,000 of them had taken up arms, leaving

---

35 "Affaire de Dijon," *Le petit journal*, November 12, 1870, 2–3; and "German Success Two Days before the Fall of Dijon" and "Military Affairs in the Vosges," *New York Tribune*, November 3, 1870, 1. Also Gaudelette, *Histoire de la guerre en Bourgogne*; and *La Bourgogne pendant la guerre et l'occupation Allemande 1870–1871*.

36 *Dépêches circulaires, décrets, proclamations, et discours de Léon Gambetta (4 septembre 1870 1–février 1871)*, 2 vols. (Paris: G. Charpentier et Cie, Éditeurs, 1887–91), vol. 2, 365 (hereafter *Dépêches . . . Gambetta*).

the complex "abandoned and almost deserted." Canzio reported that the workers had already "chosen their officers, as is their custom," and wanted to serve under one of Garibaldi's sons. Most of these armed proletarians entered the war through two battalions of the *mobiles* of Saône-et-Loire, said to number 1,730 men under an old soldier who had been in exile after the Bonapartist coup. Dumay himself served as a lieutenant in one of the battalions. Functioning as both workers and soldiers, the old strikers of Creusot took on a role new to them, their employers, the government and the society. They certainly knew whom they wished to fight for, one observer describing their offer "to fabricate mitrailleuses, cannon, or Chassepots, or to put on red shirts and fight."[37]

Shortly after, Joseph Collet, a former French member of the IWA's General Council, wrote from Neuchâtel "appealing to the Council to assist him in getting up an ambulance for Garibaldi's corps." By focusing on the military situation in France, suggested Collet, liberals might be enticed to finance the cause.[38] He was not alone in this approach.

These ties became even more important because the government had made Garibaldi even more directly dependent on support from Lyon and Marseille, though Frapolli—dismissed as chief of staff by Garibaldi—got direct control in managing the payment and supply of the recruits.

Moreover, the situation in those cities became even more intense. The capitulation of Strasbourg at the end of September and of Metz and Dijon at the close of October drastically undercut what little confidence remained in the readiness and ability of the new government to protect the great cities in the southeast of the country.

Marseille erupted. Unsympathetic dispatches "describe the excesses of the Reds as reaching a climax of violence and absurdity." Esquiros, the city's representative in the National Assembly, flatly refused Gambetta's demand for 800,000 francs, as his city opted to go its own way. Gambetta removed him from his duties as prefect. Veteran radicals such as Adolphe

---

37 "Le companies d'ouvriers," *Le petit journal*, November 15, 1870, 4; "L'Armée des Vosges," *Le petit journal*, November 16, 1870, 2; "Règlement pour les ouvriers," *Le petit journal*, December 9, 1870, 3; Molis, *Les francs-tireurs et les Garibaldi*, 68, 121. See also "État des troupes qui restent a Autun le 20 9bre 1870," Lt. A. Szezesnewiez to Garibaldi's staff, November 26, 1870, and "Le club de la ligue du droit" to Garibaldi, December 1870, in LG3, as well as November 2 communiqué from Creusot, and Dumay report, October, in LG5. Note, too, the presence of Second Lieutenant Dumay on a council of war for the Fourth Legion of the GNM. January 14, 1871, LG6.

38 G. C. Mins., *DFI*, 4 (December 6, 1870), 91.

Carcassonne emerged once more, as the city and the Ligue du Midi threatened to take control of the nation's defenses across the south.[39]

The eccentric American millionaire George Francis Train turned up offering what sounded like an easy solution. Associated with Garibaldi's efforts a decade before, he stopped while on a trip around the world that he later claimed inspired Jules Verne's *Around the World in Eighty Days*. He offered to bring over 100,000 rifles from America, with powder, bullets, and cartridges, but "a good army must be immediately formed in the South, and then advance on Paris."[40] Revolutionists at Marseille likely thought Train's plan worth exploring, though they surely did not hail him as the savior of the revolution, as he later claimed.

Train claimed to be in the thick of things. A hopeful delegation escorted him to the Opera House, "packed with excited people from the stage to the topmost boxes." As he took the stage, they chanted "Vive la République!" and "Vive la Commune!" and shouted his name "with a French accent and a nasal 'n.'" Soon, "the fire and enthusiasm of the people swept me from my feet. I was thenceforth a 'Communist,' a member of their 'Red Republic.'" He made another speech at the radical Alhambra, denouncing President Grant for encouraging American sympathies for Prussia without uttering "a word of sympathy for the valiant sons of Lafayette."[41] He had rented the entire front suite of rooms in his hotel.

Meanwhile, a Colonel Marie—almost surely the officer of that name designated to lead a newly recruited local brigade to Garibaldi—found himself in command of the local National Guard with orders to suppress the revolt. Marie declined to arrest the president of the revolutionary council, which, in turn, moved quickly to replace him, likely expecting his imminent departure to the front.[42]

Meanwhile, the revolutionary leaders turned to General Cluseret to command the military forces of the Ligue du Midi. Train later wrote

39   "A Red Republic at Lyons," *Northern Echo*, November 3, 1870, 3.

40   Train, *My Life in Many States and in Foreign Lands*, 301, 309; "George Francis Train Comes to the Rescue of France," *Glasgow Herald*, October 24, 1870, 5.

41   "George Francis Train Comes to the Rescue of France," ibid. Train, *My Life in Many States and in Foreign Lands*, 303–4, 304–5, 331–3, 334–5, 313, 301. Some in the government seem to have believed Train to be the mastermind of the Marseille commune. *Official Despatches*, vol. 1, 129, 2; 137, 2; vol. 2, 20, 2; 23, 1; 34, 1; 319, 1.

42   Greenberg, *Sisters of Liberty*, 181–2.

that he had suggested Cluseret, who himself said that he had been dispatched there by the International. Certainly, Train shared a long association with Cluseret running back through Garibaldi's circles. The former had spent the American Civil War in England, spying on Confederate shipbuilding, a project to which he recruited William De Rohan, the American organizer of the second 1860 English Legion for Garibaldi. At that time, both De Rohan and Hugh Forbes knew Cluseret, who had commanded the French Legion, with the assistance of Joseph Bordone.[43] More immediately, both Train and Cluseret had been deeply involved with the Fenians, and the same British crackdown that had landed Train behind bars in the Four Courts of Dublin had driven Cluseret back to France, from which the imperial authorities had chased him into Switzerland.

As fellow American, who enjoyed the special aid of the US Embassy, was George N. Sanders, the veteran Confederate conspirator in his self-imposed exile. Perhaps best remembered as the most likely handler of John Wilkes Booth in the murder of Abraham Lincoln, he presented himself as having organized the wartime defenses of Richmond, Virginia, though he had spent most of the Civil War in Canada. Sanders claimed that the French Army had him planning for a system of rifle pits and zigzags outside the fortifications, and assured the press that the city would be impregnable, if only the French would use the spade.[44]

Awareness of these Fenian associations may have informed the hostility of Britain's *Penny Illustrated Paper*.

> Given a shrewd attorney with some experience in the art of organizing a bubble company; a "working man" who has long left off labour, having found it more profitable to hold a committee-room in his favourite "public," where he can receive subscriptions to beery state; a professional agitator, whose knowledge of "the laboring classes," consists of an acquaintance with their usual restors after work and an artful stimulation of the enthusiasm which is more likely to operate

43 For Cluseret in Marseille, see Braka, *L'honneur perdu du Général Cluseret*, 117–29.

44 Henry Labouchere, *Diary of the Besieged Resident in Paris*, 3rd edn (London: Macmillan and Co., 1872), 28. See Yonatan Eyal, "A Romantic Realist: George Nicholas Saunders and the Dilemmas of Southern International Engagement," Journal of Southern History 78 (February 2012), 107–30.

on their immediate weaknesses; throw in a real working man or two, who, fancying they have attained political knowledge by a perusal of two or three eleventh-rate books founded principally on the fallacies of the first French Republic, and have deserted the ennobling labour that should sustain wives and children for the spurious notoriety of the debating hall—and the association is complete.

It advised everyone to regard with suspicion "leagues, societies, and congresses."[45]

Still, such caveats mattered little in the south of France. Having learned from his experience with the Fenians, Cluseret insisted on a force of at least 2,000 armed men. A few days later, the general turned up, "a splendid-looking fellow with a great military mustache," using the name "Tirez." A mass meeting of 5,000 crowded into the Hôtel du Louvre, singing the Marseillaise, when Train arrived in a blue coat with gold buttons sporting the regalia of the Fenians with Cluseret at his side. That evening, the two walked arm in arm at the head of a crowd of 10,000 at the local Cirque. The press reported this organization for the Ligue de Midi as an attempt to "form a separate and independent Republic."[46]

For a few days, power seemed to teeter precariously at Marseille.

Framing all of these developments had been the news of the collapse of the last surviving imperial army at Metz, the plots it generated, and the monarchist longings it inspired. From that point, the "Revolution of September 4th" had to define itself. Sections of the army clearly depended heavily on the resources of those large cities still in the hands of the French Republic, particularly Lyon, Marseille, and the temporary capital at Bordeaux. Then, too, the political and class resentments that spawned these democratic currents grew, in part, from the new corruptions associated with the supplying, equipping, and organizing of the resources needed to fight the war.

Through it all, what the central government of the republic ultimately required of its people differed little from the demands of the old empire:

---

45   "Apes in the Tree of Liberty," *Penny Illustrated Paper*, October 29, 1870, 274.

46   Train, *My Life in Many States and in Foreign Lands*, 302–3, 305, 306; "Nouvelles générales," *Le petit journal*, November 4, 1870, 4; Greenberg, *Sisters of Liberty*, 180, 181, 183; "A Red Republic at Lyons," *Northern Echo*, November 3, 1870, 3. See also Aminzade, *Ballots and Barricades*.

loyalty to their death and ruin, regardless of the corruption and the institutional frustration of self-government. As had been the case with the empire, the extent to which the government could do these things would turn on its ability to produce military results.

The first generation that bore the full brunt of modern war survived it as their heirs would, only in part, and muddled through with illusions ever more dense and burdensome. Later, chroniclers of the campaign would remark on the high morale of the French troops and their optimism about the future. For the French, wrote one officer, "Communists, Republicans, Imperialists, Legitimists, and Orleanists —all, as one man, renounced party, and allowed their differences to stand in abeyance until they had either sunk or swam together."[47] In practice, imperial decisions had courted the invasion, leaving the people generally little choice in the matter.

To the southwest of Paris, the *gouvernement de la défense nationale* had pinned its hopes on constructing and building a new Armée de la Loire, supplemented by a corps from Normandy, organized quickly and hopefully. Rather characteristically, the republic appointed a monarchist and politicized Catholic General Louis Jean-Baptiste d'Aurelles de Paladines. "Of all the faults of the French army during those autumn months," noted a contemporary writer, "the worst was insubordination." The new commander decided to nip it in the bud: "Soldiers, what I ask of you, above all things, is discipline and firmness. I am, moreover, thoroughly determined to shoot any soldier who hesitates before the enemy; and if it should chance that I myself fail to do my duty, I tell you to shoot me." Amused by this "direct incentive to mutiny," one commentator noted, "every soldier is at liberty to determine for himself when his commander has failed to do his duty, and is thereupon invested with the privilege of summary execution."[48] This army had one immediate goal,

---

47   H. Bonnal, *L'esprit de la guerre moderne: Le manœuvre de Saint-Privat 18 juillet–18 août 1870*, vol. 2. (Paris: Librairie R. Chapelot et Cie., 1906), 486–8; Kirwin, *La compagnie irlandaise*, 123.

48   Ollier, *Cassell's History of the War*, vol. 1, 392. See Paul Hugounet, *Les champs de bataille de 1870: Orléans. 11 Octobre 1870–11 Octobre 1884* (Orleans: H. Herluison, 1883–4); Georges Breuillac, *Campagnes de la Loire et de la Sarthe pendant la guerre franco-allemande 1870–1871, avec un autographe du général Chanzy et une carte du théâtre de la guerre . . . (9 juillet 1871)* (Niort: L. Clouzot and Paris: E. Dentu, 1871); General Barthélemy-Edmond Palat, *Campagne de la Loire en 1870–1871*.

to retake Orleans, halfway between the government-in-exile and the capital, theoretically the prelude to fighting their way north to break the Prussian stranglehold on Paris.

Remarkably, on November 9, this new force demonstrated that it might well be up to the challenge. After some minor fighting in the area, about 70,000 French soldiers threw themselves against 20,000 Bavarians at Coulmiers, west of Orleans. With an initial advantage in artillery, they used their numbers in a fierce bayonet charge that drove the Germans from the town. Two days later, the victorious French retook Orleans.[49]

This singular victory around Orleans left the beleaguered defenders of Paris—and France—what little they had left on which to hope.

---

49   "La Victoire d'Orleans," *Le petit journal*, November 14, 1870, 1.

8
Shaping a Republic:
From the South to the Capital

As the weather chilled and food became scarcer in Paris, the Anglo-American Ambulance relied more and more on Hélène Bernois, whose familiarity with the city and widespread contacts proved vital to the survival of the enterprise. The African American woman from New Orleans essentially managed part of the hospital and lavished particular attention on some of the wounded, especially those who might otherwise be viewed as hopeless. After losing a dying Zouave who had "the dusky hue of the chasseur d'Afrique," she turned to aid an "Ancient Mariner," a *mobile* who clung to life despite "no less than nine wounds in different parts of his body."[1] It hardly mattered which wounds he incurred for the empire and which for the republic.

The government, managed largely by monarchists, had declared a republic. Efforts to shape a genuinely representative model found their effort continually thwarted by the national government. These remained particularly strong in the south, which had long felt neglected by the centralizing imperial power in Paris. So, too, Giuseppi Garibaldi's Armée des Vosges found itself fighting for a government that denied them resources, authority, and, ultimately perhaps, a cause in which to hope. The war bottled these tensions in Paris itself, largely abandoned by those with means and disproportionately left to those with fewer resources to bear the bitter miseries of the siege.

---

1   Louis Judson Swinburne, *Paris Sketches* (Albany: Joel Munsell, 1875), 78–81.

The Battle over Republicanism in the South

After several popular challenges to its authority in the south of France, the central government had to respond. Gambetta telegraphed Alphonse Gent, moving that official previously assigned to Algeria to a new job as the prefect at Marseille. Well aware of their tenuous position, Cluseret and other leaders of the commune sought to avoid a direct clash, and tried to persuade Gent to share power with the outgoing prefect, the radical leader Alphonse Esquiros.[2]

Gent not only declined, but sent a detachment to search for General Cluseret. When they demanded entry into George Francis Train's hotel suite, he claimed, he and his three secretaries armed themselves with revolvers, after which he warned the officer that they would be able to "kill at least two dozen of them," should they force the issue.[3] After a short discussion outside, they left. When they returned later, they found the red flag, a French flag and a US flag displayed from Train's balcony. "Vive la République!" he heckled them, adding "Vive la Commune!"

Shortly after, someone took a shot at Gent in his carriage. In response, the troops sought to impose something like martial law on the city. According to Train, a detachment returned to his hotel, after which he decided to "die in the most dramatic manner possible," stepping out onto his balcony and wrapping himself in the flags of France and the United States, shouting down to them in French, "Fire, fire, you miserable cowards!" He said that they drew back and "marched on down the street and out of sight." Of course, as the *Observer* noted, "all statements made by Mr. Train must be taken with reservations." Still, nobody refuted the specifics of his version of events and such confrontations likely took place across the city as power teetered.[4]

What the authorities presented as a radical attempt on Gent's life may not have turned public opinion against the revolution, as has been asserted. However, the perception that this had happened likely forced much of the movement to think twice about casting their lot with those

---

2 Train, *My Life in Many States and in Foreign Lands*, 306–7.

3 Greenberg, *Sisters of Liberty*, 182–3. For Train's account, see *My Life*, 307–8

4 "George Francis Train Again" (from the *Observer*), *Freeman Journal*, November 14, 1870, 3.

who might not consult them before taking such a major decision. More substantially, 2,500 troops from Lyon steamed into the city to impose the will of the central government. Not surprisingly, coming from another city that had made its bid for power, some "serious disorder" broke out among those troops, resulting in the execution of several men as mutineers.[5] On November 13 though, Gent telegraphed the government that the commune at Marseille was no more.

Meanwhile, Cluseret himself had gone into hiding, while Train and Gaston Crémieux left Marseille together for Lyon. On the train, though, "a man, wearing conspicuously the ribbon of the Legion of Honor, entered our compartment" and picked a fight with Crémieux. The man left at one of the stops just outside of Lyon, and, when the two continued on into the city, they found themselves "confronted by six bayonets." Train quickly swallowed the slip of paper with Cluseret's address before they could stop him, and they locked him up for thirteen days.[6] Cluseret, too, wound up behind bars for a period.

In Lyon, Train's cousin and secretary, the Boston-born future mayor of Omaha George Pickering Bemis, spent a frantic week after his employer did not turn up. He got US ambassador Elihu B. Washburne at Paris to make enquiries. Eager to placate the former insurgents, the local authorities back at Marseille reportedly ordered his release, but the central government now had control of the prisoner, who soon found himself on a train to Tours.[7]

We have only Train's version of his exchange with Gambetta.[8] Underfed and sickly from his incarceration, he awaited "the Dictator's pleasure." Around him had been "men who had been waiting for three weeks; in the next rooms were those who had waited for two weeks; and in the third rooms I found officers of the army and navy, who had waited one week." When he gained admission, Gambetta left him standing until Train went on the offensive. "When a distinguished stranger calls to see

5   Allnutt, *Historical Diary of the War*, 179; "La province (d'apres les journaux etrangers)," *Le petit journal*, December 3, 1870, 3; *Dépêches . . . Gambetta*, vol. 1, 506 n.

6   Train, *My Life*, 309–10, 329.

7   Biographies of Train and Bemis are available in the Douglas County section of Alfred T. Andreas, *History of the State of Nebraska* (Chicago: the Western Historical Company, 1882), an unpaged but well-indexed version of which is online at kancoll.org. "Douglas County," Andreas' *History of Nebraska*. Sebrell's *Persuading John Bull*, did not seem to understand the relationship of Bemis to Train, 107, 203.

8   Train, *My Life*, 311–12, with the exchange at 312–13.

you, M. Gambetta, I think you might offer him a chair." When Gambetta waved him to a seat, Train continued:

> M. Gambetta, you are the head of France, and I intend to be President of the United States. You can assist me, and I can assist you." He continued, "Send me to America, and I can help you get munitions of war, and win over the sympathy and assistance of the Americans.

In response, though, Gambetta accused him of being an ally of Cluseret. "Cluseret is a scoundrel," snarled Gambetta. "The Communards call you that," shrugged Train, who soon found himself on his way out of the country.

Had he made it into Lyon, Train would have doubtlessly complained about the imposition of Gambetta's central government there. The Ligue du Midi, that alliance of the southern communites, faded as quickly as had the short-lived local radical regime there. Lyon hosted its last meeting in November.[9]

The government found itself in no position to reform the rampant corruption in the system of recruitment and supply acquisition that accompanied the reimposition of order there. As to the corruption, Gambetta never took measures to stop Luigi Frapolli and his circle from controlling much of the logistics. Garibaldi respectfully heard Gambetta make the case for reinstating Frapolli on his staff, but the general remained as unbending as the clique controlling his line of supply through Lyon. The continued lack of cooperation there also created and complicated problems bringing up assistance from Mâcon, Marseille, and other communities to the south. Nevertheless, the government repeatedly tried to get Frapolli back into a position of greater authority.[10]

Eager to establish its legitimacy, the Armée des Vosges decided to act in the wake of the inspiring French recapture of Orleans. Several hundred of them successfully overwhelmed a German garrison at Châtillon-sur-Seine far behind Prussian lines serving as a vital link of supply and communications to the Germans in recently captured Dijon. Garibaldi and his staff surmised that the Prussians would strengthen such outposts, weakening their hold on the city. Garibaldi could muster several thousand men for an

---

9   Greenberg, *Sisters of Liberty*, 180.
10 Bordone, *Garibaldi et l'Armee des Vosges*, vol. 2, 179 n., 166, 180 n.; Foule at Mâcon to GG at Autun, November 21, 1870, LG3.

offensive operation, in coordination with General Camille Crémer's division of 10,000 to 12,000 in the Gardes nationales mobilisées then lurking just to the south of Dijon.[11] A coordinated attack might carry Dijon and, with Orleans, turn the tide across the southern front.

On Saturday, November 27, Garibaldi's column, moving west out of Autun, struck a Prussian outpost a few kilometers beyond Lantenay. The Italians and a mixed group of irregulars and *francs tireurs* pushed them back and through Prenois toward Pasques, "a little village built on a rocky eminence, and surrounded with stone walls." Reinforcements came from Val de Suzon, Darois, and elsewhere. It took until early afternoon for enough support to catch up and, with artillery, to press the Germans out of Pasques, after which Garibaldi's force began to fan out in a broad arc from near Darois back through Prenois and Pasque and down toward the Ouche near Velars, facing the largest German concentration along the road between Darois and Hauteville.[12]

Despite mistaken reports that Crémer's *mobiles* just the other side of Dijon might have gone into action as well, word reached the staff that Crémer would leave them unsupported. Giuseppe Beghelli later wondered whether his superiors had been "more ignorant or more guilty" risking their attack on Dijon, under such circumstances.[13]

At this point, an attack could only be a great gamble. They had lost the element of surprise and would have no support, and they had made a long march and fought hard to get where they were.[14] Also, they

11   Bordone, *Garibaldi et l'Armee des Vosges*, vol. 2, 169–70, 171–2; "Rapport sur l'affaire de Chatillon sur Seine," January 21, 1871, LG3; "Bulletin de la guerre," *Le petit journal*, November 29, 1870, 4. Giuseppe Beghelli, *La Camicia Rossa in Francia* (Turin: Civelli, 1871), 208. See also the treatment of Karine Varley, *Under the Shadow of Defeat: The War of 1870–71 in French Memory* (Basingstoke: Palgrave Macmillan, 2008), 221.

12   "L'Affaire de Dijon," *Le petit journal*, December 1, 1870, 1; Bordone, *Garibaldi et l'Armee des Vosges*, vol. 2, 185, 187–8, 199. Beghelli, *La Camicia Rossa in Francia*, 35–6, 100, 139–40, 141, 142; Ettore Socci, *Da Firenze a Digione: Impressioni di un reduce Garibaldino* (Prato: Tipograpfia sociale, 1871), 77; Garibaldi, *Souvenirs de la campagne de France*, 48–9, 50; Bizonni, *Souvenirs d'un garibaldien*, 116. Baghino also left a short *Reminiscenze* (Genes: s.n., 1888).

13   Bordone, *Garibaldi et l'Armee des Vosges*, vol. 2, 182, 184, 186, 284; Beghelli, *La Camicia Rossa in Francia*, 124, 144, 146; Garibaldi, *Souvenirs de la campagne de France*, 52.

14   Edmond Thiébault, *Ricciotti Garibaldi et la 4me brigade: récit de la campagne de 1870–71 avec documents et cartes* (Paris: Godet, 1872), 34–5, 37–8, estimated that the army then had around 7,000 in the area of Dijon. "Dans l'est," *Le petit journal*, December 5, 1870, 1; Luigi Canessa, "The last battle of Garibaldi," at utenti.multimania.it. See also

believed in the possibility of a bold move, and many thought that it might, like the movement of "the Thousand" in Sicily, inspire a population energized by patriotic hope and a determination to fight.

Around 6:30 p.m. footsore, hungry, and discouraged men blunderered through a chilling autumn rain into the first Baden outposts, which fell back down the slopes toward Daix. There, the Germans had a makeshift barricade with four ranks of fire that flashed into the faces of their tormentors. "The only thing that surprises me is that two-thirds were not killed," recalled one of their targets. A succession of volleys followed, and the first of the *mobiles* broke for the rear. In the dark, their flight carried to the rear those units behind them until it threw everything into chaos, as, unit by unit, the attack disintegrated. As his men ignored him, one Basque officer stood helplessly in tears.[15] Hundreds disappeared.

Most of those they fought, it was later said, had been *mobiles*, but one Italian recalled of his unit, "With swords drawn and revolvers cocked, they led on a given number, and the *mobiles* marched well, stood fire bravely—in short, did their duty." In the midst of this, the radical Beghelli encountered the young pastor of the church in Prenois sobbing, and found himself moved by "the tears of that good man."[16] In the end, neither politics nor good intentions provided any effective rearguard action.

Back at Dijon, General August Graf von Werder smelled blood and sent a large force in pursuit. The next few days brought scattered skirmishes as the bits and pieces of a shattered Armée des Vosges scrambled to reorder their ranks. By November 30, only part of the army had reached Autun, where most collapsed into a fitful sleep before greeting the reinforcements that had come up. The next day, around 7,000 to

---

Aroldi, *L'ultimo dei vecchi garibaldini*, xvi; Achille Bizzoni, *Souvenirs d'un garibaldien (Campagne de 1870–71)* (Paris: Librairie de Firmin-Didot et Cie, 1892), 92; Pennazzi, *L'Armée des Vosges et ses détracteurs*, 15–16.

15   Beghelli, *La Camicia Rossa in Francia*, 145, 146, 147, 148, 150; Molis, *Les francs-tireurs et les Garibaldi*, 85–93; Bordone, *Garibaldi et l'Armee des Vosges*, vol. 2, 194, 195; Dormoy, *Les trois batailles de Dijon*, 173–9, 183–91, with relevant excerpts from Feill's account at 443–61; Bizzoni, *Souvenirs d'un garibaldien*, 64–5, 501–32; and Jessie White Mario, "Garibaldi in France," *Fraser's Magazine* (new series), 16: (October, 1877), 474–5. Mario's marvelous account appeared in three installments in this volume of *Fraser's* (October, November, December 1877), 452–77, 602–18, 720–35; Molis, *Les francs-tireurs et les Garibaldi*, 85, 86–7, 90–1; "Dijon et les garibaldiens," *L'impartial dauphinois*, December 9, 1870, 2, repeated at 6.

16   Beghelli, *La Camicia Rossa in Francia*, 158.

8,000 Germans—two Baden regiments with enough divisional troops to man the eighteen cannons and two squadrons of cavalry—attacked Autun.[17]

That Thursday, the desperate advocates of the "universal republic" found themselves literally with their backs to the wall, albeit ancient Roman walls. Not too far to the south of Autun, the political ferment of an industrial society deepened around those "rich Creusot's arsenals." There, the municipal council survived, a simple reflection of the staff of Schneider, with the support of a government convinced that its presence could maintain the production of weapons vis-à-vis revolutionary agitation. Jean-Baptiste Dumay emerged as the chair of the local defense committee, and, on September 24, Gambetta's government appointed him the provisional mayor of Creusot.[18] Although growing in strength, the radicals were not alone.

The tumultuous politics of these insurgent communities found a reflection on the field, because they provided so many of the French troops in Garibaldi's army. The thirty-man unit of Francs-tireurs lyonnais or the Francs-tireurs du Midi, turned up early. It later merged with the even smaller unit of ten volunteers in Captain Bablon's Francs-Tireurs de Philippeville to form the Francs-tireurs du Midi et de Philippeville, soon to be reorganized as the core of the Franc-Tieurs réunis.[19] .

Marseille provided two large battalions of the Corps franc de l'égalité de Marseille. Delpech, the republican insurgent from Marseille, had brought up another battalion of that body. On the other hand, the reactionary Lieutenant Colonel Jacques-Édouard-Claude Chenet had recruited ship crews from the Levant in that community into his Guerilla française d'Orient or the Guerilla d'Orient. At a crtical point, with his forces occupying the keystone position in the line, Chenet decided to

17   Thomas Joachim Alexandre Prosper Mignard, *De l'invasion de l'Allemagne dans les provinces de Bourgogne et de Franche-Comté en 1870–71* (Besançon: Marion, Libraire, and Dijon: Lamarche, Libraire, 1875), 102; and, on the numbers Frédéric Sassone, *La Savoie armée pendant la guerre franco-allemande 1870–71* (Chambéry: Bonne, 1875), 155.

18   Beghelli, *La Camicia Rossa in Francia*, 123; Pierre Ponsot, "Dumay Jean-Baptiste," in Jean Maitron, ed., *Dictionnaire biographique du mouvement ouvrier international*, 12 vols. (Paris: Les Éditions ouvrières, 1974); as well as Dumay, *Mémoires d'un militant ouvrier du Creusot*. See also René-Pierre Parize, "Savoir de soumission ou saviors de révolté? L'exemple du Creusot," in Jean Borreil, ed., *Les sauvages dans la cité: Auto-émancipation du peuple et instruction des prolétaires au XIXe siècle* (Seyssel and Paris: Champ Vallon and Presses universitaires de France, 1985) 92–4.

19   Bordone, *Garibaldi et l'Armee des Vosges*, vol. 1, 112.

march his men off the field back toward Le Creusot, confusing adjacent units and carrying some of them off the field with them.[20] His most apparent motives seem to have been his skepticism about the entire republican project and a contempt for the foreigners who had come to defend France.

Yet the line held. Garibaldi's forces, likely amounting to around 5,000 effectives, managed to repulse the Prussians, who had brought around 7,000 men to the attack. The success of the defenders might not have erased the memory of their failure at Dijon, but, as Beghelli waxed philosophically, "even in war, you have to be able to forget the failures."[21]

In a matter of weeks, the very same troops that had defended Dijon would hold the Prussian line on the Lisaine river against almost ten times what Garibaldi had could have thrown against them. Even had part of the Armée des Vosges managed to take the city—and been rejoined shamefacedly by those who had fled from the field—they would never have been able to hold it, unless Crémer brought up reinforcements in an act of cooperation that had thus far eluded them.

And such a republican triumph in Burgundy would mean little without successes elsewhere that would not only keep the Germans at bay, but drive them from Paris.

The Siege from Below

As events blighted the power of the French state, its leaders became increasingly desperate and their abilities to plan, always limited, faded into little more than a series of immediate responses. By the closing weeks of 1870, France had lost all but half a million of those it had placed in field along with their equipment and arms, including hundreds of cannons. It could not bear a continuation of those losses.

The government's survival rested, paradoxically, upon the exclusion of Paris from its affairs, but its surrender to the Germans would likely spell the doom of the national government as well. Always politicized to

20 Molis, *Les francs-tireurs et les Garibaldi*, 296; Bordone, *Garibaldi et l'Armee des Vosges*, vol. 1, 118, vol. 2, 206–11, 206, 220, 229, 226, 229; Beghelli, *La Camicia Rossa in Francia*, 171, 203, 197, 198, 200, 205; Bizzoni, *Souvenirs d'un Garibaldien*, 137.

21 "État des troupes présentes à Autun le 2 décembre," LG3; Molis, *Les francs-tireurs et les Garibaldi*, 121–5, 125–35; Dormoy, *Les trois batailles de Dijon*, 249–54.

a certain extent, questions of strategy became entirely politicized, especially evident in the defense of the largest city, Paris. The national government, governing in the absence of Paris, had mixed feelings about having to address the concerns of a liberated capital. The army's approach to its administration of the city or its use and management of the National Guard reflected this. So did the growing public mistrust of the army and the national government.

As much to migitate these pressures as to raise the siege, generals Louis Trochu and Joseph Vinoy did lead a series of sorties beyond the city walls. The news from Metz moved the army to make a disastrous foray to Bourget, but these twin disasters moved the people of Paris to march on the Hôtel de Ville at the end of October.

The International had certainly discouraged taking issue with the republic in the face of the Germans. On September 9—almost as soon as the news of a republic had reached London—Marx rushed into action before the General Council of the IWA to analyze what the war meant. Despite considerable confusion as to the details, the IWA leadership immediately began planning a demonstration in favor of British recognition of the new French republic. Marx soon reported that August Serraillier "had gone to Paris and decided to remain there," where he joined the National Guard, and the General Council started a fund to support his family. The following month, Marx added that Serraillier had sent his mother-in-law a letter from Paris by the balloon post.[22]

In London, the International appealed to the British government to recognize the French republic. They also held mass demonstrations in Hyde Park. A few weeks after the solidarity meeting there, a small squad of hungry French soldiers ventured along the Marne from Charenton in search of food. There they encountered a small mounted body that had slipped through the lines to deliver the regards of "the Liberal Association of Greenwich." Their captain identified himself as De Rohan, an aide-de-camp Garibaldi, who had turned up to assist the new French republic.[23]

---

22   G. C. Mins., *DFI*, 4 (September 6, 9, 13, 1870 Special Meeting), 56–8, 59, 60. See also G. C. Mins., *DFI*, 4 (July 26, 1870), 31–7; (August 2, 1870), 37–42; (August 9, 1870), 43–6; (August 16, 1870), 47–8; (August 23, 1870), 49–50; (August 30, 1870), 51–5; 4 (Sept. 6, 1870), 55–9.

23   For the Hyde Park demonstration of support addressed by Beesley, Odger, Weston, and others associated with the IWA, see "The French Republic and the London Working Class," *Darlington Northern Echo*, September 12, 1870, 6. Also see G. C. Mins., *DFI*, 4

William De Rohan came as "delegate of the democracy of England." He brought a document from London sanctioned by that immense meeting which had been held in favour of France, and implied that this meeting represented public sentiment in Britain. On behalf of the government, Jules Favre expressed his sincere thanks "for the sentiments which have been so nobly expressed in the name of the English nation." De Rohan then opted to stay to defend the city and, after recovering from a wound received south of the city, he took charge of a battery.[24]

The International did take some modest action in defense of the republic. At first, even the most radical residents of the city—those who had opposed the arrogant imperial war of Napoleon III—fell into line behind a defensive republican war. The International, trade union bodies and serious republican groups formed committees of vigilance in each neighborhood. These, in turn, established a Republican Central Committee of the Twenty Arrondissements.

In a very important sense, the International exercised a broad influence in Paris. This came, in large part, from its participation in new mass organizations such as the Légion garibaldienne or the Ligue républicaine de défense à outrance. Both of these grew very rapidly with deep roots among the workers of the capital.[25] However, the very rapidity of that development reflected a potential weakness, in that the democratic

---

(September 6, 13, October 18, November 29, 1870) 58, 61, 73–4, 90; for the delegation, Mr. Alexandre Bay, J. S. Floyd, and Merrimann, "Sympathy with the French Republic" (*Daily Telegraph*), *Daily Alta California*, October 12, 1870, 2. P. Christian, *Histoire de la guerre avec la Prusse et des deux sièges de Paris, 1870–1871*, 2 vols. (Paris: Legrand, Troussel et Pomey, 1872), vol. 2, 15–16; *Journal de Siège de Paris*, 3 vols. (Paris: Librairie générale, 1874), vol. 1, 339, 451.

24   Henry Labouchere, *Diary of the Besieged Resident in Paris*, 3rd edn (London: Macmillan and Co., 1872), 75. The correspondence occupies two columns in the *Journal officiel de la République Française*, but, when the *Daily News*, October 7, 1870, 6, reported the story, it added that "M. de Rohan's residence in England is, I should imagine, in the vicinity of Tooley Street." This journalistic joke referred to a parliamentary petition in the name of "the people of England" that supposedly came from three tailors on Tooley Street. See Herschel Gower, *Charles Dahlgren of Natchez: The Civil War and Dynastic Decline* (Nashville, TN: Richland Press, 2005), 200, 222; "War Miscellany," *Sheffield Daily Telegraph*, November 15, 1870, 8; "Admiral De Rohan. An Extraordinary History Elicited in a New York Civil District Court," *New York Sun*, September 22, 1879, 3.

25   Martin P. Johnson, *The Paradise of Association: Political Culture and Popular Organizations in the Paris Commune of 1871* (Ann Arbor: University of Michigan Press, 1996), 31–2, 38–9, 73, 169. For a discussion of this in a broader context, see Martin Breaugh, *The Plebeian Experience: A Discontinuous History of Political Freedom*, trans. Lazer Lederhendler (New York: Columbia University Press, 2013), 173–98.

skills needed to function there remained, of necessity, new and poorly exercised.

By late October, though, members of the International, such as Cluseret and others, participated in the attempted rebellion. Most importantly, though, one of the living legends of the revolutionary movement, Auguste Blanqui, reemerged as a leader of this resurgent popular movement. A free man under a general amnesty, he had established La patrie en danger, and led several armed demonstrations against the government over the previous year, including an August attempt to seize weapons from the government. The authorities quickly identified him as one of those responsible for the rising of October 31.

Blanqui's comrade in this had been the journalist Auguste-Jean-Marie Vermorel. Vermorel's collaboration with the most radical of the socialists obscured some of thse most fundamental of his beliefs. The author of Les hommes de 1851 and Les Vampires, he compiled studies of the humanist writer Estienne de La Boétie, and leaders of the French Revolution of 1789—André Boniface Louis Riquetti de Mirabeau, Pierre Victoria de Vergniaud, Georges Jacques Danton, Jean-Paul Marat, and Maximilien Robespierre.[26] It was a revealing preoccupation.

On one level, Jacobinism had been a grand historic failure and there existed no reason to expect that it would be otherwise. Beyond the rather narrow circles of pioneering theorists, old enlightenments and shadows defined the contours of a seemingly accessible future. From below, the movement developed a common denominator that sounded increasingly like Jacobinism, something aimed at the goal of a radical republic, pursued primarily in the elimination of the aristocracy, its collaborators, its potential collaborators, and those who could be collaborators. Anyone wielding any kind of power within the envisioned revolution might have the power to damage it, creating a version of revolution fully capable of justifying the reported self-imolation of the revolutionists.

The army responded to the bid for power with lead, a precedent for its policies over the coming weeks and months. A major motive for most of the fighting around Paris that followed aimed at providing an outlet,

---

26 Auguste Vermorel, *Les hommes de 1851; histoire de la présidence et du rétablissement de l'empire* (Paris, Décembre-Alonnier, 1869), and *Ces dames: Portraits de Malakoff, de Zou-Zou, de Risette, photographiés par Pierre Petit* by Vermorel, A. *(Auguste), 1841–1871* (Paris: Eugene Picic, [1860]).

a political safety valve to diffuse popular mistrust of the intentions of the government and the military from reaching the point of a rising. Only a few days later after the October debacle, skirmishing erupted before the Fort de Nogent, and thereafter some skirmishing would take place every few days

After a month of this, on November 29, Trochu moved a large force against the Prussian lines over the flooded valley of the Marne. He lost 1,300 almost immediately along the flooded river bottom, but they secured beachheads east of the river in the villages of Champigny. By December 2, Prussian reinforcements threw the French back into the city. The Germans lost over 3,000 men, but inflicted three times that number of casualties on the French.

Periodic skirmishes continued for weeks. On December 19, a portion of the defenders had ventured out once more to Bourget. In the second battle of Bourget, they overwhelmed the Prussians and secured what could have become a serious breach in the encirclement of the city. Two days later, the reinforced Germans in that corner of the line retook it and reestablished their hold over the area. The following day, their artillery opened on the city's defenses at Avron, though not yet on Paris itself.

No matter, though, the German bombardment resumed on December 27, 28, and 29, and again with the New Year.

As the siege wore on, it made Paris more allies, even unexpected ones. Captain Louis Rossel and other officers who had survived the disaster at Metz began to feel something very similar in Paris. Later, in the month of January, he wrote to General Crémer, reminding him that they had not acted to save the army at Metz in October. "We must ourselves take the lead."[27]

From above—or from below—Paris faced serious questions, and the answers differed.

Contemporaries described this as increasing class tensions. "The bourgeois and the working man worship different gods," wrote a British newspaperman, "and have hardly two ideas in common." Another described defenders as drawn from those "who threw down their arms and surrendered themselves unwounded" or "maltreated their officers

---

27 Gerspach, *Le Colonel Rossel*, 52; Devaureix, *Souvenirs et observations sur la campagne de 1870*, 419–20.

and became openly mutinous at Sedan," predicting that others would come back from their captivity in Germany to enjoy a life of leisure on their pensions.[28]

The burdens of the siege in Paris fell disproportionately upon the laboring classes. French elites could disproportionately afford escape to the countryside in the days between Sedan and the arrival of the Prussians. After the siege, those with connections, or the cash to make connections, could always find their way through the lines.

As winter swept into the city, Paris waited in suffering for rescue from outside. Increasingly, the shortages and poverty of the siege had already closed the cafés and driven the remaining population into their homes. The people grew less and less patient.

Although Paul Déroulède, the conservative officer of the *turcos* at Sedan, had slipped to Belgium during the battle, and returned to Paris where he worked himself into a lather about "the military mutiny in the streets of Sedan," immediately associating it with the rebelliousness of the Parisian crowds. On October 6—the day after the demonstrations in Paris itself—garrison troops at Charenton station outside Paris actually did come near to mutiny. When two enlisted men refused to obey direct orders from a newly promoted officer, matters escalated, and other enlisted men refused to arrest them.[29] Such incidents had already become ubiquitous.

The movement at Paris reflected the particular cosmopolitanism of the greatest metropolis on the continent. Leó Frankel, a Hungarian Jew with Prussian citizenship, had been long involved in the ADAV before coming to Lyon. He then moved on to Paris, where he worked as a jeweler, and wrote on events there for various socialist papers back in the German-speaking world. In the city, he not only held membership in the International but also helped to organize German and Hungarian workers in the captial.

Among the many Poles and Russians drawn there was Élisabeth Dmitrieff. Incarcerated in her youth in the notorious Peter and Paul Fortress at St. Petersburg, she read Nikolai Chernyshevsky's *What Is to*

---

28 "Letter of Besieged Resident in Paris to *Daily News*, October 10, reprinted as 'The War," *Bradford Observer*, October 25, 1870, 3, cols. 2–4; "The War. III," *Fraser's Magazine*, new series, 2 (November 1870), 658.

29 Déroulède, *1870*, 256, 259; and "Juridiction militaire," *Le petit journal*, January 30, 1871, 3.

Be Done? (1863), and determined to find a way to contribute to what she saw as a coming Russian revolution. She managed to get permission to go abroad to a university, where she soon found herself drawn into revolutionary politics and the exile that often went with it.

The siege brought women generally came to the fore in ways they had not done before. Louise Michel, born out of wedlock to a serving maid, came to Paris from northeastern France. A few years earlier, she had opened a school famous for its progressive methods, and came to know Victor Hugo, Blanqui, and other radicals. In 1869 her Société pour la revendication du droits civils de la femme, with close ties to the Société cooperative des ouvriers et ouvrières petitioned the government for civic equality for women.

The crisis also offered unanticipated openings for Bernois, the African American from New Orleans with the Anglo-American Ambulance.[30] Demonstrating skills not previously exercised, she become one of the practical administrators of the project. One of the white Yankee college boys with whom she worked noted that she "did indeed bow and cringe to a few superiors, and probably she had her reasons for it, but she made distinctions on the grounds of like and dislike all the same." She faced down "certain ladies who had opposed her entrance to the Ambulance, on the pretext of color." "From her bitter life experience," continued her admirer, "she had learned to penetrate almost unerringly into the hearts and intents of men, and to conceal her own designs in turn." Her commanding personality found her supervising some white, as well as black, assistants in the enterprise. However, as everything in Paris grew scarce, her familiarity with the city and widespread contacts became increasingly essential to the survival of the enterprise.

The exigencies of the war and siege posed new challenges and thrust greater responsibilities on her.

---

30   For this sketch of her, see Swinburne, *Paris Sketches*, 75–8, 79, 80–1, 82–3, 103–4. Note that the recorded dialect of a black attendant hints broadly that he had come from the western hemisphere.

Reversals and the Grand Scheme

The French had a few, very brief, glimmers of possible success. On November 9, at sea near Havana, the French *Bouvet* damaged the German *Meteor*, which sought refuge in that neutral Spanish-governed Cuban port. Of real importance, on November 28, General Joseph-Constant Crouzat's Armée de la Loire with 60,000 men attacked fewer than 10,000 Prussians at Beaune-la-Rolande, roughly thirty miles from Orleans and only about sixty-five miles south of Paris. Wave after wave of his Garde mobile failed to drive the German veterans back from the stone walls south of the village, and inflicted fewer than 900 casualties on the well-protected enemy. The French lost over 8,000, including the painter Frédéric Bazille and electrical engineer Alexander Siemens. The bloodshed ended only when the ranks of the French Army refused to repeat these pointless attacks.

Over the next few days, several sweeping Prussian counterattacks pushed the the Armée de la Loire west and retook Orleans, dividing the French forces in the valley. That to the west—under General Antoine Eugène Alfred Chanzy—remained particularly active, and French casualties, including prisoners, tallied in the tens of thousands. With an eye toward Garibaldi's army, one of the more pious of the beaten explained the outcome as a divine effort to teach his fellow Catholics an object lesson in the threat of infidelity to military success.[31]

Desperate measures were needed. With the Armée de la Loire severely battered and the Armée du Nord held at bay, the government pinned everything on a final offensive by a new Armée de l'Est. Assigned merely to reoccupy Dijon, the Armée des Vosges seemed destined to play no further role in the war. However, the course of the war through the first weeks of January 1871 did not leave them marginalized, so the conduct and size of Garibaldi's force, controversial from its large proportion of foreign volunteers and its radical and secularist leadership, came to be a battleground over which later political conflicts would rage.

---

31   General Antoine Eugène Alfred Chanzy, *La Deuxième Armée de la Loire*, 4th edn (Paris: Henri Plon, 1872); Barthelémy-Edmond Palat, *Campagne de la Loire en 1870–1871: Josnes, Vendome, Le Mans* (Paris, Nancy: Berger-Levrault et cie, 1895); Pierre Lehautcourt, *Études de tactique appliquée: Bataille de Bapaume (2 et 3 janvier 1871)* (Paris: Henri Charles-Lavauzelle, 1901). Also Moltke, *The Franco-German War of 1870–71*, 192; Vizetelly, *My Days of Adventure*, 174; Kirwin, *La compagnie irlandaise*, 17.

The government calculated that it likely had resources for only one more major offensive. This gave rise to a bizarrely messianic hope that a single drive might yet save the nation, should God or the gods be on the side of the tricolor. It shifted two corps from the Armée de la Loire to the east of France by train. Around them, the authorities cobbled together a new Armée de l'Est. The plan was to make a rapid thrust east to Belfort, picking up the thousands of besieged soldiers there, after which they would turn north and liberate Paris.

This made complete sense to the bureaucrats and aspiring bureaucrats poring over maps hundreds of miles away. The Ministry of War, after all, presided over a secular church founded on an innate faith in Napoleonic genius. And some leaders of the nominal republic remained less than enthusiastic about bringing the troubling politics of Paris into the deliberations of the government.

Still, those with their feet firmly planted on what would soon be freezing terra firma tended to have questions. The longer the campaign lasted—the greater the distance it had to cover—the more it would be facing a French version of the Russian winter that had frozen the ambitions of the original Napoleon. Then, too, the longer the march was, the more certain it that those massive, well-supplied, well-reinforced German armies would mobilize and act against it.

There were other considerations, as well. The defenders of Belfort, however heroic, would have experienced several months of siege, and were unlikely to be able to gather up their munitions, equipment, and supplies to join in a forced march through the snows to the capital. And, if they were—if all of them were—the combined numbers were still not going to match those that had been trying repeatedly to break the siege of Paris from the outside (or inside). If those earlier, less battered and demoralized armies had been unable to do so, why would anyone seriously think that the Armée de l'Est would be able to do so? And, if it could break the siege of Paris, what would prevent the massive, well-supplied, well-reinforced German armies from simply repeating their earlier successes?

Fortunately for the ministry, they had spent over half a century cultivating a general command unlikely to share their questions. Garibaldi's headquarters pointed out to the government that it made more sense to concentrate everything it still had in the south for the largest possible drive on Paris over the shortest distance. Insights that made complete sense offered by foreigners were probably doomed from the onset.

Then came the choice of which well-connected failed general would get the final command. One might think that a republican official would have had to try hard to find a worse choice than General Charles-Denis Bourbaki, the monarchist conspirator who had, a few weeks earlier, been planning the overthrow of the republic in the interests of the Bonapartists. His appointment to command the Armée de l'Est provided yet another demonstration that the new republic would do nothing to dislodge the institutional power of the imperial army and the Church.

Winter was already upon them before Bourbaki's forces gathered at Besançon.[32] Around the New Year, the French force got into position at Villersexel, in anticipation of holding it for the expected passage of Borubaki's army. On January 9, the advance of the Armée de l'Est arrived, even as did 15,000 of Werder's Prussians. Filing through an unguarded pass, they rapidly overwhelmed the positions, cutting off the bridge over the Ognon. By early afternoon, they had captured the chateau, though the French eventually got around 20,000 men into the fight. Their afternoon counterattack devolved into confused street fighting, but recaptured the chateau. Fighting sputtered on into the night until the Prussians withdrew in the early hours of the next morning.

Bourbaki's men also managed to retain their hold on Esprels and Autrey-le-Vay. More particularly, they hold on to Villers-la-Ville to the east of Villersexel. This left the way to Belfort open to them, though Werder had only fallen back some twenty kilometers north along the Lisaine river, with more German troops moving into the area and coming in off the roads every hour.

Eager to better concentrate his forces, Bourbaki did not resume his march until January 13, during which time much of the rest of the Prussian Army turned up. By then, the Germans had gathered about 40,000 men entrenched into positions along the Lisaine river, centered at Héricourt, only about fourteen kilometers from Belfort.

∾

---

32   Barthelémy-Edmond Palat, *Campagne de l'Est en 1870–1871: Nuits, Villersexel* (Paris: Berger-Levrault, 1896). Yves Chenut, *La dernière chevauchée des vaincus* (Besançon: Editions Cêtre, 2008); and the forthcoming Quintin Barry, *Last Throw of the Dice: Bourbaki and Werder in Eastern France 1870–71* (Solihull: Helion and Company, 2018).

Those in the ranks understood the problem better than those at the helm of government. One day in Autun, Giuseppe Beghelli listened as a well-informed Basque major at the Hôtel de la Poste ticked off what France had already lost: an emperor, six marshalls, 110 generals, and several armies' worth of enlisted men.[33] The war the empire had so needlessly declared looked as though it was on the verge of inflicting a humiliating defeat for the republic unless a miracle could turn the tide of war . . . on the Lisaine, if not the Seine or the Marne.

Meanwhile, Bernois and her colleagues in Paris greeted the New Year with "a grand banquet" to accompany the great fire they decided to build for a brief spate of mid-winter comfort. When all took their chairs, she presented a unique menu.

Ambulance Américaine
Avenue Uhlrich 36
Directrice Mme. Bernois.
Potage au chien
Pâté de chat
Rat sauté aux champignons
Gigot de chien
Oignon à la sauce blanche
Pomme de terre au naturel
Salade laitue
Tarte du Carin
Gelée aux cerises
Café.

Except for the dog, cat, and rat, it represented a real feast, the work of a mistress of organization and scavenge.[34]

It was as makeshift as the defense of the republic, and as hopeful as the prospect springtime in Paris.

---

33   Beghelli, *La Camicia Rossa in Francia*, 112.
34   Swinburne, *Paris Sketches*, 139, 140.

9
The Coming of Winter: Despair, Starvation, and Exposure

The winter of 1870–1 found hundreds of thousands of soldiers and civilians trudging endless days through the ice and snow from the Loire to the Alps. The weight of numbers alone meant that, notwithstanding their individual or collective wills, they descended on small rural communities like packs of ravenous wolves, consuming what they could find of the food and firewood. Their uniforms did not matter. Whether they called it *Winter* or *hiver* mitigated nothing about the cold or the hunger. The death and suffering moved growing numbers of those serving the new French government to draw conclusions about orders of their "betters" that accomplished nothing and was of no real benefit to themselves, their families or anybody like them. The shimmering old republican visions had become new "republican" truths that felt very imperial.

They still fought under the banner of the eighteenth-century tricolor but for aspirations that reached beyond it. The war entered 1871 with serious and desperate campaigns through the Somme valley centered on Amiens, the Loire around Orleans, and vicinity of Dijon in Burgundy. However, the designated focus of the last great French offensive was aimed at relieving Belfort, to be followed by a drive on Paris. The diplomats confirmed a particularly troubled peace that reflected the quiet that came over many thousands who simply had no reason any longer to shoot at each other.

From the Somme to the Loire to the Ouche

Hopeful saviors of Paris—and France—gathered in three corners of the country. To the northeast, Louis Léon César Faidherbe had cobbled together an Armée du Nord and churned terrain that had hosted the Hundred Years' War and would later inspire so many twentieth-century nightmares. Something of a lower-middle-class outsider from Lille, he had held commands in Algeria and Guadeloupe before taking a position as governor of French West Africa. After the crushing of the imperial armies and government, he drew together the scattered garrisons in the region, adding a large number of raw recruits.[1]

From mid-November, Faidherbe had probed the Prussian positions, hoping to take advantage of any openings left them or, at the very least, to draw off enough Prussians from the capital to permit success from elsewhere. From mid-November, he had led a series of campaigns around Saint-Quentin and in the valley of the Somme. His counterpart, General Edwin Freiherr von Manteuffel, remained a particularly reactionary Catholic monarchist famous for having crippled a liberal pamphleteer. On November 27, Manteuffel's army pushed the French from Amiens in the battle of Villers-Bretonneux.

However, the French patiently prepared a counterattack. On December 30, Faidherbe's army drove a Prussian reconnaissance in force toward Querrieu back to Amiens. Three days later, 22,500 Germans ventured beyond the Hallue river, inflicting several thousand more casualties, most being French prisoners. Later that month, the Germans encircled and besieged a French garrison of several thousand men at Péronne.

Faidherbe's army gathered fresh troops and supplies at Doullens and Bapaume. After concentrating a force estimated about 43,000, they turned back on the Germans in hopes of relieving Péronne. On January 3, 1871, the outnumbered but more experienced and better-organized Prussians failed to dislodge the French from Faidherbe's positions around Bapaume. Nevertheless, the battered French retreated, leaving the garrison at Péronne to surrender on January 10.

---

1   Alain Coursier, *Faidherbe: 1818–1889: du Sénégal à l'Armée du Nord* (Paris: Tallandier, 1989). See also Quintin Barry, *The Somme 1870–1: The Winter Campaign in Picardy* (Solihull: Helion & Company, 2014).

Under direct orders from the government, Faidherbe gathered everything he had for one desperate last try to retake Saint-Quentin. On January 19, his troops threw themselves against the Prussians under August Karl von Goeben. Prussian casualties ran to 2,400 and French to 3,500 with another 9,000 captured. Saint-Quentin effectively ended the war northeast of the capital.

During these weeks, the French made another attempt to save Paris from southwest. By December 8, the Prussians who had retaken Orleans enjoyed greater successes to the south of the Loire, leaving their hold on the strategic city stronger than ever, as General Chanzy's army scrambled farther west to place miles of long and icy roads over rugged terrain between themselves and the Germans and the latter's vital lines of supply.[2]

Chanzy's men wound up at Le Mans, a community with now unusable rail connections to Nantes, Brest and Paris. On the way, thousands of their exhausted, shivering and demoralized comrades slipped away into the woods. For their part, the Germans pursued them with little enthusiasm, clashing with the French on December 15 at Vendôme, some fifty miles west of Orleans and roughly halfway to Le Mans.

The government had hoped that Chanzy would be able to reverse the Prussian successes, launch his own relentless drive east, and retake Orleans. A large French column did ambush two German battalions on December 27 at Trôo, but success eluded them when they pressed the attack at Vendôme on December 31 without any success. On New Year's Day 1871, the Prussians organized a counteroffensive, and began pushing the French back toward Le Mans.

By January 6, German troops approached the Huisne river before Le Mans. Three days later, the French struck at Ardenay-sur-Mérize and managed to hold their own through the snow until night. The fighting resumed on January 10, fading into several days of severe fighting as the Germans turned the French flanks on the Huisne. The Germans captured thousands of prisoners, and virtually disintegrated Chanzy's army, though the battle left the victors too exhausted to take full advantage of the situation.

The fighting in this area engulfed the Mobiles de Gers. The republic had called these two battalions into existence with that political controversy

2   Antoine Eugène Alfred Chanzy, *Campagne de 1870–1871: La deuxième Armée de la Loire Atlas* (Paris: Plon 1871).

that plagued their organization. Within days, local officials had reported "3,000 very good, very solid *mobiles*," though only half were armed and those with refurbished muskets dating back almost to the Napoleonic wars. The raising and mobilization of this force became embroiled in the tensions between the old imperial officials and the demand for republican appointees, as well as the hard questions about the capacity of the central government to organize their defense. Conflicts continued into December, even as the local *mobiles* entered the war. At the center of this struggle to get the men supplied and fit for the field was Louis Lartet, the son of a veteran republican and rationalist of 1848 who had sought human identity in fossils. Despite good connections, he functioned as the quartermaster sergeant among the *mobiles*.[3] The two battalions from Gers formed the 85th Regiment of the *mobiles*, which, at points, bore the full brunt of aggressive Prussian attacks.

The battle around Le Mans claimed 25,000 killed or wounded among the French, and another 50,000 deserted in its wake. It also proved to be, by far, the costliest battle for the Mobiles de Gers, which lost 336 casualties in the course of the campaign, most at Le Mans. When the Confederation Army had recovered enough to catch up with Chanzy's shattered army on January 21 about thirty miles southwest of La Mans, at La Flèche, Lartet and his regiment fought there one last time.[4]

In the course of all this, war had removed scores of Lartet's outfit into eternity where they were as irretrievable as the people whose ancient bones he had unearthed at Les Eyzies. Then, only a week later, his father, Édouard Lartet, the giant of early paleontology, died, the cause ascribed to a deep depression at the fate of his country.[5]

---

3   *Enquête parlementaire sur les actes du Gouvernement de la la défense nationale* (Versailles: Cerf et Fils, 1875), part 3, vol. 1, 305–6, 306 ff.

4   Aristide Martinien, *Corps auxiliaire créés pendant la Guerre 1870–1871, première partie: Garde nationale mobile* (Paris: Librairie Militaire Edmond Dubois, 1897), 27; and his *État nominatif, par affaires et par corps, des officiers tués ou blessés dans la deuxième partie de campagne* (Paris: Henri Charles-Lavauzelle, 1906), 145, 151; Mobiles du Gers, Gers, *Bulletin de la Société archéologique, historique, littéraire & scientifique du Gers*, 1940, 46–66; and 1975, 189–92; and "Parcours d'un garde mobile du Gers durant la guerre de 1870–1871," October 30, 2008, at marciac.typepad.com.

5   A. Lavergne, "Louis Lartet," *Revue de Gascogne*, 41 (1900), 177; and Émile Cartailhac (resident member), "Éloge de M. Louis Lartet, Membre libre de la Société Archéologique du Midi de la France Prononcé à la séance du mardi 43 février 1900," *Mémoires de la Société archéologique du Midi de la France*, 16 (1908), 13–14.

Activities to the southeast of Paris resolved the impact of radicalism on the war's course. Into December, discontent among the *francs-tireurs* plagued the division of General Camille Crémer, who had declined to participate in the proposed joint attack on Dijon the previous month. The government decided "that all the troops acting under his command" would both obtain rations and serve under him, but some refused his orders, insisting that they would function independently. On December 18, Crémer made his own attempt on Dijon, hitting General August Graf von Werder's troops below the city at Nuits-Saint-Georges. For three hours, Crémer sent General Garibaldi urgent appeals for help. Before elements of the Armée des Vosges hurried toward Beaune and Nuits, Crémer had already withdrawn to the south. Not long after, the ministry reassigned Crémer, leaving the *mobiles* nearest Dijon under General Victor Pellissier.[6]

Within days, the Germans had abandoned Dijon to dash east after General Charles-Denis Bourbaki's drive on Belfort, and Pellissier reoccupied the city with some of his *mobiles* from nearby Auxonne. The Ministry of War immediately began pressing Garibaldi to move the army from Autun to Dijon, even as the winter freeze and heavy snowfall blocked the roads and the government itself had requisitioned the available supplies and transport for the Armée de l'Est.[7]

The Armée des Vosges likely took something like 6,500 to 6,800 men at Dijon, having sent its second brigade off toward Langres. This figure jibes with some generally ignored contemporary estimates, including one German account.[8] Contradictory records

6   On the night of December 18–19, see Pennazzi, *L'Armée des Vosges et ses détracteurs*, 22; Beghelli, *La Camicia Rossa in Francia*, 241–2; Garibaldi, *Souvenirs de la campagne de France*, 65–6; *Dépêches . . . Gambetta*, vol. 2, 383–4; Victor Pellissier, *Les Mobilisés de Saône-et-Loire en 1870* (Macon: E. Protat, 1878), 68–9.

7   Beghelli, *La Camicia Rossa in Francia*, 276, 279, 289; Bordone, *Garibaldi et l'Armée des Vosges*, vol. 2, 216, 224, 272, 274–5, 294–5, 295–6, 296; and vol. 3, 334, 448–9. Fabricius, *Kämpfe*, 42, 49; Pierre Lehautcourt, *Campagne de l'Est en 1870–1871* (Paris: Berger-Levrault, 1896), 258; Molis, *Les francs-tireurs et les Garibaldi*, 206; Dormoy, *Les trois batailles de Dijon*, 339–40; Bordone to minister of war, January 20, 1871, LG3. Eugène-Désiré-Édouard Sergent, *Grenest: L'Armée de l'Est, relation anecdotique de la campagne de 1870–71* (Paris: Garnier frères, 1895); and Julie Favre, *La vérité sur les désastres de l'armée de l'est et sur le désarmement de la Garde nationale* (Paris: E. Plon, Nourrit, 1883).

8   Wenzel, *1871: Vor Dijon* (Berlin: Carl Zieger Nachf., 1892), 27. For German accounts, see Karl Baudach, *Das 8: Pommersche Infanterie-Regiment No. 61* (Berlin: A. Bath, 1878); and Hans Fabricius, *Die Kämpfe um Dijon in Januar 1871 unter die Vogesenarmee* (Bromberg: Verlag der Mittler'schen Buchhandlung, 1897).

reflected a vast gap between what was there and what was presumed to be there.

Garibaldi positioned most of these available forces to the north and northeast of the city along the road to Paris and Troyes, with others along the approaches from the west and east. On the morning of Saturday, January 21, Major General Karl Friedrich von Kettler's infantry brigade—with some divisional detachments of cavalry and artillery—came in three columns from the north with a large reserve. A small group of mostly boys, sent from Saint-Étienne near Lyons to labor on the defenses, and some of those factory workers from Le Creusot in the Mobilisés de Saône-et-Loire, met the Germans around Hauteville. Fighting became very severe around Messigny and Asniers. General Józef Hauke-Bosak, the Polish revolutionary, lost his life attempting to stem the German advance in the Bois du Chêne near Darois.[9]

Another Prussian column swept in from further west, capturing Daix just beyond the slopes of Talant, the heights on the edge of Dijon itself. At one point, a Basque company rushed behind an old stone fence along a vineyard, and one of the men put his beret on the ground next to him, placed his allotted sixty cartridges into it, and began methodically loading and taking carefully aimed shots at individual Germans that came into view. Shortly after noon, as the Italians formed to the right of the Basques, the English woman Jesse White-Mario spoke to Giorgio Imbriani, a friend and comrade of the future anarchist Errico Malatesta. Shortly after their charge had been driven back, she heard that Imbriani had been "killed at the first shot." By mid-afternoon, most Italians had entered the fray, and Antonio Orense, the Spanish republican, fell wounded at the head of his Compagnie espagnole and was initially believed dead. Havana-born Count Luigi Penazzi had fought in several of Garibaldi's earlier campaigns before having settled in Alexandria, where he recruited about sixty men into the Chasseurs égyptiens, all but

9 On Dijon, see Sassone, *La Savoie armée pendant la guerre franco-allemande*, 259–86; Molis, *Les francs-tireurs et les Garibaldi*, 176–84; Pellissier, *Les Mobilisés de Saône-et-Loire*, 87, 103–4. On the movements against and defending Dijon, see maps in Eligiusz Kozłowski, *General Józef Hauke-Bosak: 1834–1871* (Warszawa: Wydawn. Ministerstwa Obrony Narodowej, 1973). On the engineers, see also Gauckler to Freycinet, January 21, 1871, LG3. Gauckler to de Freycinet, January 21, 1871. Baudach, *Das 8*, 55, 57–8, 61, 57; Wenzel, *1871*, 15–16, 18, 19–20, 21–2, 23–4, 24–6, 27; and note particularly Claude Kayser, *Messigny-et-Vantoux: 21 janvier 1871, 8 septembre 1944* (Messigny-et-Vantoux: C. Kayser, 1982).

destroyed in the fighting near Daix.[10] Diverse radical republican aspirations from across the Western world—and beyond—bled out in the valley beyond Dijon.

Meanwhile, some of these mixed units attacking Daix shifted behind the village to the edge of the plateau at Hauteville, where three rank-and-file Zouaves burst from the woods, surprising the Germans there. In short order, Major Luigi Perla's Légion italienne de Cacciatori di Marsala retook Hauteville, along with some of the *francs-tireurs* from North Africa, as well as the Mobilisés de Saône-et-Loire.

Those mobiles took responsibility for defending Hauteville. They thwarted several counterattacks before realizing how untenable their situation was and withdrawing after dark. The surgeons and nurses had occupied the mayor's home as a temporary hospital, and clearly raised the red cross above it. After the firing had stopped and the exhausted medical team had finished treating the wounded, the women began preparing some food for them. Suddenly, Prussians, clearly unnerved by the continued outbreaks of episodic gunfire around them, forced entry. One of the officers told her in French that he knew they had concealed *francs-tireurs*, and she "let them search; they found none." Nevertheless, the Germans shot Dr. Morin twice in the head and once in the chest before they "finished him off with the bayonet." When Dr. Milliard made a run for it, they shot him just outside. They also left four of the nurses for dead. In addition, they shot a twenty-year-old woman "through the heart, but accidentally." Before leaving the village, some of the Prussians returned to the house to strip and rob the wounded.[11]

Garibaldi's army had been fortunate the previous Saturday. Had the Germans actually brought the nearby brigade of Major General Wilhelm Karl Albert du Trossel into a simultaneous attack on Dijon from the northwest, they would have likely overwhelmed the Armée

---

10   Pellissier, *Les Mobilisés de Saône-et-Loire*, 104; Molis, *Les francs-tireurs et les Garibaldi*, 183–7. For Imbriania, see Mario, "Garibaldi in France," 465, 612–13, 614; Socci, *Da Firenze a Digione*, 131, 144–5, 152, 155, 156, 201; Beghelli, *La Camicia Rossa in Francia*, 298–9, j301, 303, 304, 305, 306.

11   "Notes from Dijon," *Daily News*, February 7, 1871, 6; Pellissier, *Les Mobilisés de Saône-et-Loire*, 107–8. See also "Murder of French Military Surgeons by Prussian Soldiers," *Medical Times and Gazette: A Journal of Medical Science, Literature, Criticism, and News*, 1 (February 11, 1871) 167; Julius Von Gosen and Georg Hirth, *Tagebuch der Deutsch-Französischen Krieges 1870–1871*, 3 vols. (Leipzig: Verlag von g. Hirth, 1871–4), vol. 3, 5065.

des Vosges. It had already designated a fallback position from the city on the heights of Talant and Fontaine. This would likely have kept any German hold on Dijon tentative, but only for a while. Indeed, the Germans could have had the same result had they brought troops into play on Sunday.

The Prussians abandoned on Sunday much of what they had taken on Saturday. Scouts reported that the Germans had left Plombières, Pasques, Prenois, and Lantenay. The French had retaken Daix and Hauteville. Nor did sorties out of Dijon not explain all of Sunday's clashes, in which the Prussian artillery and dragoons had been ubiquitous.[12] In the end, the Germans did not renew their attacks, because they had repositioned themselves and, certainly, consulted with superiors.

However, Kettler's shift to the north and northeast of Dijon permitted cooperation with those troops back along the road to Langres between Selongey or Orville and Is-sur-Tille. Other reports indicated German forces active across a broad swath of the countryside beyond Dijon. Beyond the French right, a scouting party of the *francs-tireurs* from Béarn observed German movements about twelve kilometers past Val-Suzon—indeed, beyond Vitteaux at Bligny-le-Sec. Some of the Béarnais wanted to ambush the Prussians at Saint-Seine-l'Abbaye, but their officers refused to permit it, out of a fear of reprisals.

The Germans shifted because they were well aware of what the French had not been informed of.

The Fate of the Final Efforts

The French government had put all its eggs into the basket of Bourbaki, who had already scrambled them. Bourbaki's Armée de l'Est had started from Besançon, about 100 kilometers east of Dijon. Twelve days before the first attack on Dijon, part of General Werder's XIV Korps had met the French relief expedition less than thirty miles short of Belfort at the village of Villersexel and its bridge over the Ognon. They had travelled

---

12 "The War," *Daily News*, January 25, 1871, 3; "The Fighting at Dijon," *Daily News*, February 3, 1871, 6; "Operations in the East," *New York Tribune*, January 25, 1871, 1. On the casualties, see Garibaldi to Ministry of War, January 22, 1871, LG3.

over 60 kilometers northeast of Besançon, and still had about forty-six more to go before getting to Belfort. Werder's men dug defenses into a strong line along the Lisaine river, from near Héricourt down to Montbéliard. These Germans—the ones who had done so well on the defensive against Garibaldi in November, held their own against attacks by Boubaki's army from January 15 through 17. The roughly 40,000 Germans successfully thwarted a French Army of about 110,000. Vigorous Prussian thrusts at his lines of communications and supply continually backed the last major French Army through the snows toward the Swiss border, an ordeal which, with the earlier fighting, reduced the French Army to around 84,000.[13]

Bourbaki spent several days gathering his army and withdrawing south with the Germans in pursuit. Ten kilometers south of Héricourt, Paul Déroulède secured Montbéliard, at the Allaine river, the last crossing before Switzerland. Shed of his Turcos after Sedan, he had made his own way to Paris from Belgium, and took a new assignment in the Loire as part of unit sent to slog its way through the snow and ice under Bourbaki.[14]

The Ministry of War, in this exigency, demonstrated its genuine character. Having refused Garibaldi's suggestion to move his army close enough to support Bourbaki's movement, it now accusingly telegraphed the embattled little army at Dijon: "You have given Bourbaki's army no support, and your presence at Dijon has had no effect on the enemy march from west to east. In short, fewer explanations and more action, that's what we want from you."

The institutional cynicism this represented could hardly have been deeper. The idea that the failure of the Armée de l'Est was the responsibility of the foreign volunteers in the Armée des Vosges could scarcely be more absurd. No commander—however young, pious, or French—could have deployed his tiny force in such a way as to keep a massive army 150 kilometers away from being driven up into Switzerland. More tellingly, Villersexel came twelve days before the fighting at Dijon, and the fighting on the Lisaine ended before Saturday's attack on Dijon.

---

13   Le Mesurier, *Feeding of Fighting Armies*, vol. 1, 268. Varley, *Under the Shadow of Defeat*, 222, 221.

14   A. Henri Canu and Georges Buisson, *Monsieur Paul Déroulède et sa Ligue des Patriotes: La vérité* (Paris: Albert Savine, 1889), 10.

If the after-the-fact explanations from the armies and governments involved are to be believed, Manteuffel's advance, engaged in the pursuit of Bourbaki, continued to pull the rest of the long German column into the mountains for nearly a week.

Worse, the government failed to inform anyone about the stunning defeat of the Armée de l'Est, particularly those along the Lisaine river. Although the defenders of Dijon realized that a massive force of Germans had gone east to stop Bourbaki, "we cannot guess whether they will or will not return in overwhelming forces to crush us." They increasingly suspected that "they will probably pay us out on their return. In any case they will probably keep sufficient numbers round Dijon to hinder us, on the one hand from attacking them en route, on the other from going to the assistance of Bourbaki."[15] Fortunately for their piece of mind in Dijon, they did not realize that Bourbaki's drive had already ended in disaster.

Garibaldi's men and officers had simply been left in the dark. They reported "no news" of military developments in the north or with Chanzy in the Loire valley to the west, while they heard only rumors about the Armée de l'Est. One of these had Bourbaki's forces "surrounded, and unless he be a genius, which he has not yet proved, his only chance of saving his army is via Switzerland. We are cut off from all communication with him."[16] Yet the Ministry of War had not been and the telegraph ran sure to Dijon.

In fact, much of Manteuffel's massive army had remained closer to Dijon than the Lisaine. After January 18, pursuing the retreat of the Armée de l'Est faded in its urgency. At this point, Manteuffel ordered General Eduard von Fransecky's II Korps at the tail of the column to make new deployments east and southeast of Dijon.[17] Garibaldi concluded, quite correctly, that the concentration of troops near the city would not withdraw without further attack.

Garibaldi and his staff correctly reasoned that the Prussians

---

15 "The Fighting at Dijon," *Daily News*, February 3, 1871, 6.

16 "Notes from Dijon," *Daily News*, February 7, 1871, 6; Molis, *Les francs-tireurs et les Garibaldi*, 204, 206; Varley, *Under the Shadow of Defeat*, 222.

17 Wilhelm Rüstow, *The War for the Rhine Frontier 1870: Its Political and Military History*, trans. John Layland Needham, 3 vols. (Edinburgh and London, 1871), vol. 1, 203, a translation of his *Der Krieg um die Rheingrenze 1870/1: Politisch und militärisch dargestellt* (Zurich: Schulthess, 1871); Mario, "Garibaldi in France," 611.

blocked on Saturday, January 21, would not leave without another serious effort to capture the city. By Sunday night, his troop reported from as far as Ventoux and Messigny that the Prussians had likely redeployed to approach the city from the north and northeast.

After repositioning, the Germans launched an even larger assault on Monday, January 23. As earlier, the presence of Prussian cavalry and artillery—divisional troops—testify to an engagement of more than just Kettler's infantry brigade, of which he committed both regiments. This would have been a serious breach of protocol without keeping a reserve, in the event of a French counterattack. Parts of the rest of General Otto Rudolph Benno Hann von Weyhern's division—now free from the pursuit of Bourbaki—remained just beyond the far side of Dijon. French scouts reported them around Mirabeau, along what had been the main route of Manteuffel's army.[18]

Around 1 p.m., a well-formed Prussian force advanced around La Charmette, closing on the Château Pouilly, north of Dijon. There, about 200 soldiers from Marseille, with sixty of the Compagnie des Ours Nantais and around sixty Mobilisés de Saône-et-Loire held the ground until their ammunition began to run out. Most of those who subsequently abandoned Pouilly—some "as fast as their legs could go"—stopped when they reached the French line re-forming just to the south.[19]

Meanwhile, Garibaldi hurried forward with the news that, from the heights over the city, he could see another German column moving in from the northeast, and likely to converge at a factory about 1,400 meters beyond the old city gates. Perhaps 1,200 to 1,500 rushed to meet an assault at the convergence point of the 6,000 Germans to decide the result of three days' battle. The day the war came to the factory of Amédée Bargy found him, like Schneider from Le Creusot, quite absent. About 400 men filed into the factory "with instruction to prepare the

18   J. Lucien Bonnams, "Les anciens plans de Dijon," *Mémoires de la Société bourguignonne de géographie et d'histoire*, 25 (1909), 428.

19   Garibaldi, *Souvenirs de la campagne de France*, 103, 104 and 104 n., 105, 109; Bizzoni, *Souvenirs d'un garibaldien*, 241–3, 261, 263–4; Charles Félix Édouard Wyts, "Operations militaires a l'Armée des Vosges. Raport," 6, LG 3. See also J. Ledeuil d'Enquin, *Tribataille de Dijon: Épisode du Château de Pouilly (23 janvier 1871)* (Beaune: Henri Lambert, 1894); L. Semme, October 3 and December 20, 1893, and A. Abelin, March 20, 1894, LG3.

room for a desperate defense." The troops outside to their right formed along a wall covering a field on two distinct levels.[20]

Ahead of them, gray columns braved the icy winter wind of Burgundy and moved into view with seemingly irresistible efficiency. As they drew near, the Germans came in waves, charge after charge pushing back the flanks on either side of the factory. The defenders dropped the assailants in waves. Desperation bolstered the Armée des Vosges until, between 3 and 4 p.m. coughing soldiers could begin emerging from the small door in the rear of the factory.[21]

In the aftermath came a rare event in the war—the French capture of a Prussian battle flag. The old iconoclast Giuseppe Beghelli remained unimpressed, bluntly reminding his readers of the lives lost to save the flag or to bring it down. He deplored such obsessions as "an old-fashioned habit and nothing else." It stirred the hearts of those fighting for home and firesides. In contrast, he saw himself and his comrades as "not soldiers of a nation, of a Government or of a faction. We were soldiers of humanity." They not only fought for France, but to advance the cause of "a unique principle for the Republic," which transcended national flags.[22]

For the next two hours, the fighting continued to the north of the city, but the tide had clearly turned there as well. The depleted numbers of the Italians made a bayonet charge, an effort saved by the several hundred of the Mobilisés de Saône-et-Loire, with others in support. In that closing push, the small mounted force available to the Armée des Vosges mounted a cavalry charge.[23]

---

20   Dormoy, *Les trois batailles de Dijon*, 371, 373; Thiébault, *Ricciotti Garibaldi et la 4me Brigade*, 93, 94; Garibaldi, *Souvenirs de la campagne de France*, 108, 109–10; Roger Gauchat, "L'urbanisme dans les villes anciennes," *Mémoires de la Commission des antiquités du department de la Cote de'Or*, 23 (1947–53), xxx; Gauchat, "Les quartiers extérieurs de Dijon," *Mémoires de la Commission des antiquités du department de la Cote de'Or*, 25 (1959–62), 312; and Goussard, *Nouveau guide pittoresque du voyageur à Dijon*, 3rd edn, rev. and augm. (Dijon: Vve Decailly, 1861), 403.

21   Dormoy, *Les trois batailles de Dijon*, 371; Garibaldi, *Souvenirs de la campagne de France*, 109, 110, 111, 112, 113. Molis, *Les francs-tireurs et les Garibaldi*, 198, 199–200, 201, 202, 204.

22   Beghelli, *La Camicia Rossa in Francia*, 177, 355; Thiébault, *Ricciotti Garibaldi et la 4me Brigade*, 97; Garibaldi, *Souvenirs de la campagne de France*, 114. See also "La prise du drapeau du 61e poméranien," in Maurice Loir and George Duruy, *Au drapeau! Récits militaires extraits des mémoires de G. Bussière et E. Legouis . . .* (Paris: Hachette, 1897), 246–50.

23   Aroldi, *L'ultimo dei vecchi garibaldini*, 167; Pellissier, *Les Mobilisés de Saône-et-Loire*, 103, 104, 105; N. Morin, *1870–71: La deuxième batterie d'artillerie de la garde*

Helmuth von Moltke later wrote dismissively of the fighting at Dijon, but the official reports of his own army reflected serious losses. Saturday's losses ran to 400 killed and wounded with a similar number taken prisoner, variously given as 400, 430, or "some 500." Monday's losses ran almost as high in dead and wounded, but with fewer taken prisoner. Dormoy's estimate indirectly placed their losses at roughly a thousand.[24] Not counting whatever losses came on Sunday, the fighting more than literally decimated the Prussian forces.

The casualties in Garibaldi's army could hardly have been less disastrous. The battle effectively destroyed several of the units. One Franco-Spanish company lost a quarter of its effectives. The smaller Egyptian body suffered proportionately even more. Only about thirty of the Genoese riflemen remained to fight. High casualties also shredded the mobilisés of Saône-et-Loire, Aveyron and Isère.[25]

Last Gasps

The successes before Dijon became eclipsed as everything had fallen apart for the designated saviors of the country. An Irish officer with Bourbaki's Armée de l'Est minced no words in his description of the retreat of his "clueless, and in many cases shoeless," soldiers through the ice and snow over a devastated countryside that offered no subsistence. "Bread nor wine could not be had for any price, nor for any cause," he wrote. The wounded, frostbitten, and dying crowded into almost every cottage available, while abandoned equipment, broken wagons, and dead and dying horses and men littered the frozen woods and fields on their headlong climb to the Swiss border. "For about half a mile the dead men were as thick as berries," he continued, "and not a few wounded, crawled into the shelter of the ditch, which, in too many cases, they

---

nationale mobilisée de Maine-et-Loire à l'armée des Vosges (Angers: impr. de L. Hudon, 1894), 5, 7; Socci, Da Firenze a Digione, 177–8. On the orders of the day, see "The Defeat of the Prussians by the Garibaldians" (from the Indépendence belge), Reynolds Newspaper, February 5, 1871, 3.

24   Dormoy, Les trois batailles de Dijon, 383, wrote of 1,700 casualties in the clashes of January 21–3.

25   Pellissier, Les mobilisés de Saône-et-Loire, 143–45, 146–8. Molis, Les francs-tireurs et les Garibaldi, 188.

probably never left alive." Reflecting what must have already circulated among the high command, he and other officers grumbled bitterly that the fate of their massive army had been the fault of Garibaldi's unreliable and distant foreigners, whose paltry few thousand had failed to protect Bourbaki's distant army so that it could win the war as planned.[26]

By January 26, things had become so bad for Bourbaki that his staff began taking measures to keep him away from weapons. Around 7 p.m. that night, a gunshot in his quarters startled his underlings, who rushed in to find him slumped over his desk, his head and face covered with blood. They rushed him to a surgeon who located and removed a single shot lodged in the temporal muscle controlling the jaw.

As in the field or in his monarchist schemes, Bourbaki had failed miserably.

This left his second-in-command, General Justin Clinchant, to finish the negotiations with the government of Switzerland. From February 1 to 3, the Swiss military counted 87,000 men—some sources say 84,000—on their long, cold deadly march into Switzerland. French soldiers crossed the frontier and surrendered their arms at Les Verrières, an event memorialized in the Bourbaki Panorama in Lucerne. They faced internment for several weeks, but had rest, warmth, and food. The Swiss management of this helped secure their reputation as a competent neutral power in a world of European conflict and rivalries.[27]

Bourbaki's collapse—with the reversals at Amiens in the north and Le Mans in the southwest—left Paris in a hopeless situation. In a feeble all-too-late effort at cooperation, General Louis Trochu issued a final call to the unwashed masses of Paris after four months of siege and starvation. Desperate armed city dwellers made a series of desperate attacks, even capturing St. Cloud on January 19, though this breakthrough, too, bogged down and those who had won it retreated heartbroken back into the city.

---

26   Kirwin, *La compagnie irlandaise*, 216–17; Le Mesurier, *Feeding of Fighting Armies*, vol. 1, 268.

27   Émile Davall, *Les troupes françaises internées en Suisse à la fin de la guerre franco-allemande en 1871: Rapport rédigé par ordre du Département militaire fédéral sur les documents officiels déposés dans ses archives* (Bern: Librairie Max Fiala, 1873); Jacky Edouard, *L'occupation des frontières suisses en 1870–71 et l'entrée en Suisse de l'Armée française de l'Est* (Neuenburg, 1914); Aymon Galiffe, *L'occupation des frontières par les troupes suisses en 1870–71* (Lausanne: Revue militaire suisse, 1917).

Within days, the military authorities in Paris used the Breton *mobiles*—some of whom had earlier refused to serve under Garibaldi—to fire on angry members of the National Guard who had marched on the Hôtel de Ville. Over the next few days, the authorities had banned republican clubs and suspended seventeen newspapers, even as the Prussians bombarded Paris with large-caliber Krupp siege guns, prompting its surrender on January 28.

The peace talks agreed to the cession of Alsace and Lorraine to Germany, with an indemnity of 5 billion francs. The stubborn defense of Belfort had won an exemption for their city from cession to Germany. With the armistice, the Prussians sent trainloads of food into Paris and obtained a partial occupation of the Champs-Élysées area, a victory parade, and the collection of all the scattered artillery raised by public subscription.

Back in Burgundy, Garibaldi and the radicals waited for some word of the war's end. After their victory of Monday, January 23, the city's defenders realized that the Prussians still remained in the area—and in growing numbers. The French government, for its part, responded as though it still had big plans for the Armée des Vosges. Events had left Garibaldi the senior surviving commander in the field, charged with what remained of fifteen French divisions, perhaps around 50,000 men, at least on paper. None of these scattered numbers meant much in terms of more men, powder, and cartridges at Dijon. Nevertheless, even in the face of the enemy, the old imperialists and the Church hierarchy found themselves as eager as any Prussian leaders to ensure a humiliating defeat for Garibaldi and his radicals.

At the close of Sunday, January 29, elements of General Weyhern's division skirmished with Garibaldi's outposts and scouts along the way before stopping at the Burgundy Canal well south of the city. Fortunately for the defenders, the Germans moved very cautiously, and more than the below-freezing temperatures cooled their enthusiasm for combat. After all, the Germans actually knew about the armistice and shared an entirely reasonable unwillingness to be the last man killed in a war that had already ended.[28] The arrival of more Germans from the campaign in

---

28   Hermann Ludwig Wilhelm Karl Alexander Friedrich von Wartensleben, *The Campaign of 1870–1871: Operations of the South Army in January and February 1871*, trans. Charles H. Wright (London, H.S. King, 1872), 82, 102–3, 107–8; Pelissier to Freycinet, January 31, 1871, LG3. For material on the subject covered in this section, see

pursuit of Bourbaki's army surely enhanced the desire among the Germans to bring their war to an end as quickly as possible.

Finally, on Monday, January 30—a week after the successful military defense of Dijon—Garibaldi and his staff sent a delegation to meet directly with the growing German force lurking beyond the city. This time, to their great credit, the Germans frankly told them the truth— that the guns had fallen silent everywhere across France except the Côte d'Or, the Jura, and Doubs, which had been explicitly excluded from the armistice. Garibaldi immediately telegraphed for confirmation to his government, which did not respond until the evening, when it shared the news without offering any explanation. "What had really happened remains a mystery," wrote one veteran. "No matter how one racks one's brain to find an excuse for the French government," wrote Cesare Aroldi, "one cannot avoid the conclusion that they deceived Garibaldi and his poor army in a most contemptible way."[29]

Otto von Bismarck had specifically insisted on leaving open the option to definitively crush Garibaldi and demolish his army. The Iron Chancellor had flatly refused impassioned pleas from the French government to permit Bourbaki's surrender to spare his army the ordeal of having to climb into Switzerland. As to Garibaldi's army, Bismarck snarled that he regarded the revolutionary as a brigand. "I want to get my hands on Garibaldi!" he insisted, "to parade him through the streets of Berlin, with a sign round his neck saying, 'This is Italian gratitude!'" The Prussians had also threatened more generally to treat the meddlesome foreign radicals as *francs-tireurs*, criminals rather than soldiers.[30] Bismarck entertained the fantasy of using the war to crush radicalism of any sort for a generation, and the French authorities found themselves thinking along the same lines.

Through the night of January 30/1, German pickets heard heavy rail traffic moving south from Dijon. With first light, they found that the

---

Molis, *Les francs-tireurs et les Garibaldi*, 222–6; Dormoy, *Les trois batailles de Dijon*, 393–6. Also Le Mesurier, *Feeding of Fighting Armies*, vol. 1, 268.

29   Bordone to minister of war, January 30, 1871, LG3, Aroldi quoted in Viotti, *Garibaldi*, 182–3; Bordone marked urgent to delegate of war, January 30, 1871, LG3; Bordone to chief of staff, Bordeaux, January 31, 1871, LG3. Also Viotti, *Garibaldi*, 183.

30   Julius von Pfulgk-Harttung, *The Franco-German War,1870–71* (London: Swan Sunnenschein and Co., 1900), 617–18 n.; Molis, *Les francs-tireurs et les Garibaldi*, 205. Lieutenant-Colonel Theodor von Bernhardi recalled dining at Bismarck's on the evening of the armistice; Viotti, *Garibaldi*, 182, citing *Aus dem leben Theodor von Bernhardi*, 9 vols. (Leipzig: S. Hirzel, 1894–1906), vol. 9, 483 n.

Armée des Vosges had somehow shipped out their wounded by train, slipped their artillery back to the station and entirely disappeared into the night, steaming or marching toward Chagny, some sixty kilometers to the southwest. At 7 or 8 a.m., the Germans reached the railyards, capturing some civilian railroad workers and possibly a few stragglers.[31] By then, the army had moved well beyond reach of the Germans and was well on the way to the safety of the department of Saône-et-Loire.

After they had failed to betray the Garibaldians in the field, the French government quietly sent orders to the authorities at Lyon and Marseille to hurry them out of the country. The republic reportedly sent William De Rohan to represent it at the new Italian capital at Florence. In the end, though, the government took a sharp turn politically to the right, and he found himself "shelved in favour of a candidate whose aristocratic name appears to suggest a widely different order of ideas."[32]

From this point forward, the responsibility of the government would be the traditional ritual of disarming those to whom it had lied. The Spanish volunteers in the Armée des Vosges well knew that war between France and Germany over the succession in Spain had failed miserably even to resolve the crisis at home. When demobilized, they did not want to return their arms, pleading for a chance to carry their weapons back over the Pyrenees to fight against the tyranny at home. A sympathetic Ettore Socci thought that their stubbornness fringed on mutiny, and they took some persuasion before they stacked arms and "decided to disband peacefully." By the end of the month, in the Jura, the *mobiles* of Hautes-Alpes went into "complete insurrection"; gunfire in the streets of Lons-la-Saulnier, ending in the arrest of two of the ringleaders.[33]

---

31   Wartensleben, *Operations of the South*, 106; Socci, *Da Firenze a Digione*, 228; Thiébault, *Ricciotti Garibaldi et la 4me Brigade*, 111; Garibaldi, *Souvenirs de la campagne de France*, 126–7; Morin, *1870–71: La deuxieme batterie d'artillerie de la garde nationale mobilisee de Maine-et-Loire*, 8–10; Quintin Barry, *The Franco-Prussian War, 1870–71: After Sedan, Helmuth von Moltke and the Defeat of the Government of National Defence* (Solihull: Helion & Company, 2009), 402. Among the small units appearing briefly in the staff tally sheets was a Compagnie du chemin du fer, Fourth Brigade ("Noms et Grades"). 95 only on tally sheet of January 19.

32   "Italy," *London Standard*, April 8, 1871, 5;

33   Socci, *Da Firenze a Digione*, 266; *Rapport fait au nom de la Commission d'enquête sur les actes du Gouvernement de la défense nationale* (Versailles: Assemblée nationale, 1874) vol. 2, 784.

Other revolts marked the end of the war. Officers complained of December mutinies among the *mobiles* of Auch and Placentia, and the government advised them to act with caution, using the gendarmerie rather than troops to arrest the leaders. Mid-January brought troubles and talk of "sedition and violent resistance" among the *mobiles* of Toulouse and Gers.[34] One cannot but wonder whether Louis Lartet pondered now this fitted into the long, evolutionary history of human progress.

So ended one of the bloodiest, shortest, and most decisive conflicts in European history. It quickly overturned the dominant power on the continent. This inadvertently made a French republic and created a German Empire. From the relative safety of Tours and Bordeaux, the republican government stalled the cession of Alsace and Lorraine, but, with Paris in a throttlehold, surrender would be inevitable. Officially, it took the Germans nearly 45,000 dead and 90,000 wounded, while the French lost nearly 139,000 dead, 143,000 wounded, and 475,000 prisoners to the Prussians. Over 11 percent of German participants became casualties, while over 83 percent of French participants did. With some exaggeration, a French paper claimed that the government had been left with "only the debris of an army, without guns, without officer, without discipline. Revolt and mutiny had themselves done their work."[35]

Victory had crowned Bismarck and the Prussians with a world-historic success. They won their new united German Empire, one Prussianized from birth. Created in the Hall of Mirrors at Versailles, it reflected the tormented imperial ambitions of France from the Bourbons through the Bonapartes. So it was that a strutting French Empire had bullied its oppressed German neighbor until it knocked France into a nominal republic and took up the mantle of an imperial German juggernaut. With his characteristic sense of irony, Marx observed that the people of France gained from their defeat by getting a republic, while "the Germans would become what the French have been."[36]

---

34 *Dépêches . . . Gambetta*, vol. 1, 464; *Réponse au rapport de M. Alfred Monnet, sur les marchés passes dans la Haute-Garonne pour l'habillement et l'équipement* (Paris: Hanchette Libre, 1872), 10.

35 'La Chasse de Marly: Encore L'Armée de Versailles," *Le Constitutionnel*, June 2, 1871, 3.

36 "Prussification de l'Allemagne," *Le petit journal*, November 29, 1870, 1; G. C. Mins., *DFI*, 4 (September 6, 1870) 58.

That said, the wonderfully modern new war—full of rhetoric about republicanism—came to a very traditional end, worthy of Klemens von Metternich. The emergent new structure of the Great Powers would cooperate to maintain order. In the wake of the war, and despite all their losses, the Germans withdrew their forces to the east of the city, to be withdrawn as soon as France held a new election to ratify peace terms and make its initial payment of the war indemnities.

The Germans would also expedite the repatriation of the 200,000 French prisoners of war it held, earmarked for possible use in the French government's armed pacification of the country.

PART IV

War for the People: The Revolution

10

The Springtime of Peoples Revisited: The Specter of a Social Republic

On April 3, tens of thousands people left Paris to reenact their past. Many who marched on Versailles to bring their government back to the capital walked consciously in the footsteps of the great 1789 march of the women to bring *le roi à Paris*. By all indications, they expected their new republic to yield, as had Louis XVI. Although uniformed, armed, and emerging from a long siege, the citizens of Paris who ventured beyond the city walls felt assured that they would not be fired upon. With many believing that they had undertaken more of a political march than a military expedition, numerous civilians joined the outing. Everybody enjoyed the relative abundance of food and wine outside the walls, and some wandered off to picnic or find cheaper bread or wine or even just to pick flowers before rejoining the column, if not their own designated unit. Most seem to have expected nothing when the army opened fire on them.

That Monday, the Communards of Paris marched from the eighteenth into the twentieth century. The government—stressed by war, defeat, and the painful failure of its own republicanism—had abandoned the people of the capital to their own devices. With the end of the war, the new working class of such cities emerged no longer as mere specters haunting Europe but as the embodiment of the terrible decisions of their government. A sacrament of war, with its age-old sacrifices, offered nothing less than the transubstantiation of the national community.

The Birth of the Commune

Citizens at the capital demanded a better defense and a more vigorous attempt to break the siege, organizing the Republican Central Committee of the Twenty Arrondissements on January 7. Paris, however, could do nothing to keep the French government from accepting the German insistence on a special election and a new government to ratify the peace terms: the cession of Alsace and Lorraine and war indemnities. France held those elections on February 8, and Paris voted to send Giuseppe Garibaldi and Victor Hugo, along with León Gambetta, among their representatives. What Socci called "the malignant breath of provincial reaction" filled the new assembly with old monarchists. Meanwhile, the Germans held a victory parade in Paris, foreshadowing the humiliation that came seventy years later.

Garibaldi headed to the assembly, still at Bordeaux. He believed that the cost of the reparations for war should be borne by those who had voted in its favor, especially the imperialists and the priests; he wanted an appeal to international arbitration for any such indemnities. He also hoped to protest the exclusion of his army and others from the armistice. However, when he rose to speak, the reactionaries who had agreed to their exclusion shouted him down. "What is all this rubbish?" yelled Adolphe Thiers. "This 'rubbish,'" came a voice from the gallery, "is Garibaldi, and he's worth more than the lot of you together." Effectively barred from speaking, the general walked out and left for Marseille and Caprera. So ended the war, with old Orleanists and Bonapartists purging their "republic" of republicans.[1] Notwithstanding the old promise of the universal republic, the new kind of "republic" represented the will of the governed not by simply implementing it but by arrogating to itself the power to be selective about who they would represent.

Those mobilized to fight the war remained openly discontented, particularly in the southeast. On March 7, members of the 10th Battalion

---

1   Viotti, *Garibaldi*, 183–4; Belot and Bermond, *Bartholdi*, 162–3; "General Garibaldi," *The Times*, February 16, 1871, 5; Thiébault, *Ricciotti Garibaldi et la 4me Brigade*, 131; Socci, *Da Firenze a Digione*, 256; Viotti, *Garibaldi*, 183; Pellissier, *Les Mobilisés de Saône-et-Loire*, 123–4, 133–4; Garibaldi, *Souvenirs de la campagne de France*, 131. See also Berrand Taithe, *Citizenship and Wars: France in Turmoil, 1870–1871* (London and New York: Routlege, 2001).

of the Mobiles of the Seine actually threatened to hang their commander, though the army quelled the mutiny without serious consequences. When the government assigned General d'Aurelle des Paladines to take charge of the National Guard, battalion commanders responded with a memorial requesting the right to elect their commander in chief.[2]

Most dramatically, radical Parisians began taking matters into their own hands. They overran prisons and released political prisoners. More dangerously, they began rounding up the cannons, bought through public subscription, and concentrating them on the heights of Montmartre, at the far end of the city from Versailles.

After making its peace with the Germans, the national government moved back from Bordeaux as far as Versailles on March 10. It balked at immediately returning to Paris, which still continued to live under martial law and to suffer from the shortages and impoverishment of the siege. In addition, it realized that the recent vicious repressiveness in Paris had only deepened mistrust of government and radicalism among its people. This understanding did not prevent them from voting to cancel pay for the National Guard and to end the moratorium on rents and payments of commercial bills. The guard, grumbled one conservative, "mutinied for the sake of the franc and a half a day which they would lose if disbanded."[3]

The French authorities had certainly shaped the preconditions for insurrection, though a successful revolution was a different matter. Many had fled the city during the brief interlude after the armistice. Others faded away when the pay dried up. The political culture hardly improved. On March 11, the government suspended another half dozen republican papers. The army had already assumed the authority to sentence insurrectionist leaders to death *in absentia*, particularly Auguste Blanqui and Gustave Flourens for their role in the attempted rising the previous October. On March 17, the authorities arrested Blanqui at the home of a physician friend at Bretenoux in Lot.

Flourens remained at large. Sarah Bernhardt traveled in similar bohemian circles and found him charming. In hindsight, though, she claimed to have found him as "a mad sort of fellow, full of dreams and Utopian follies." He "wanted every one to be happy and every one to

---

2 Allnutt, *Historical Diary of the War between France and Germany, 1870–1*, 384.
3 Ibid., 417.

have money, and he shot down the soldiers without reflecting that he was commencing by making one or more of them unhappy."[4]

Nevertheless, it was neither Flourens nor Blanqui who seriously challenged the power structure. Some 1,325 delegates representing 215 of the 270 battalions of the Garde nationale officially founded their Federation on March 15 and called for a "democratic and social republic." The new *fédérés* also appointed thirty-two members to a Central Committee, including Adolphe Assi and Eugène Varlin, veterans of the struggle at Le Creusot, as well as Nicolas Faltot, and other old Garibaldians.[5]

Two days later, the 67th Battalion elected Assi, a lieutenant in the 192nd Battalion of the National Guard, to be their commander. He pitched in on the practical efforts to protect the city. On that same day, Thiers set policies leading to a confrontation at Montmartre.

Early on March 18, at around 2 a.m., General Joseph Vinoy sent two brigades of his division under generals Jacques Léonard Clément-Thomas and Claude-Martin Lecomte to retake the artillery at Montmartre. Vinoy may not have ventured to take cannons from the Prussians near Sedan and, in trying to take them from the people of Paris, failed to provide horses to bring the guns down from Montmartre. As troops arrived early in the morning, women and children blocked their way, and the soldiers fraternized with the population.

When the commanders ordered the troops to fire on the civilians, the men refused. This refusal to obey a direct order left the soldiers vulnerable to trial and execution. In self-defense, they seized Clément-Thomas and Lecomte and took them a short distance from Montmartre, presumably arguing and getting little reason for hope that the generals would relent. In the end, soldiers killed both of them. There is no indication that the regiments themselves held a hearing and came to a collective conclusion, so this act most likely represented the work of individuals.

---

4   Sarah Bernhardt, *My Double Life: Memoirs of Sarah Bernhardt* (London: William Heinemann, 1907), 220,

5   Alleman, Andignoux, Arnaud, Arnold, Assi, Babick, Barroud, Bergeret, Billioray, Blanchet, Castioni, Chouteau, Clémence, Duval, Eudes, Faltot, Ferrat, Fougeret, Gauthier, Geresme, Gouhier, Groslard, Josselin, Jourde, Lisbonne, Lucien, Maljournal, Moreau, Mortier, Prud'homme, Ranvier and Varlin. See also Deleurmoz, *Commune(s)*, 86.

Civilians had no involvement in this and the Commune did not even exist at the time. Nevertheless, Thiers and the government would hold the Commune responsible for it, along with every other crime real or imagined said to take place in the city, and the entire city would be deemed responsible for the Commune. Most immediately, he ordered the official bodies in the city to withdraw to Versailles. Within hours, the Central Committee of the National Guard scheduled the election of a Commune a week later to serve as the city government.

On March 26, 275,000 Parisian voters returned a large radical majority. The Communards moved into the Hôtel de Ville, and mounted their red flag. It formed nine commissions to run the city, and would operate closely with the Central Committee of the National Guard. On March 30, it reimposed the wartime moratorium on the payment of rents and debts.

The Commune chose Blanqui as its president and Garibaldi as their commanding general. In response to the summary execution of communards, they also seized hostages, including the Archbishop of Paris, Georges Darboy, to insure Blanqui's safety and offered to release all of them for Blanqui's release. The clergyman twice wrote to Versailles personally, urging them to agree to an exchange, but the government would have none of it. For his part, Garibaldi wrote, "I should have been proud, if health permitted, to share the glory and the dangers."[6] Karl Marx later mused that Blanqui could have provided the movement a sorely needed leadership.

The course of the Commune reflected the rapidity of the crisis that brought down the old order and the natural inexperience of the movement's leadership. There is little evidence to believe that Blanqui or Garibaldi would have changed any of that. Both saw revolution as requiring a small vanguard to seize power and implement some fundamental changes before handing power to the masses. Most of the leading Communards saw themselves within the old Jacobin tradition, and tried to lead accordingly. Jacobinism, the most explicitly

---

6   A hostile biographer, J. T. Bent, later quipped that "Garibaldi's sword had been rejected by a pope, trifled with by a constitutional king, and was now insulted by a republic: so he thought he had nothing left for him to do but to embrace the cause of the most extreme revolutionists." J. T. Bent, *The Life of Giuseppe Garibaldi* (London: Longmans, Green, 1882), 285; "The International Society," *New York Times*, October 16, 1871, 4.

revolutionary current to wield power in the original French Revolution, represented the effort of an organization within a minority social class to displace another minority class that ruled the country.

The later concept of creating a workers' state—of leading the majority class to take the reins of civilization—required something very different. Of course, the members of that majority class had no opportunity to distill a civil culture of self-government around leaders they wanted. Most likely had little coherent knowledge of the candidates running.

Worse, the revolution taking shape in Paris started with a battered and depleted National Guard. Toward the end of March, estimates placed the strength of those 215 insurgent battalions at only 75,000 to 90,000, with another 100,000 in reserve. By early April, a more realistic guess ran to fewer than 40,000.

What would dramatize these shortcomings began to gather west of Paris.[7] The Seine flows from Paris into a large loop to the southwest before turning sharply north and northeast from the capital. The road running roughly west from the city intersects the river again at Neuilly on the right bank, opposite Courbevoie on the left with Asnières a bit farther downriver beyond Courbevoie. By the last hours of March, government troops had begun probing the defenses there.

Position often mattered more than numbers in such fighting. Smaller numbers on the defensive could often hold the line against a greater force. Colonel Louis Rossel, the engineer, had understood this almost instinctively. After his bitter experience at Metz, he had reported for garrison duty at Paris. When the government abandoned the city to the Germans without a fight, he wrote his resignation letter from the army and turned to the Commune. As the two sides approached each other west of the city, Rossel planned to lead 2,000 men from Neuilly into Courbevoie along the line of the railroad, but found that "at least two battalions were completely drunk, and others complained of not having eaten."[8]

With a base on the west bank of the Seine at Courbevoie, Flourens decided to lead an expedition from Paris to Versailles on April 3. They

---

7   Marie-France Sardain, *Défenses et sièges de Paris: 1814–1914* (Paris: Economica, 2009), particularly "Le deuxième siège de Paris (18 mars–28 mai 1871)," at 161–230.

8   *Rossel's Posthumous Papers, Translated from the French* (London and Paris: Chapman and Hall and E. Lachaud, 1872), 68–9, 76. Also Devaureix, *Souvenirs et observations sur la campagne de 1870*, 419 n.

intended to venture forth to demonstrate the need for new arrangements between Paris and the rest of France. They might have expected some resistance and maybe a bit of gunfire. However, they believed that most of the uniformed and armed fellow citizens to their front wanted no war, and that the few who did generally would find little encouragement.

Mont-Valérien glowered down from the highest point in that area, as still it does. During the siege, it had been a key to the city's defenses. With the surrender, the French government handed the position over to the Prussians, who had since given it back to the Versailles government. Representatives of the Commune had asked the army to allow the National Guard to garrison the place. The commander there would not do so, but assured them that he would never use the advantage of the position to fire on Parisians.

The Commune apparently believed the army.

The guns of Mont-Valérien waited patiently until much of the column wending its way out of the city got within range and sight. Then they opened fire. Prussian royals may have had qualms about bombarding Paris and its people, but there is no indication of hesitation by the French government. So the long-range shells of a coming twentieth century crashed into the last hopeful midst of eighteenth-century republicans.

Flourens and Émile Duval, at the head of the column—now separated from the rest of the expedition—made a mad dash against the government's infantry that did not end well. Wounded and maimed, one account had Flourens stretching out his arms, shouting to the hesitating soldiers, "Shoot, shoot! I should not have spared you!" Government troops tossed his butchered body into a cart and hauled it back to Versailles.[9] Duval died the next day.

Behind them—back toward Courbevoie and the river—much of the rest of the Communard force had been unprepared and misled as to what to expect. They virtually disintegrated and made their way east toward the bridge in hopes of getting back to the city. That evening, Gustave Cluseret stood observing it all near the river. The veteran of the efforts at Lyon and Marseille had few illusions but had only recently been appointed to assist in the Commune's defense. The evening of the third, he "did what [he] could" to minimize the panic and keep enough

---

9 For a version of his death, see Bernhardt, *My Double Life*, 220,

of an organized force to resist the government troops.[10] Before the end of the day, Cluseret would be reorganizing the Communard army, such as it was.

Nothing but civil war could follow. No individual—no group of individuals with any substantive power—could prevent it. And, should such a war take place, the laboring poor of Paris would fight the government of the ruling elites that had exercised a class dictatorship over them, their country, and their world.

Commune Movements

Neither the International nor any other radicals had overthrown the government. It had rather collapsed under the weight of its own corruption and arrogant obliviousness. It had ruthlessly foisted upon society a series of decisions that proved entirely self-destructive of the institutions essential to its survival. it showed itself to be incapable of any rational reflection upon—and correction of—the turn bourgeois republicanism had taken.

That said, the IWA rallied to the cause of the Commune almost as soon as it got news of its establishment. On April 8, the General Council in London issued its "Address to the People of Paris" declaring support. However, the Commune itself would be gone before the document could be widely circulated.

None of this mattered in Paris, of course, where members of the IWA had already thrown themselves into the work of establishing the Commune, contributing their special concerns about mobilizing the wider society for support. They also reached out to the insurgent movements that had broken out elsewhere in the country. Even before the proclamation of the Commune, they had sent Charles Amouroux and others to find allies beyond the capital. On March 24, the delegation had reached Lyons. From there, Amouroux had sent Captain Montcharmont and Saint-Hillaire to Saint-Étienne and Leblanc continued to Le Creusot. Saint-Étienne had established the commune followed by more to the south—Marseille, and other communities.

---

10   *Procès-verbaux de la Commune de 1871*, vol. 2, 503. For Cluseret's oft-neglected role in the Commune, see Braka, *L'honneur perdu du Général Cluseret*, 139–78.

Three years before, the imperial authorities had suppressed a move for local government at Toulouse—only about a third the size of Marseille—resulting in three days of rioting, but the war and national developments had revived the movement. Rebellion also broke out at Narbonne, and, on a lesser scale, at Limoges, Guéret, and the Nièvre, even as active republican agitation stirred Grenoble and Mâcon.[11]

At Le Creusot, Jean-Baptiste Dumay and others led a battalion of some 800 of the guards to the Hôtel de Ville, where they fraternized with the company of infantry and cuirassiers holding the place, and arranged its peaceful transfer. After they raised a red flag, Dumay declared himself "no longer the representative of the Government of Versailles, I am the representative of the Commune of Le Creusot." A provisional government of thirty-two people began to plan the democratic election of a permanent government, the decisions of which "would be immediately subjected to the appreciation of the people in public meeting or by way of posters." Penhoat sent a delegation of officers to Creusot to report on what had really taken place.[12]

On March 27, a train with a thousand soldiers steamed into Le Creusot and took charge. They prohibited meetings, and issued arrest warrants, dispersing several demonstrations, though the red flag still waved for another day. When the flag came down, the army arrested several of the commune's leaders and drove the rest into Switzerland. Dumay remained in hiding locally until the April 30 municipal elections. By then, the government had seized 700 rifles and 20,000 cartridges from the workers. In the election, the fugitive ran against Henri Schneider, the son and heir of Eugène the industrialist, but the results proved remarkably close and the announced count was greeted with suspicion. Still, the young Schneider became the mayor over the bones of the workers' commune there and kept the office for the next quarter of a century. The local courts processed the prosecutions of twenty-two leaders of the insurrection, condemning half a dozen *in*

11 Ronald Aminzade, *Ballots and Barricades: Class Formation and Republican Politics in France, 1830–1871* (Princeton: Princeton University Press, 1993), 215; Greenberg, *Sisters of Liberty*, 9, 48, 138, 139, 141, 210, 225, 262.

12 On involvement at Le Creusot by some remaining elements of the Armée des Vosges, see Penhoat, March 27, and Chief of staff to minister of war, March 16, 1871, both in LG3. At least part of the widely scattered Forty-Second Mobiles from Aveyron garrisoned Le Creusot, as well as Mâcon.

absentia, sentencing Dumay to forced labor for life and the rest to deportation.

Lyon also teetered. Garibaldi, who had returned to Italy, left his son Ricciotti to linger there long enough to monitor the prospects for the new commune movement. "I authorize you to take a hand," he wrote, should the movement show any prospect of resuming the war or regenerating the republic. Garibaldi promised that, in the event, "I will go immediately to join you." However, he cautioned his son against involving himself in simple political rivalries among the French. Both sides in Lyon sent delegations to court Ricciotti, who concluded that the conflict excited class tensions simply for political purposes and kept his forces out of the city, insisting that they would return to Italy shortly. Nevertheless, as he noted, the government later issued an arrest warrant "against any member of my family who would dare step foot in France."[13]

At Lyon, an orchestrated wave of support for the government swept a mass reception for veterans of the siege of Belfort against the exhausted insurrectionists there. A few days later, on March 28, the authorities had gotten into a position where they could crush the movement for a new commune. At nearby Guillotière, barricades went up at the end of April as a crowd estimated at 20,000 to 25,000 confronted the arrival of two columns of infantry, but the troops eventually moved against the barricades and deployed artillery against that symbol of republican government, the Hôtel de Ville.

As the Thiers government thugged its way back into power at Le Creusot and Lyon, the jackboots hit the cobblestones across France. Communard delegate Albert May had gone to Toulouse, but the authorities crushed the local insurgency on March 27. That brought down the revolt at Narbonne the next day.[14] Armed Legitimists and Bonapartists—now calling themselves "republicans"—wrote much the same story in crushing the popular bids for power at Saint-Étienne and Limoges.

The press reported the commune "re-established in Marseille, where, it is said, the Mayor and General Prefect have been made prisoners." In fact,

13 Garibaldi, *Souvenirs de la campagne de France*, 133–4, 134–5.

14 On the repression in Creusot, even as Paris saw "the arrest of persons implicated in the Commune disturbances continues daily," see "France," *The Times*, October 24, 1871, 5; Greenberg, *Sisters of Liberty*, 10, 138, 140, 141, 246, 262; Frederick Engels, "The Bakuninists at Work: An Account of the Spanish Revolt in the Summer of 1873," *MECW*, vol. 23, 581–98.

Gambetta's man in the city, Alphonse Gent, resigned as prefect in disgust over peace terms, and voters there reelected Alphonse Esquiros to the National Assembly. The mayor tried to stop the national authorities from taking the local National Guard to Versailles, and their march to the station on March 23 ended in a mass demonstration that cheered Garibaldi along with Esquiros and their own civic guards. The crowd stormed the prefecture, raised the red flag, and established a new local government of republicans and moderate Blanquists, socialists, and members of the IWA. From the balcony of the Hôtel de Ville, Gaston Crémieux declared their solidarity with Paris, and tried without success to steer the movement away from direct confrontation with the national government.[15]

At Marseille, on April 3, the army declared a state of civil war, cancelled plans for an election, and marched 6,000 or 7,000 soldiers into the city. They bombarded the city from Notre-Dame de la Garde—later called "Our Lady of Bombard." Two days later, the army prevailed in a ten-hour fight over the prefecture, claiming a loss of 30 dead and 50 wounded, while killing about 150 insurgents and taking 500 prisoners. The next day, the reactionaries through the city exacted revenge and shouted, "Vive Jésus!" and "Long live the Sacred Heart!" On April 8, the army arrested Crémieux, the only revolutionary leader who had not fled the city, and gave him a short trial behind closed doors before condemning him. "All the republican societies have been disbanded," gloated one report, "and the red flag has vanished from the city."[16]

The gap between the capital and the rest of the nation widened. Prosper-Olivier Lissagaray, future editor of *Le tribun du peuple*, recalled that "one of our friends arrived—one of the most timid men of the timid provinces. His kith and kin had escorted him on his departure, tears in their eyes, as though he were descending into the infernal regions." He asked the Communards about the rumors circulating about them in the countryside. "Well," replied one, "come and search all the recesses of the den."[17]

Yet while the Parisians might bring a country cousin into the city to give them an insight into the city's responses, the government had the

---

15   Bordone, *Garibaldi et l'Armée des Vosges*, vol. 3, 347; "France," *New York Times*, March 26, 1871, 1. See also Greenberg, *Sisters of Liberty*.

16   "The Commune a Failure at Marseilles," *New York Times*, March 31, 1871, 1.

17   Prosper Olivier Lissagaray, *History of the Commune of 1871*, trans. Eleanor Marx Aveling (London: New Park Publications, 1976 [original 1886]), 233.

power, the printing budget, and the institutional authority of the army and the Church to present anything it wanted to the country with little risk of contradiction.

Few people in the leadership of the Commune would have understood this in a more visceral way than Cluseret, who emerged as the new delegate of war after the fiasco of April 3. He knew the realities of politics in the south better than any of the other leaders in Paris, having been intimately involved in the efforts of Lyon and Marseille to chart a course more helpful to their defense during the war. And Cluseret understood the position of the insurgency in the most starkly realistic terms.

The US ambassador, Elihu B. Washburne, clearly reflected his government's quiet sympathies with the Prussians and then with Versailles. He complained that even though he had gotten many of the wealthier of his countrymen out of the city, "we still have here a large number of Americans." One of them recalled of Cluseret "the feeling of security entertained by all Americans in Paris while he remained in power."[18] Still, Washburne cordially detested him for his radicalism, implying that Cluseret only claimed to be a US citizen and even used scare quotes to suggest that his former rank in the US army was not real.

However, the general personally got the ambassador in to see the imprisoned archbishop. The general wisely scoffed at the idiotic policy of seizing individual hostages, when the Commune "held such infinitely more valuable hostages as, say, the banks of Paris." He wanted to release everybody. " 'I don't want to take one life unnecessarily," he assured one hostile observer. He added that foreigners enjoyed Cluseret's "extremely liberal policy towards us"; Englishmen and Americans particularly "have never gone about Paris with so little annoyance or fear of arrest."[19]

No matter.

Cluseret struggled mightily to centralize the military authority, an obvious task more easily said than done. Other members of the council, neighborhood associations, even private citizens of Paris could formulate and attempt to implement their own initiatives. For example, Louise

---

18   Elihu B. Washburne to Fish, April 6, 1871, in *Franco-German War and Insurrection of the Commune: Correspondence of E. B. Washburne* (Washington, DC: Government Printing Office, 1878), 178; Fetridge, *Rise and Fall of the Paris Commune*, 199.

19   Fetridge, *Rise and Fall of the Paris Commune*, 199.

Michel, the head of the Montmartre Women's Vigilance Committee, planned to slip through the lines to Versailles on her own and attempt an assassination of Thiers.

In the end, hostile observers, politicians, and often later scholars generally find Cluseret one of the more enigmatic (and easily vilified) of the Commune leaders. Those who do not simply ignore his efforts describe them as those of an aspiring dictator. One chronicler depicted a general of "insatiate ambition, greedy of power," who has "gradually and steadily gathered all power into his own hands, and has made no secret of his resolution to resist and resent all interference on the part of laymen in what he considers the all-absorbing question of the moment, the effectual defense of Paris." He even described Cluseret as someone who could be bribed based on the fact that he made decisions according to "practical" considerations.[20]

For his part, Cluseret and many of the Communards understood the internal as well as external threats to the project's survival. Those who had been seriously involved in trying to unpack eighteenth-century republicanism into the nineteenth century understood the immense pitfalls of the self-regarded reincarnated Jacobins that dominated the Commune—the willful reenactors of a Lost Cause.

Their predominance in the elected offices of the Commune reflected the very limited civic life and experience of the working-class electorate under the regime in which they had lived for a generation. Lack of experience also thwarted electoral efforts. Most who went to vote had never heard of the candidates and had little idea what agendas they might pursue. This became evident in the quality of their leaders, who— to be entirely fair—had had little preparation themselves for governing a city. In revolutionary circumstances, the masses can learn quickly, but they had had only a week between the call for elections and the voting in March.[21]

Too make matters worse, officeholders under the Commune frequently translated that old Jacobin faith in the power of the *levée en masse* into a simplistic dismissal of the value of experience. This made the critical matters of the city's defense an arena for political and personal

---

20   Ibid., 199–200. Braka, *L'honneur perdu du Général Cluseret*.

21   See also April 16 elections reported "Commune de Paris," *Journal officiel de la République Française*, April 19, 1871, 324–5.

rivalries. Those who brought experience and expertise to the Commune's defense, such as Rossel, found themselves with anything but a reliable officer corps or a disciplined, trained defense force.

These political considerations, as well as the military circumstances, had earlier persuaded Marx and the IWA General Council back in London to urge Parisians not to attempt to seize power.[22] However, the revolutionists are the last to get to pick and choose when and where revolution takes place. The insurrection had become a successful revolution when the government abandoned Paris and, subsequently, chose to wage a civil war against the vilified urban rabble. Once that happened, the choice was simply whether to take an unprecedented opportunity or to leave those masses, urged for generations to stand up for themselves, to their own fate. On April 8, the General Council realized this and issued an "Address to the People of Paris" declaring their support for the Commune. In doing so, it followed the lead of its comrades present within the city.

What the Commune needed in order to solve these problems of disorganization or dogmatism was time and experience. The immediate challenge of its leadership was to buy that time.

The Politics of Military Defense

April in Paris offered Cluseret what he had not had at Lyon or Marseille. Behind him, he had a relatively more stable revolutionary authority that would buy him some time and accord him a role that better reflected his experience and inclinations. Within hours of taking general charge of the defenses, he began issuing orders aimed at sealing the city.[23]

In doing this, Cluseret deployed the available insurgent units of the army with that idea that he, like Trochu during the earlier siege, had a

---

22   Eugène Dupont, Secretary of the International (General Council) for France, wrote the same on September 7, 1870. V. I. Lenin not only drew on Marx and Engels but G. Weill, *Histoire du mouvement social en France 1852–1902* (Paris: s.n.n.p., 1904) for his understanding of the Commune.

23   *Procès-verbaux de la Commune de 1871*, vol. 2, p. 503. Also Victor Hugo, "Three Adventurers: Cluseret, Osman Digna and O'Danne," *New York Tribune*, February 4, 1889, 3. An occasional correspondent of the *Tribune*, "Three Adventurers: Cluseret, Osman Digna and O'Danne," *New York Tribune*, February 4, 1889, 3.

large, organized Garde nationale in support. In truth, though, Trochu had rarely taken the National Guard seriously as a military force. In an economy crushed by the war, its primary function had been to subsidize the poorest of the city to minimize civic disorders.

It took several days for the full reality of the situation to sink in, after which Cluseret turned quickly to the training of his forces. On a good day, he might be able to train, equip, and dress 9,000 to 10,000 men, but he had no means of keeping most of them to their duty. He soon found, "I was deceived in this case. This is because I was not in Paris during the siege. If I had known the state of the National Guard, I would not have taken responsibility of this organization."[24] Cluseret rather quickly revised his numbers to a more realistic 25,000 to 30,000, adding later that he never had never been able to get more than 6,000 at the front.

Despite all the problems, though, Cluseret immediately located and began reinforcing the crossing between Courbevoie and Neuilly, the approach most readily accessible to the *versaillais*. He immediately mistrusted those who had managed the bloody political theatre of April 3 at Courbevoie. One of these, General Jules-Henri-Marie Bergeret, in command of the crossing at Courbevoie, began changing the orders Cluseret issued to his troops in the field.

Cluseret replaced Bergeret with Jaroslaw Dombrowski, who secured the line at Neuilly, with brother Ladislaw holding neighborhoods to the right. However, Bergeret not only tried to keep his old assignment, but tried to unseat Cluseret, complaining that he had taken American citizenship in preference to French and had fought to sustain slavery against liberty in the war there. It fizzled out but absurdities of this kind continually distracted the Commune and burned its limited time.

This unevenness also characterized the quality of the actual work of defense. While much of the defense force turned out to be essentially paper organizations, others bore a much greater portion of the fighting than others. For example, the 101st battalion from the Mouffetard neighborhood in the Thirteenth Arrondissement under Jean-Baptiste Sérizier came under fire almost continually after April 3, supported later

---

24 *Procès-verbaux de la Commune de 1871*, vol. 2, 502; Edward S. Mason, *The Paris Commune: An Episode in the History of the Socialist Movement* (New York: Macmillan, 1930), 208–9.

by the 175th and 176th. "Day and night, their guns hot, they had roamed about the trenches, the villages, the fields; the Versaillese of Neuilly, of Asnières, ten times fled before them. They had taken three cannons from them, which, like faithful mastiffs, followed them everywhere." Lissagaray described them as "undisciplined, undisciplinable, wild, rough, their clothes and flag torn, obeying only one order, that to march forward, mutineering when inactive" for "their rage was their only commander."[25]

On the afternoon of Friday, April 7, the government troops decided to take the bridge to Neuilly away from them. "At none of the encounters between the Prussians and the French around Paris did I see more severe fighting than on Friday evening at the Courbevoie end of the bridge of Neuilly," wrote an observer with the government forces. The artillery from Mont-Valérien lobbed shells at the Communard batteries near Porte Maillot while the *mitrailleuses* sprayed the streets. By 3:30, elements of the army with generals J. Charles Péchot and Pierre-Marc Besson moved on the Communard barricades there and in the middle of the bridge. More Communards hurried forward from the Bois de Boulogne with more sandbags. The government, nevertheless, gained the bridge, where a caisson exploded, killing Besson on the spot. Later, they found a badly wounded Péchot elsewhere. "During the fight no fewer than twenty-one officers were killed or wounded on the Government side. The bridge and the entrance of the Avenue were strewn with dead and wounded insurgents."[26] Any expectations on the part of the government that it would easy to retake Paris died with them.

In Paris, the passage from Monday's outing to Friday's battle marked an epoch.

Next to the river crossings west of Paris, government troops pressed strongly against the defenses southwest of the city, along the left bank of the Seine. Generations before, the village of Issy had grown well beyond the city walls around the old Château de Issy, the seat of the princes of the Conti or Condé branch of the Bourbons. Thirty years before, the government had built Fort Issy there to protect that approach to the city walls. The Prussians had

---

25 Lissagaray, *History of the Paris Commune*, 281–2.

26 Fetridge, *The Rise and Fall of the Paris Commune in 1871*, vol. 2, 122–3. Reprinted in Ollier, *Cassell's History of the War*, 393.

simply blasted the area during the siege, and reduced much of it to rubble.[27]

The several hundred men the Commune had sent to hold the fort soon came under serious attack by the Versailles troops.[28] After a desperate struggle in the village of Issy, the insurgents fell back under cover of the forts, which kept up strong fire to protect their retreat. The *mitrailleuses*, with which the barricades were armed, also opened fire on two strong columns of troops which were marching on Issy. Dombrowski passed on reports that "the situation presented no gravity; that Paris could preserve its confidence; that the attack of the Versailles forces, which had been expected for two days, would not succeed."

On the night of Tuesday, April 11, the government waged a particularly violent night attack on the gates of the southwest. The Enfants de Paris— along with the 208th and 179th battalions—threw back this assault. Over the next few hours, Issy repulsed three successive attacks with heavy losses, and the defenders in the trenches before Fort Vanves were similarly successful.

Veterans of Garibaldi's ventures assumed responsibility for the Commune at all levels. The emergence of Cluseret deepened a confidence he did nothing to dampen. His field commander, Dombrowski, had raised troops for Garibaldi during the war in the south. Assi the leader of the factory workers at Le Creusot had fought with Garibaldi in Italy and now brought to bear his experience organizing the manufacture of armaments for the insurgents.

Also of high rank in the defense of the city, Napoléon La Cécilia had been a captain of engineers in the Thousand. In 1859, he had been a professor of mathematics but left to fight for freedom under Garibaldi. Since then, wrote one chronicler, "he has taken part in every revolutionary plot or intrigue." In the recent war, he had fought in the Loire valley, emerging as a colonel of the *francs-tireurs* of Lipowski, and the Commune made him the chief of staff for General Émile Eudes, the Blanquist.[29]

---

27   Sardain, *Défenses et sièges de Paris*, particularly "Le deuxième siège de Paris (18 mars–28 mai 1871)," 169. The Italian version of Conde, Conti, was adopted by Hugh Forbes's family.

28   Quotes in this and the following paragraph from Fetridge, *Rise and Fall of the Paris Commune*, 125–6.

29   J.-L. Menard, *Émile Eudes, 1843–1888: Général de la Commune et blanquiste* (Paris: Dittmar, 2005); Fetridge, *Rise and Fall of the Paris Commune*, 502.

It was noteworthy that Cluseret's ascent to authority in the Commune's defense brought a number of others into its deliberations. He released Rossel from a jail cell, where someone's accusation had temporarily sent him. A well-trained and experienced officer, Rossel resented the corruption of the government and its surrender to the Prussians, though his politics remained a crudely formed, romanticized, if practically distant, appreciation of "the people." He may well have had "a deeply exaggerated appreciation of his own importance," and thought he should have a field command. When Cluseret assigned him to organize a military court, Rossel convinced himself that he was being sidelined. In fact, Cluseret needed to bring Rossel's professionalism to bear in this effort to discipline the defending forces.[30] Nevertheless, Rossel did his duty well, gaining a reputation as severe in his efforts to build a military force that could meet that of the government.

Cluseret, the old abolitionist and bohemian, also helped bring into the government Sainte Suzanne Melvil-Bloncourt. Reelected as the deputy for Guadeloupe, he could have taken his place with the government at Versaille, but the France he aspired to help govern met in the Hôtel de Ville. The presence of this black radical in the Commune leadership virtually embodied the persistent desire for the universal republic.

At headquarters, Cluseret lived awaiting reports he desperately needed and rarely got. He continually sent orders to units that could not be found and scrambled for news from units that seem to have disappeared. He found himself regularly gasping for air in the dire realities of the smoke of combat west of the city and in the Hôtel de Ville where dwelt the abstractions of Fourier and Blanqui, mingling under the grandfatherly puffery of "Jacobinism." Meanwhile, those with a soldier's eye knew that, within walking distance of this rebellious hopefulness, waited the two largest armies in Europe.[31]

---

30   Rossel was arrested but released by Cluseret on April 2. Someone later told Rossel that they had forced his assignment to a military role in the Commune on Cluseret, which persuaded Rossel that Cluseret had "at bottom . . . a certain jealousy of me." The obvious usefulness of Rossel to Cluseret indicates the absurdity of this. *Rossel's Posthumous Papers*, 79–80, 83, 84–7.

31   M.W.H. wrote two pieces: "Some New Books: Gen. Cluseret's Memoirs—The Truth about the Paris Commune" and "Some New Books: Minister Washburne's Recollections," *New York Sun*, August 21, September 4, and October 16, 1887, all on p. 4.

Cluseret understood that they stood on the brink of a massacre of world-historic proportions in what had been the most important city in Europe for generations. He had organized a credible defense of the city out of the disorganized and chaotic forces that had just paraded their fatal vulnerability at Courbevoie, but the government forces grew by the day and would be inching ever closer, around both Neuilly and Issy.

Upon taking charge of the city's defense, Cluseret reached out to open negotiations. Thiers's "republic," which had negotiated with the Prussians, declined to hold talks of any sort with the people it claimed to represent. The French government simply had no interest other than bleeding the city.

Some informal representatives of the government did approach the Commune. One of Gambetta's Masonic brothers, Luigi Frapolli, made the case. Despite his checkered record in recruitment and supply at Lyon, Cluseret thought him "an honest man and a gallant man" and heard him out. Frapolli urged him to weigh certain concessions the Commune might wring from Versailles against risking the loss of everything, assuring him of a general amnesty for the insurgents. Cluseret, however, felt that Paris could hold out indefinitely and doubted the promise of amnesty. He believed that Frappoli's strongest argument was that the Commune would excuse the reconstruction of the military establishment.[32]

Cluseret also proposed talks with the Germans. On April 10, Bismarck told General Georg Alfred von Fabrice, the governor general of occupied France, to hear out any overtures, with the understanding that they would be forwarded to Berlin.

On April 26, Cluseret rode out to Fort Aubervilliers to meet with Baron Friedrich von Holstein.[33] Born to a Prussian military background, the baron had been in the foreign service for years, though his last assignment, to Washington, ended after a particularly undiplomatic

---

32   Gustave Paul Cluseret, *Mémoires du Général Cluseret*, 3 vols. (Paris: Jules Lévy, Éditeur, 1887–8), vol. 2, 120–1, 125. The three volumes cover *Le second siège, Les derniers combats* (of the Commune), and *La fin de l'empire*.

33   Cluseret, *Mémoires*, vol. 2, 1–5, 7–9, 10–14. See also Norman Rich, *Friedrich von Holstein: Politics and Diplomacy in the Era of Bismarck and Wilhelm II* (Cambridge: Cambridge University Press, 1965). See also Braka, *L'honneur perdu du Général Cluseret*, 153–4.

affair with the wife of Cluseret's old benefactor, Senator Charles Sumner. The negotiations between the two remained remarkably frank.

Cluseret acknowledged "the delicacy of the position in which we stand towards one another." "You are dealing with no riot, nor even with an insurrection, but simply with a municipal revolution. It is in the name of the municipal council of the city of Paris, defending its rights, that I have come to confer with you." He said that the Commune wanted nothing from the Germans but their neutrality. Holstein suggested that releasing the archbishop would strengthen the case. Cluseret agreed to do what he could to arrange this.

He also tried to disabuse the Germans of their nostalgia for a French monarchy. "There is no species of monarchy which can, I will not say, maintain itself in France, for none can do that, but even try to maintain itself without a promise of revenge." Cluseret agreed that they would not be able to exact their revenge:

> A people only fights for what it loves, and the French people *hates* the castes that govern it. As to the officers, they only fight for their pay. Put their pay at stake, and they will fight for it as dogs fight for a bone. Reassure them upon that point, they'll let themselves be taken prisoners and will yield up their swords.

France, "to give the semblance of reality to these bellicose professions, will be forced to ruin herself in armaments, compelling you to do the same." "The army, paid by the people to serve against you Germans, would in reality serve only against itself, and that is what we all are interested in preventing."

The triumph of Versailles would mean nothing but "perpetual disquietude" for Germany. Already, argued Cluseret, the Kaiser and his high command had won such victories that it would become hard to persuade their armies that they were still needed in the field. He reminded Holstein, "Why, already you can hear the clamors of your soldiers, furious at being kept so long in France."

Holstein agreed that "we are in a hurry to get home. Discipline is suffering."

Morale had fallen in sections of the German Army. Back in Burgundy, when Jesse White Mario and other medical personnel from Garibaldi's army passed through the lines, one of the Prussian officers asked why Garibaldi would fight against him, describing him as "a great man and a good one at any rate." This represented more than the still-glowing embers of 1848 because younger Germans drew lessons from the war. When Paul Déroulède told a young Saxon that his wounded brother needed a doctor, he responded, "Ah! we hurt your brother? What do you want, it's war!" He quickly added, "It's the fault of Napoleon and of Bismarck." Nor should it be forgotten that Germans in Paris had taken up arms for the Commune.[34]

"How, then, will it be?" asked Cluseret,

> When this situation becomes chronic, [when it] shall force you to keep under the colors the men whom the public interest summons to the fields or to the workshop? Your parliaments, no doubt, will stand by you, but who will stand by your parliaments? I tell you that you will see the germ of revolution introduced into Germany.

The baron, slated to become governor general of occupied France, pressed as to whether the Commune would contest Alsace and Lorraine militarily. "We want more than that but we would get it in another way."

Twenty-three years after Marx and Engels described the fearful hobgoblin of revolution, the ruling class and its French and German governments saw it very clearly, even if many of the communard leaders did not. Cluseret found himself in an increasingly intense tussle with the governing bodies of the Commune. He complained that he had found the War Office with nothing necessary to fight a war. As he tried to cobble them together, the governing institutions refused to sanction his proposed military court and left him no gendarmerie or other means to enforce his orders.[35]

Bismarck and the Germans found nothing in their talks with the Commune that offered more than cooperation with the plans of the French government. Through it all, Bismarck cooperated actively with the French efforts to build yet another army, one aimed at inflicting mass death on other French people. The Germans facilitated the return

---

34   Mario, "Garibaldi in France," 610; Déroulède, *1870*, 192; and Mareike König, "Les immigrés allemands à Paris 1870/71: Entre expulsion, naturalisation et lutte sur les barricades," in Sylvie Aprile, Quentin Dupuis, Jacques Rougerie, *La Commune et les étrangers* (Paris: Génériques, 2010), 60–71.

35   *Procès-verbaux de la Commune de 1871*, vol. 2, 499, 500.

of tens of thousands of French prisoners held by the Prussians. Moreover, the Prussians continued to allow people into Paris through the gates they controlled north and east of the city. What drew these new people to the capital was not tourism but the promise of the Commune. Knowing full well what the French Army would do, Bismarck had reasons as strong as Thiers's to hope that as many radicals as possible would crowd into the city.

What followed, he hoped, would destroy radicalism for generations to come.

11
Actors versus Reenactors: April 28–May 21, 1871

The disaster of April 3 would not be the last attempt of the Commune's leadership to reenact the history of revolutionary activities in Paris. For some days in late April, the local Masonic lodges had struggled with the issues of the insurrection. In the end, the more political of them brushed aside the objections of the Grand Orient to present themselves as an appeal to the government. In the end, on Saturday, April 29, a reported 15,000 Masons gathered on the Place de la Bastille and marched through the city, up the Champs-Élysées to Porte Maillot. They marched out to the government lines. Gunfire from the *versaillais* killed two Masons, but the delegation continued into Courbevoie to make their appeal. Some officers who were members of the order were not without sympathy for the message. Nevertheless, the government officially ignored their appeal and the Freemasons returned to plant the flag of the order on the barricade of the Commune.[1]

As the drama of ritual Masonic appeals unfolded along the Seine west of the city, more pernicious efforts were made to resurrect the ghosts of the previous century. Events turned most dramatically on the developments around Fort Issy, southwest of the city, over the Seine and downstream. In response to disaster there, the Jacobin wing of the Commune's leadership insisted on the organization of a Committee of Public Safety.

---

1 Marc Viellard, *Les francs-maçons et la Commune de Paris* (Paris: Éditions maçonniques de France, 2003), 93–9. Also see Cluseret, *Mémoires*, vol. 2, 56–65.

The subsequent efforts of the Commune to function became structurally inseparable from the necessity imposed on it of defending itself.

The Transformative Removal of Cluseret

On Friday—the day before the Masonic parade—Cluseret came out to Fort Issy to inspect the physical condition of the badly battered installation and arrange any necessary repairs. He passed over the ramparts and visited the upper bunkers temporarily in use to house the gunners. He also checked the supply of munitions, noting enough shells for 3,000 shots. He made sure that the fort had about a hundred gunners and sent more engineers.[2]

The garrison included several hundred guardsmen of the 107th Batallion under the command of a thirty-year-old railroad engineer, Léon Guillaume Edmond Mégy. Nominally a member of the International, he had earlier stood trial for shooting a policeman, and had close ties to the Blanquists.[3] An honest, politically serious figure, Mégy had done well in a position for which he had little experience.

Cluseret returned to the city. After putting in more busy hours at the War Office, he went to bed at around two o'clock and rose expecting another normal Saturday. In short order, though, he got a dispatch from Jaroslaw Dombrowski reporting an "armistice concluded with the enemy. On the whole line, that the hostilities were suspended." With his military court nobbled and military decisions made without even consulting him—although he would be held responsible for them—he sent his resignation to the executive of the council. Shortly after, word came from the southern front that the enemy had surprised two barricades between Vanves and Issy.[4]

---

2 *Procès-verbaux de la Commune de 1871*, vol. 2, 499. Cluseret's account of what happened in April is quite straightforward, if short, and was given in his hearing, which included many members who would have happily challenged him if anything he stated had been challengeable. For the material used here, see ibid., 498–500.

3 Edmond Mégy noted in *Journal officiel de la République française sous la Commune*, hereafter cited as *J.O. s.L.C.*, April 18, 1871, la Ville de Marseille, L'Insurrection du 23 mars 1871 et La Lois du 10 Vendémiaire an IV (Paris: Typographie Georges Chamerot, 1874), 6–7, 57, 57–8 and n., 68. On Mégy, see Cordillot, *La sociale en Amérique*, 304–7. Bernard Noël, *Dicionnaire de la Commune*, 2 vols. (Paris: Mémoire du livre, 2001), vol. 2, 89–90.

4 *Procès-verbaux de la Commune de 1871*, vol. 2, 485, as well as the rest of his testimony.

Then came the frantic and desperate appeals from Issy. These stunned Cluseret. As he put it, only hours before, Mégy had described his garrison as "in the best spirits," but now claimed to need thousands of men to strengthen a fort with 500. Cluseret sent word that he would be bringing reinforcements personally.

Back at Fort Issy, Mégy and his men watched as government troops took positions that had kept them and their artillery from getting closer to the fort itself. He sent Cluseret the first of several pleas for reinforcements. They held on, as the barricades and rifle pits protecting the fort kept the troops at some distance, but being under shot and shell must have been entirely nerve-wracking. As would be common for soldiers in masonry forts, it must have seemed at times as though a few well-placed blasts would bring down the walls. And every time they ducked for cover and raised their heads again, it seemed as though the *versaillais* had inched their way a bit closer to the fort.

At this point, Staff Colonel E. Leperche, who had been at Metz with Louis Rossel, dispatched a messenger to Mégy and his officers. He gave the garrison fifteen minutes to surrender, after which they would be "allowed to live where they please except in Paris." Should they not surrender, he threatened, the government would put the whole garrison to the sword.[5]

This seems to have been what really unnerved Mégy. In the absence of any reinforcements, concern for his men overrode his military instincts. As the walls rattled around them, he consulted his officers and came to a decision to abandon the fort.[6]

It is unclear whether Mégy and his men had actually evacuated the fort completely. A muddled anti-Commune account reported the fort "on the point of surrendering" when General Walery Antoni Wróblewski, a veteran of the Polish revolt seven years earlier, turned up to relieve him, reassigning the post to General Émile Eudes with orders to hold the fort until death. The same source reported that it was Cluseret himself who "first came to the rescue of the abandoned fort."[7]

Cluseret quickly began drawing what he had available to a rendezvous

5 Fetridge, *Rise and Fall of the Paris Commune*, 202–3.

6 *Paris-Commune, le siège Versaillais: Avec commentaires, détails historiques et documents officiels* (Paris: Degorce-Cadot, [1871?]), 134–5.

7 Fetridge, *Rise and Fall of the Paris Commune*, 197–8.

at the École militaire. He had about 300 members of the 137th battalion, and added some artillery and as many others as he could bring with him. He noted that his fellow Garibaldian, General Napoléon La Cécilia, had organized other reinforcements, as did some other officers.[8]

Their march from the École militaire to Fort Issy likely took a bit over an hour, though they faced a delay at the city gates. Several hundred of the guard, willing to defend their own neighborhoods, refused to go beyond the city walls. This represented exactly the sort of issue Cluseret had tried repeatedly to address only to find the Commune's government unwilling to support his views. At this point, he could do nothing but make a quick reassignment of officers to take the unwilling back to duty in Paris.

Certainly, though, reinforcements arrived a few hours after the crisis began. Some of the command at Issy seem to have remained there, if dispirited and demoralized. One account described Cluseret finding the fort abandoned, except for a sixteen-year-old in tears, sitting on a powder keg ready prepared to blow up the magazine when the government troops entered the fort; Cluseret embraced him.[9] The reality could well have been less dramatic.

Whatever transpired at Issy, Cluseret managed to sort it out and returned to the War Office, where he found that, fortunately, no other emergencies had broken out. At this point, representatives of the executive committee ringed the headquarters, placing guards at the exits, implying a fear that Cluseret might bolt, and entered to remove from office the fellow whose resignation they had just declined to accept.[10]

In fact, Cluseret's arrest had nothing particularly to do with him, but with a political struggle within the Conseil de la Commune. Jules Miot and others of the Jacobin-inclined majority pointed out that they, like their predecessors of 1793, were under threat and that the proper response would be to delegate power to a Comité de salut public. Cluseret, like some others of the IWA, did not understand the value of such a

---

8   Ibid., 205.

9   *Paris-Commune, le siège Versaillais*, 134–5; Rupert Christiansen, *Paris Babylon: Grandeur, Decadence and Revolution. 1869–75* (London: Pimlico, 2003), 329.

10   Cluseret's enemies also asserted that generals Zadlo-Dombrowski and Wróblewski both sent in their resignations on account of Cluseret's mismanagement, but on hearing of his arrest withdrew them. Fetridge, *Rise and Fall of the Paris Commune*, 198.

measure. Aping a failed strategy torn from its historical context might not have been a particularly good plan, but it was, at least, something. The elected council voted forty-five to twenty-three to delegate power to an institutionalized "revolutionary dictatorship." True, this did absolutely nothing to halt the erosion of their position, but nobody really knew how to do that with certainty or wanted to gamble on defeat. As a recent historian has written, the general "had done absolutely nothing except oppose the creation of the committee and failed to beat the odds and improve the Commune's increasingly impossible military situation."[11]

Cluseret's arrest aimed at breaking even the most minimal concentration of any centralized military authority. Miot pressed his imprisonment on the flimsiest grounds, backed by allies who said that, while nothing had been proved, Cluseret needed to be incarcerated as a precaution. To be sure, Jaroslaw Dombrowski, Rossel, and Wróblewski found working under Cluseret frustrating, largely because his orders seemed to be regularly reversed or contradicted. Nevertheless, they had no sympathy for Miot's power grab, and Rossel expressed astonishment at the charge the Cluseret had "attempted to excite some corps against the Commune. The general, who has always been friendly towards me, was absolutely incapable of doing anything of the sort, or even of thinking of it." Prosper-Olivier Lissagaray rightly scoffed at "the ridiculous impeachment" of Cluseret, describing Miot's "evidence" as mere gossip.[12]

The goal of the Jacobin current had not been the mere removal of Cluseret as a possible competing military focus of power, but the forestalling of any discussion of future strategy. This seemed to preclude bringing him to trial. They reportedly confined him for a while at the Conciergerie and at Mazas. The latter would have paradoxically landed him with the Archbishop of Paris and other hostages. After a few days of captivity, another IWA member, Charles-Ferdinand Gambon, visited Cluseret, reporting the general sick and his cell unhealthy. Cluseret told him that "he had not yet seen anyone, and asked to be questioned."[13]

It became increasingly obvious that many in the council hoped to

11   John Merriman, *Massacre: The Life and Death of the Paris Commune of 1871* (New Haven: Yale University Press 2016), 121.

12   Fetridge, *Rise and Fall of the Paris Commune*, 205; and Lissagaray, *History of the Paris Commune*, 246.

13   *Procès-verbaux de la Commune de 1871*, vol. 2, 478 n.; and, *Journal officiel de la République Française*, May 7, 1871, 63.

restrict traditional military authority in the interest of establishing what they saw as a kind of unquestionable executive carved from the General Council. Figures such as the sixty-two-year-old revolutionary journalist Charles Delescluze hoped to authorize a new Committee of Public Safety, a final homage to their Jacobin illusions. Part of this involved securing control over the essential tools for the city's defense, though they actually had little idea what they needed to do with them. By this strained logic, the stronger defense of Paris would not be served by even the most modest successes of Cluseret's War Office in the defense of Paris.

It represented a possibly symbolic response to what was taking place across France. On the very day of the crisis at Issy, the government at Versailles held municipal elections across the country. As marginalized by this voting as in the previous February election of the national government, Paris watched with awe as the imperial figures running the country walked it through the ritual of republicanism. Radicals in the Eleventh Arrondissement hung black in mourning that election, though it had returned some modest gains for moderate republicans, as opposed to the old imperial politicians.

The Commune Defining Itself

In the absence of Cluseret, responsibility for the defense of the city fell to Rossel. As of April 30, the Garde nationale still claimed impressive numbers, with battalions organized into twenty legions consisting of 162,651 troops with 6,507 officers. Those available for active centralized defense might have been little more than the roughly 10,000 men in thirty-four irregular brigades. The units reflected the diversity of the Communard army: *tirailleurs* of the Marseillaise; the Polish Chasseurs; and legions of Italian, Alsatian, and Belgian Communards.[14]

Rossel likely shared Cluseret's sense of the actual numbers involved in the defense of Paris, but he accepted the assignment. He added, "I require your most absolute co-operation in order not to succumb under the weight of present circumstances." He sent Dombrowski to Neuilly to take command on the right bank, and assigned Wróblewski to take

---

14   Christiansen, *Paris Babylon*, 329, 330 n.

charge of the troops and defenses on the left bank of the Seine, including Issy. La Cecilia became the general of the centre with Bergeret and Eudes in command of the two reserve brigades; Rossel also set Citizen Napoléon Gaillard to take up a version of Cluseret's old project, "the construction of a second line of barricades immediately inside the fortifications, as well as a third at the Trocadero, Montmartre, and the Panthéon."[15]

In terms of Issy, Rossel arrested Mégy for abandoning the fort, which he turned over to Eudes. They reinforced the position with a barricade running across the front of the fort and at the foot of the slope in front, armed with a few more pieces of artillery. They also had two insurgent gunboats cannonading the heights of Meudon and Brimborion to their front.[16]

On Monday, May 1, Rossel responded to his old colleague Leperche, who had threatened to slaughter the garrison: "The next time that you venture to send us so insolent a communication as your letter of yesterday, I will have your messenger shot, in conformity with the usages of war." Unfortunately, the young Communard officer who carried Rossel's message did not know its contents. When he asked about it, Leperche told it was an order to have him shot, and sent the courier to Versailles.[17]

That very night, the army advanced on the station at Clamart, located on high ground overlooking the fort. Hundreds defended the station, though most had stood down after sunset, and the soldiers moving toward them through the dark identified themselves as National Guard before rushing them with bayonets. Later claiming that some of the Communards were army deserters, the attackers gave little quarter, quickly butchering around 200 of them. A simultaneous night attack on the Château of Issy—which had already changed hands several times—met similar success. Almost immediately, Communard guns opened on these positions. Daybreak on Tuesday saw spirited Communard counterattacks that ultimately failed. And the garrison at the fort soon had to throw mattresses into position for protection. The government

---

15 Fetridge, *The Rise and Fall of the Paris Commune in 1871*, 202–3, 217. Raymond Huard, "Napoléon Gaillard chef barricadier de la Commune, 1815–1900," in Alain Corbin and Jean-Marie Mayeur, eds., *La Barricade. Actes du colloque organisé les 17, 18 et 19 mai 1995* (Paris: Sorbonne, 1997).

16 Fetridge, *The Rise and Fall of the Paris Commune in 1871*, 204.

17 Ibid., 202–3, 205–6.

also launched attacks to the east, around the redoubt of Moulin-Saquet, and to the west of the city.[18]

While the French Army grew larger, better-equipped, and more experienced by the hour, the Commune could only hold on, at least for the present.

In this strange, if very temporary, stasis, that old creative spirit of Paris reemerged within the revolutionary insurgency. Readers still sat at the long tables, immersed in their work at the Bibliothèque nationale. People still toured the Louvre, admiring the artwork, even as the distant thunder of artillery rumbled outside the door. Communards protected the holdings of the Palais de i'industrie, even when it came under fire from the government artillery.[19]

Newspapers still circulated freely, though pro-government papers tended to wink out of existence. On May 5, the Commune suspended seven pro-Versailles newspapers, but Lissagaray briefly surveyed some of what remained:

> The *Officiel* is little asked for; the journalists of the Council stifle it by their competition. The *Cri du peuple* has a circulation of 100,000. It is the earliest out; it rises with chanticleer . . . Only buy the *Père Duchêne* once, though its circulation is more than 60,000 . . . Here is the doctrinaire journal *La Commune*, in which Millière sometimes writes, and in which Georges Duchêne takes the young men and the old of the Hôtel-de-Ville to task with a severity which would better fit another character than his. Do not forget the *Mot d'ordre* . . . It was one of the first to support the Revolution of the 18th March, and darted terrible arrows at the Versaillese.[20]

Many of the Communard leaders came from the literary tradition of bohemian life, and others, such as Cluseret, painted in addition to trying to make revolution. Born to a titled Legitimist, Victor Henri Rochefort, Marquis de Rochefort-Luçay, had made repeated efforts to break into the literary world and, in the process, clashed regularly with the authorities. Most famously, Victor Hugo, who had declined election to

---

18   Ibid., 206–7, 210.
19   Lissagaray, *History of the Paris Commune*, 236.
20   Ibid., 233–4.

the Commune himself, declared his sympathies for the effort.[21] The repressiveness of the old order drove such figures to the Commune.

Gustave Courbet proved remarkably astute politically. A painter and sculptor of the "realist" school, he had sought to bring a hard-nosed portrayal of the material world into the stylized romanticism of the contemporary art world. Concerned with the political uses of public spaces, he had long criticized the Vendôme Column and its celebration of Napoleonic glories and empire. When the Commune leadership decided to take down it down, Courbet had the responsibility of protecting and salvaging its artistic features.[22]

In terms of challenging official monumentality and public space, it is worth noting that Eugène Viollet-le-Duc narrowly missed being on the barricades of the Commune himself. The former head of the imperial efforts to restore, among other things, the walled city of Carcassonne and the keep at the Château de Vincennes, he had not left the city with Adolphe Thiers. In fact, he remained to study the siege and produced a scholarly account of the effectiveness and deficiencies of the fortifications of Paris. Only when it looked as though Viollet-le-Duc might be drawn into the National Guard himself did he slip out of Paris to a small apartment in Pierrefonds.[23]

The photographer and aeronaut Nadar, became closely identified with the Commune. His friend Pierre-Jules Hetzel hoped to continue publishing, even as his typesetters marched off to fight for the Commune. The author of fanciful tales of the possible futures opened by technology, Jules Verne visited Paris several times during these weeks, looking for Hetzel and checking on the well-being of his relatives there.[24]

In the absence of the institutions that had stifled them, new initiatives emerged. By mid-May, neighborhood associations began to federate to assure a more direct influence on the government. Any power they got

---

21   Roger Lawrence Williams, *Henri Rochefort, Prince of the Gutter Press* (New York: Scribner, 1966), particularly 104–8; Megan Behrent, "The enduring relevance of Victor Hugo," *International Socialist Review*, 89 (May 2013), at isreview.org.

22   Timothy J. Clark, *The Absolute Bourgeois: Artists and Politics in France, 1848–1851* (Berkeley: University of California Press, cop. 1999); and Fabrice Masanès, *Gustave Courbet* (Cologne: Taschen, 2006).

23   See Georges Poisson and Olivier Poisson, *Eugène Viollet-le-Duc* (Paris: Picard, 2014).

24   Butcher, *Jules Verne*, 214–15.

would foster the serious democratization and decentralization of the Commune.

The condition of women changed very dramatically. Even a most reactionary French thinker about military logistics conceded the value of mobilizing armed women, even if "solely for the defence of fortified towns." Women, he continued, could "give an excellent exhibition of endurance, of courage, and we believe of capacity for fighting. There would always be the advantage to the defence of being able to draw upon such reserves, which could never be employed upon offensive operations by those engaged in the attack."[25] Circumstances forced on Paris the most expansive view of the role of women in war, even more so than in Garibaldi's innovative army.

More importantly, though, the women of Paris began to organize to shape the future for which the people fought. They took a direct hand in the efforts to convert the empty and quiet workshops to communal uses. Women such as Élisabeth Dmitrieff, Louise Michel, and others became essential to the popular mobilizations. However, they also began pressing for concerns distinctive to them.

Many came to see the Commune as socialist or anarchist, reflecting its embrace of distinctive principles of government and its efforts to implement them. It extended the moratoriums on rent and on the payment of debts imposed by the siege (and set aside by decree of the government at Versailles). It also separated church and state, eventually secularizing education and abolishing the distinction between legitimate and illegitimate children in the distribution of National Guard pensions.

Those who described the Commune in such terms had tangible class arguments. The revolutionary authorities set 6,000 francs as the maximum annual salary for any member of the government, about the same as a skilled worker. It forbade employers from imposing penalties and deducting them from wages. It projected the seizure and reopening of the workshops and formally requisitioned vacant lodgings for the use of those who did not have them. It took action directly to ban night work in bakeries and formally decreed a preference for cooperatives in supplying government contracts and sanctioned worker participation in governing the conditions of their work. A few days later, it opened

25 Le Mesurier, *Feeding of Fighting Armies*, vol. 1, 259.

discussions with the existing trade unions to over the seizure of abandoned workshops.

However incomplete or even aspirational many of the more far-reaching proclamations and measures were, tangible changes did take place:

> 1,500 yards from the ramparts, and a few steps from the War Office, a hundred ordnance pieces remain inert, loaded with mud. Leaving on our right the War Office, that centre of discord, let us enter the Corps Législatif, transformed into a work-shop. Fifteen hundred women are there, sewing the sand sacks that are to stop up the breaches. A tall and handsome girl, Marthe, round her waist the red scarf with silver fringe given her by her comrades, distributes the work. The hours of labour are shortened by joyous songs. Every evening the wages are paid, and the women receive the whole sum, eight centimes a sack, while the former contractors hardly gave them two.[26]

Then, too, the Commune reportedly discussed the abolition of formal standards of French grammar and spelling, as well as purging words such as king, duke, sir, servant, conscription, and so on from the dictionary.[27]

Issues of grammar aside, Rossel continued to fight an uphill battle to get cooperation from the council and its leaders, who—as with Cluseret—withheld the kind of power that any military command defending a major city would have to have. When, on May 9, the encroaching government forces seized Fort Issy, Rossel's sense of help-lessness overwhelmed him and he resigned in disgust. The Commune responded by replacing him with Charles Delescluze.

Meanwhile, Cluseret finally heard the seven charges made against him. Miot and Delescluze had gathered everything against him that they could find. The prisoner answered them in writing, but the Committee of Public Safety secured its power on May 15, and its supporters had enough power to repeatedly forestall his requests for a formal hearing.[28]

At no point did the Commune have the freedom to be able to seriously

---

26   Lissagaray, *History of the Paris Commune*, 238-39.
27   Fetridge, *Rise and Fall of the Paris Commune*, 141.
28   *Procès-verbaux de la Commune de 1871*, vol. 2, 478 n.

work out its own destiny or imagine much of what that would be, but that almost seemed inevitable in the context of its times. The war for the people was certainly no less mismanaged and misdirected as that earlier war for the republic or that for the empire. Those who directed the earlier conflicts passed on much of their cost in blood and treasure to the people. A war for those people would not have the option of passing on its cost.

And it would not have the institutional wherewithal to bury its mistakes or place the blame for them on the treachery of foreigners.

The later influences of the Commune abroad reflected the cosmopolitan demographics of Paris and the movement on its behalf. The government reported foreigners among the thousands of prisoners taken, and one suspects that those falling into the hands of the French Army were likely killed in larger proportions. The defense of the city would arguably never have been as strong as it was without the large number of militarily experienced Poles, though neighboring countries provided large numbers of Belgians, Dutch, and Swiss, as well as Italians and other veterans of Giuseppe Garibaldi, while Spain and Portugal also contributed fighters, as did Wallachia and Hungary. Smaller numbers of Russian, Austrian, English, Irish, American, and African Communards also took up arms, with handfuls of Greeks, Swedes, Danes, and Turks, with a couple of Brazilians, some identified simply as "Asians," and eight "miscellaneous." The director of manuscripts at the National Library under the Commune was Egyptian.[29]

Most notably, a significant cluster of Germans fought for the Commune. They might have done so as a more coherent force but for the flight of German civilians from Paris, which also disintegrated the German-speaking section of the IWA there.[30]

---

29   For the numbers, see *Le rapport d'ensemble de M. le Général Appert, sur les operations de la Justice militaire, présenté a l'Assemblee nationale* (Versailles: Imprimeurs de l'Assemblée nationale, 1875), 263, cited in Thomas March, *The History of the Paris Commune of 1871* (London: S. Sonnenschein & C. 1896), 348. See also Fetridge, *Rise and Fall of the Paris Commune*, 479–80. See also Christopher John Marshall, "A Revolutionary Crucible: French Radicals, Foreign Expatriates, and Political Exiles in the Paris Commune," PhD dissertation, University of Minnesota, 2014. See also Deleurmoz, *Commune(s)*, 38–44.

30   König, "Les immigrés allemands à Paris 1870/71."

Holding the Line

Across the line, the military of the government, even in defeat, had managed to raise a large army. Certainly, many of its new recruits did come from the more reactionary rural districts, but troops from these areas had also demonstrated a capacity to act in their own interests. Most immediately, during the first few weeks of their conflict with Paris, the authorities came to a rapid agreement with the Prussians, who began releasing war prisoners. In short order it would be building an army of 130,000.[31]

The new Reich proved only happy to be rid of the prisoners.[32] Even before the fall of Metz, the Germans held 131,577 unwounded French prisoners with between 20,000 and 50,000 sick or wounded in German hospitals. Metz came close to doubling that, and Sedan added yet again a similar number. The captors had already separated those from Alsace and Lorraine and organized them for agricultural work.

The German authorities often permitted the prisoners to roam freely through their towns, having no money or resources to effect a serious escape. A writer from Stuttgart described them as moving

along the street like shadows, Zouaves, Line, and Turcos, attired in the garments they have been able to pick up on the field of battle; the capote of one regiment and the kepi of another. Frequently the capote or the pantaloons have been pierced by a hostile ball, and they carefully preserve this souvenir; for the rest they are always very clean, and bathe every day.

To keep order among themselves, they also hand-picked a body of "tall and fine gendarmes, who walk the streets in uniform, always two by two, as in France."

Rumors of a prison revolt periodically terrified the German authorities. At one point, the rumors caused a serious panic at Cologne, where

---

31   Mason, *The Paris Commune*, 209–10. Lissagaray, *History of the Paris Commune*, 298; Christiansen, *Paris Babylon*, 359–65; Alistair Horne, *The Terrible Year: The Paris Commune 1871* (London: Macmillan, 1971), 135–6; Frank Jellinek, *The Paris Commune of 1871* (New York: Grosset & Dunlap, 1965), 360–3; see also Stewart Edwards, *The Paris Commune 1871* (Chicago, IL: Quadrangle Books, 1973).

32   For this and the following paragraphs on the prisoners, see Ollier, *Cassell's History of the War*, vol. 1, 423.

troops had to restore order among the civilians. The apparent source of the rumors had been the "riotous manifestation" in the camp when new prisoners arrived from France.

On the other hand, there might have been something to the rumors. At one point, the authorities responded to some alleged insubordination by removing 500 Turcos and Zouaves from Wahn Heath, just south of Cologne, to the citadel at Wesel. The subsequent search for weapons through the camp came up with sixty-four revolvers and a thousand daggers.

Those desperate enough could accept a return to duty in France, where equally desperate veteran officers stood ready to command them. Arsène Lambert, who had charge of the Maison de la dernière cartouche near Sedan, returned to take revenge for his capture by the Germans by shooting Parisians. Paul Déroulède, back from Switzerland, prepared to launch a new career that would carry him into the jihad against Dreyfus and a duel with Georges Clemenceau.

The heroes of the world-historic defeat of France would now take their revenge on the irreligious foreigners and ungrateful poor of the city. Among them, favoritism and politics informed their selection. The new army had no room for the scapegoat of Wissembourg Auguste-Alexandre Ducrot, the independent-minded old curmudgeon François Certain Canrobert, or the lower-middle-class Louis Faidherbe—or for Charles Auguste Frossard, so personally associated with the old imperial family. Perhaps, too, they might not have entirely trusted Louis Jules Trochu, who had commanded the defense of Paris against the Prussians.[33]

The army began chalking up a series of victories along the southern approaches to the city in early May. It not only took Issy, but the redoubt of Moulin-Saquet, near Fort Ivry and Fort Vanves, in the second week of the month. Moreover, Mont-Valérien threw shells not only at Porte Maillot and the avenue de la Grande-Armée, but also at Point du-Jour and Muette.[34]

Still, the particular loss of Issy left the southwestern approaches to the city largely unprotected. It meant the government could avoid the bottlenecked attempt to force a crossing of the Seine downriver at

33   Robert Tombs, *The War against Paris 1871* (Cambridge: Cambridge University Press, 1981).
34   "Mount Valerian," *Le petit journal*, April 29, 1871, 2.

Neuilly, for example. Instead, it could move more safely and without risk of detection through the Bois de Boulogne to the very gates of the city.

In the middle of May, Lissagaray walked along the defenses at the western end of the city.[35] He looked up the Champs-Elysées as far as the Place de l'Étoile and the Arc de Triomphe, noting that the shells from Mont-Valérien and Courbevoie landed there often enough to keep the street largely deserted. Defenders had walled up the main arch and built a strong makeshift barricade, where they had begun to mount guns.

The government artillery from Mont-Valérien, Courbevoie, and Bécon had thrown 800 shells into the area. It reduced to ruins virtually everything beyond the Arc de Triomphe to the right, the neighborhood between the avenue de la Grande Armée, and the Ternes. Here and there he sighted "human salamanders" lurking in the ruins. To defend the Porte-Maillot, the Commune had three batteries with a total of a dozen guns manned by only ten men.

To the south, near the gate of La Muette, Dombrowski himself waved his *képi* and taunted the troops approaching through the Bois de Boulogne. He had made his headquarters in the Château de la Muette, although shells had riddled all the rooms. Those around him took courage from his fearlessness under fire. "Stay there," he told one particularly hard-pressed detail, "if you are not destined to die there you have nothing to fear." Farther along, the shelling had almost emptied the ramparts near the river and the nearby railway.

On Wednesday, May 17, the government brought forward and masked new batteries that placed most of the city within range. On Saturday, they unmasked 300 naval guns and siege pieces, the salvos of which would announce the beginning of the end.

All this drove the already challenged leadership of the Commune to pointless brutalities that accomplished nothing for the city. It voted to authorize the threatened killing of hostages, and suspended more papers in Paris.

On Thursday, the National Assembly ratified the Treaty of Frankfurt. It had come time to settle the troubles in Paris. In the night, government troops crying "Vive la Commune!" approached, then attacked the outpost at Cachan south of the city, continuing east almost to the

---

35   Lissagaray, *History of the Paris Commune*, 236–38.

Hautes-Bruyères. Nearby, Communards noticed Dominican monks signaling the enemy and incarcerated them at Fort de Bicêtre.

More menacingly, on Friday, May 19, the government resumed its push from the west. In fact, several of the gates through that part of the wall had stood virtually undefended. When told this, the council promised to respond and concluded that it had done its duty, giving the matter no further thought. Fortunately, the Commune had established its strongest fortifications internal to the city walls along the west side, commanded directly from the Château de la Muette.

Here and there in the city, residents had removed and piled the cobblestones into barricades and even impressive little miniature forts. They had yet to construct any serious defenses at Montparnasse, the Panthéon, or Montmartre. Importantly, the decentralized character of the defenses dotted the city with barricades, sometimes the products of neighborhood spontaneity and often disconnected from any other defenses. After seizing power, the Committee of Public Safety complained that, with tens of thousands of guards and millions of francs, they could not find sufficient labor to remedy these problems. The council debated abstractions, while the Committee of Public Safety issued more romantic proclamations, which moved nobody.

The numbers, moreover, indicated severe weakness, reflecting the ongoing flight of individuals and small groups from the still-hungry and economically depleted city. Cluseret later concluded that, in his absence, the Commune had allowed its numbers of reliable effectives to fall to 12,000 by May 20. In fact, he said that he had never had more than 6,000 available for service at the front. An internal Commune source frankly estimated that, at this point, they had lost 4,000 men, killed or wounded, and 3,500 prisoners. They had a couple of thousand under arms from Asnières to Neuilly, with perhaps 4,000 in position from La Muette through the wall fronting Issy to Vanves.[36] There remained other armed Communards, but they waited in their communities.

The increasing vulnerability of Paris had simply become too great a problem to resolve—and, hence, too painful to face.

Perhaps some awareness of this depressing state of affairs encouraged them to give a more sympathetic response to another plea from Cluseret in his cell. On May 19, he wrote, reminding his comrades that they had

---

36   Mason, *The Paris Commune*, 208–9.

fought together against preventive detention under the old order. "As a member of the Commune, I am entitled to my Seat," he wrote. "As a child of Paris, I have the right to defend my native city. As a man, I have the right to justice."[37] Yet they stalled.

On Sunday, May 21, however, the body faced the alternatives of either giving Cluseret a hearing or facing the likely fruits of the military reality it had helped to shape. Picking the least onerous alternative, the Jacobin artist Alfred Billioray—actually a newcomer to politics—hosted a discussion that regularly threatened to become entirely absurd. The neo-Jacobins had compiled every conceivable charge it could argue. It repeated stories that people had caught Cluseret sleeping on the job, and it transpired that he had taken to spending the night in the War Office to be on hand for any particular developments. At one point, as US ambassador E. B. Washburne tried to get a number of wealthy Americans out of the city, someone suggested that an American was "worth a million" and Cluseret's citizenship came up, giving rise to a rumor that he was negotiating a bribe.[38]

In fact, agents of Versailles seem to have been regularly moving through the city offering bribes to anyone. They surely approached Cluseret and others, as may have agents of their political enemies seeking to discredit them. At one point, they approached Dombrowski, who went straight to the council and proposed that they use it to lure the government troops into a trap. Again, instead of considering Zadlo-Dombrowski's suggestion, the committee turned to speculating as to who might actually be being bribed.

Indeed, the political opponents of Cluseret and the IWA stalled making the only reasonable decision about him by setting aside the hearings to hear a proposal from Lyon and other cities in the south of France to stop or forestall the civil war. The republican authorities at Lyon had hosted representatives from sixteen municipal councils—the number suggesting an attempt to revive the old Ligue du Midi—to attempt to save Paris. It voted to "affirm the Republic as the only legitimate and possible government," and "communal autonomy" as its only solid basis. They proposed an immediate cease-fire and the dissolution of both the National Assembly and the Commune, to be

---

37   May 19, in *Procès-verbaux de la Commune de 1871*, vol. 2, 420.
38   *Procès-verbaux de la Commune de 1871*, vol. 2, 486, 501, 504; Cluseret, *Mémoires*, vol. 2, 97–105.

followed by new elections that would fairly include Paris.[39] It represented the last hope of Paris, perhaps, but stirred remarkably little interest among the leaders of the Commune and carried no traction into its reception by the government at Versailles.

As radicals in the leadership of the Commune questioned the loyalty of other radicals, informants of the government confirmed that the gates of Montrouge, Vanves, Vaugirard, Point du Jour, and Dauphine were actually entirely deserted. Orders to concentrate the troops were immediately issued. Remarkably, Lissagaray later scoffed at the government claim that they had fought their way through the gate of St. Cloud, which he said had been wide open for three days, "and General Douai had crept in very modestly, man by man, introduced by treason."[40] Of course, this posed the question as to how it had been allowed to remain "wide open."

Meanwhile, the Germans remained visible at various points, armed and looking down into the city. The Prince of Saxony commanded the army that still cut off Paris from the rest of the world along the north and east. They had covered the outskirts of the capital from the line of the canal at St. Denis across the broad sweep of the old walls north of the city and swinging down towards Charenton, where the Marne entered the Seine southeast of the city. As tensions between Paris and Versailles grew worse, egress became more difficult. Foreign journalists—and surely many others—got out on the rail lines or along the rivers.[41]

On one level, it reached beyond politics to a matter of life and character. Lissagaray, that romantic revolutionary, wrote as one "who has breathed in thy life that fiery fever of modern history, who has painted on thy boulevards and wept in thy faubourgs, who has sung to the morning of thy revolutions and a few weeks after bathed his hands in powder behind thy barricades." He wrote that he

can hear from beneath thy stones the voices of the martyrs of sublime ideas and read in every one of thy streets a date of human progress, even he does less justice to thy original grandeur than the stranger, though a Philistine, who came to glance at thee during the days of the Commune. The attraction of rebellious Paris was so strong that men hurried thither

---

39   *Procès-verbaux de la Commune de 1871*, vol. 2, 504, 504 n.–505 n.

40   Lissagaray, *History of the Paris Commune*, 243–4, 247.

41   Ibid., 294–5.

from America to behold this spectacle unprecedented in the world's history—the greatest town of the European continent in the hands of the proletarians. Even the pusillanimous were drawn towards her.

He added that, from this point forward, "the prolongation of her resistance could now only serve to bear witness to her faith."[42]

Beneath the romanticism, though, everyone still in the city—but particularly the radicals—faced a decision of the most visceral nature. Notwithstanding the dunderheads in the Hôtel de Ville, the working poor of the city—fueled by desperation and hope—were actually under arms and in rebellion. They had done so in the face of a much larger, well-organized and professionally led military force—actually, two of them. Even if they downed arms and surrendered, the army entering Paris would begin a bloodbath with the full sanction of the government. Neither the rest of France nor the Germans nor any other nation would be in a position to prevent it. And, in fact, orchestrated cheers would praise the slaughter of the people as the salvation of civilization.

Every radical in the city had to decide whether they would fight or not. Nobody who understood the situation could believe victory to be any more likely than for St. Denis to rise from the dead and stroll through Paris with his head under his arm. Politically, nothing obligated those squinting at the enemy fires across the line to accept their martyrdom.

On the other hand, any who took the smart option would have to live with the memory of having left the people and their experiment to their fate.

---

42   Ibid., 233, 271.

12

La Semaine Sanglante: The Foundations of Modern Western Civilization, May 21–28, 1871

Adolphe Assi hurried through the dark to check the defenses along the Rue Beethoven at the west end of Paris. Although the lights had been put out, he saw some of his comrades along the wall, slumped and silent. As he drew near, his horse began losing its footing and stopped dead in its tracks. Assi looked closer and realized that large pools of blood and viscera coated the cobblestones. At that point, soldiers rushed from the shadows, bayonets flashing. The *Versaillais* who had just overcome the street's defenders seized Assi, who, rather unusually, lived to tell the tale of his capture.[1] Through that third week of May, thousands—tens of thousands—did not.

That single *semaine sanglante* bloodied the history of every neighborhood, every square, and every street, of the old city. In the first few days, some 130,000 well-armed, well-equipped soldiers, cynically lied to about what they were facing, had stormed into what had been the premier metropolis of the Western world to reclaim Paris for "Property, Order, Religion." Everyone who cared to look could have seen the final end, and it came with a vengeance.

Other Western nation-states uttered not so much as a hollow protest.

---

1 Lissagaray, *History of the Paris Commune*, 247–8.

The Beginning: Sunday, Monday, and Tuesday

On the morning of Sunday, May 21, the artillery of General Félix Douay, began lobbying shells against the salient at the Point du Jour, on the Seine at the city walls southwest of Paris. At that point, troops moved through the Bois de Boulogne to the gates of Auteuil and St. Cloud, which had been abandoned and their vulnerability signaled by agents. Adolphe Thiers, Patrice de MacMahon, and the other movers and shakers of this operation sent orders for the batteries to fall silent as their soldiers quietly slipped into the city, often singly, until enough had gathered within the walls to begin their operations.

Thiers and his government informed the rest of France and the world that they had delivered an ultimatum to the Commune, offering them the opportunity to surrender and save their lives. The lies dutifully sent out to the world, they sent the first of their troops into Paris to continue to do what they had already been doing on the outskirts. Gunfire erupted sporadically as the soldiers stopped along their way to shoot groups of surprised and captured members of the National Guard or civilians dragged from their homes.

Word of this reached the Hôtel de Ville from across that quarter of the city. Earlier reports to Charles Delescluze, General Cluseret's successor, apparently went missing or did not register, but Jaroslaw Zadlo-Dombrowski's message from La Muette broke the council's preoccupation with the trial of Cluseret: "The *versaillais* have entered by the Porte de St. Cloud. I am taking measures to drive them back. If you can send me reinforcements, I answer for everything." Under pressure to make a rational choice, the Committee of Public Safety voted to acquit Cluseret by a vote of twenty-eight to seven, before deciding that, before acting on any news from the front, they would need more information.[2] They also decided that the city's defenders could take any necessary action in their own neighborhoods.

As the rest of France heard reports from Thiers that the retaking of Paris had begun, Delescluze and the authorities in the city cherry-picked among contradictory reports to convince themselves that nothing serious had taken place. Their ignorance at the Hôtel de Ville of the position

2   *Procès-verbaux de la Commune de 1871*, vol. 2, 509; Fetridge, *Rise and Fall of the Paris Commune in,* 290.

of government troops went beyond geography. They took the opportunity to send the army an appeal to fraternalism, recalling how the troops had refused to fire on the people at Montmartre on March 18.

> The people of Paris will never believe that you could raise your arms against them. When they face you your hands will recoil from an act that would be a veritable fratricide. Like us, you too are proletarians. That which you did not the 18th March you will do again. Come to us, brothers, come to us; ours are open to receive you.[3]

Needless to say, they did not.

Paris in general remained oblivious to its coming ordeal. Nathalie Lemel and the Union des femmes at the Hôtel de Ville labored on a founding document for a Federal Chamber of Working Women. That Sunday evening, thousands attended a benefit concert at the Louvre for the widows and orphans of the city, even as shells began falling a few hundred yards away. Scoffing at the government's earlier threat to attack the city, a staff officer invited the audience to return "next Sunday, to the same place, to our second concert for the benefit of the widows and orphans." Later that night, though, the city's defenders realized the gravity of the situation, but hesitated to issue an alarm for fear of causing a panic. Some did begin to pore over the maps and plan a defense, a study long overdue.[4]

Through it all, wave after wave of soldiers swept through the gates, silent and veiled by the night, until their numbers allowed for a division into two columns. General Justin Clinchant--who had been Bourbaki's second-in-command—headed off along the tracks just inside the city walls, quietly seizing one position after another. Another movedin the direction of the Trocadéro.[5]

This ignorance—willful in the case of the council—left those defending the western outposts exhausted and without reinforcements. By midnight, the more fortunate of these had made their way back to Zadlo-Dombrowski's headquarters at La Muette. Across the front, people in small groups defending small neighborhood barricades fell

---

3   Lissagaray, *History of the Paris Commune*, 264.
4   Ibid., 244, 247, 248.
5   Ibid., 247.

back. On the river, sappers had begun to take key defensive positions. By the early hours of Monday, the army held the gates of Passy, Auteuil, St. Cloud, Sèvres, and Versailles, as well as the inner periphery of the western and northwestern city walls with the adjacent Fifteenth and Sixteenth Arrondissements.

By dawn on Monday, the army had its talons deep into the city. It had moved field artillery onto the rise of Chaillot, near the Trocadéro and on the Étoile, near the Arc de Triomphe. Without the walls, the defense of the Commune now relied mostly on makeshift neighborhood barricades. Early that morning, meanwhile, the political architects of this disaster at the Hôtel-de-Ville resorted to what they had done with Cluseret, grilling Dombrowski about the ease with which the *Versaillais* entered the city. With a quavering voice, the general objected to being treated as a traitor. "My life belongs to the Commune," Dombrowski insisted.[6] And so it would.

The paragons of decentralized democracy could not agree whether to inform the people of the state of their city, which effectively represented a decision not to inform them. However, the committee did agree to plaster the city with its proclamations denouncing military discipline and urging the people to organize their own neighborhood defenses. In the absence of information or a general plan, this left the Commune's artillery at Montmartre and, on the left bank, at the École militaire largely unused.

Throughout, those who did have a general plan—the army—continued to pour soldiers into the city. Those of Félix Douay took the barricade at the Arc de Triomphe without a struggle and continued cautiously along the Champs-Élysées into the heart of the city. To Douay's left, Clinchant's corps advanced toward the Parc Monceaux. Still farther in that direction, Paul de Ladmirault led his corps along the interior of the walls to the north, putting itself to the rear of the *fédérés*. Uninformed of their precarious situation, the battalions at Neuilly, Levallois-Perret, and St. Ouen found themselves cut off from the city and fired upon from behind.[7]

---

6   For the day, see Ibid., 261–72; Christiansen, *Paris Babylon*, 351–4; Horne, *The Terrible Year*, 125–7; Jellinek, *The Paris Commune of 1871*, 324; Edwards, *The Paris Commune 1871*, 245–8.

7   Lissagaray, *History of the Paris Commune*, 250–1, 254.

By mid-afternoon, resistance across the city intensified as the people of Paris in general finally learned of the extent of the danger that threatened them. In addition, though, the army's butchery seemed to leave them no options, and the military had confined the Communards into a shrinking territory. Not a few in the government of the Commune reassured themselves that the appearance of the troops would provoke a general rising in the city, leading to victory. A large barricade at the entrance of the St. Jacques Square on the Rue de Rivoli protected the Hôtel de Ville. Similar structures went up across the center of the city. On the left bank, they barricaded the Boulevard St. Michel and virtually fortified the Panthéon.[8]

On Tuesday, the people at Montmartre realized that Ladmirault's men had unexpectedly moved around the wall and were about to attack their own neighborhood. Ladmirault's cavalry commander, Gaston de Galliffet, jockeyed for position in hopes of capping a brilliant career slaughtering Russians, butchering Mexicans, and, far less effectively, bloodying Germans with the wholesale murder of unarmed and disarmed Parisians.[9]

The Communards there had almost nothing to resist them with, in part because their neighborhood sat at the far end of the city from Versailles. The Commune had sent General Napoléon La Cécilia to prepare a defense, but nobody knew him or paid much attention. Louise Michel, the head of the Montmartre Women's Vigilance Committee, and Élisabeth Dmitrieff had a core of twenty-five women to defend the neighborhood. As it became clear that troops were moving in on them, others joined the women. They had every advantage of the terrain, but not enough to keep a well-trained, massively larger military force from overrunning their positions. By mid-morning, Communard teamsters carrying munitions there found the enemy already on the heights, where it engaged in virtually indiscriminate slaughter and plunder.

Driven to the foot of Montmartre, Michel met a very tardy Dombrowski, sent by the Committee of Public Safety to save Montmartre. In the late morning, enthusiastic autonomists who did not recognize him arrested him and carried him before the Committee of Public Safety. To its credit, the committee actually accorded him a comradely

---

8 Ibid., 254–5, 256.
9 André Gillois, *Galliffet: Le fusilleur de la Commune* (Paris: France-Empire, 1985).

welcome when he was returned to them. Still, the courtesies accomplished nothing for Montmartre, though he arrived in the area in time to encounter Michel in the midst of her labors.

Resistance proved much stronger around Montmartre than on its heights. Dmitrieff sent word to the mayor of the Eleventh Arrondissement urging the armed women in the neighborhood to "come immediately to the barricades." For hours, 120 women held a barricade against Clinchant's soldiers at the Place Blanche (near the later site of the Moulin Rouge). When forced back, they retired to a more secure position along the Pigalle, defending it until about two o'clock. The government troops dragged their leader before an army officer who discharged his revolver in the face of his prisoner; leaving his soldiers to finish him. To the east, Dombrowski fell, mortally wounded, on the Rue Myrrha.

On the other, southern end of the line, on the left bank, General Ernest de Cissey had command, with General Joseph Vinoy in reserve. A handful of Communards held on stubbornly near the Montparnasse Cemetery until they ran out of cartridges, at about the same time as the army took Montmartre. However, it took them late into the afternoon to dislodge the *fédérés* near the Légion d'Honneur. Elsewhere on the left bank, Walery Wróblewski and others had prepared a series of defensive positions, particularly the Butte-aux-Cailles to the south of the Panthéon.

Late in the night, distant flames reddened the façade of the Hôtel de Ville, aided by gaslight, torches at several nearby barricades, and some bivouac fires. In one room, they displayed the corpse of Dombrowski in preparation for his funeral. In the lower lobbies, exhausted fighters sought a fitful sleep alongside the groans of the wounded and dying. The remaining members of the Central Committee had already issued their peace terms: "Dissolution of the Assembly and of the Commune; the army to leave Paris; the Government to be provisionally confided to the delegates of the large towns, who will have a Constituent Assembly elected; mutual amnesty."

The leaders still hoped, and Delescluze still signed bombastic proclamations, but the thousands of men, women, and children sleeping in short, shallow bursts on their arms at the barricades had even less room for illusions. Never able to count on reinforcements and always short on munitions, they now found themselves thrown on the meager resources of their neighbors for food. At three o'clock, a sleepy officer with the small detachment at Notre-Dame, turned up at the Hôtel de Ville, requesting permission to move the hundreds of sick and wounded near the cathedral to a safer position.

In the night, the Commune authorities sent Zadlo-Dombrowski's body from the Hôtel de Ville to the Père Lachaise. *Fédérés* at the Place de la Bastille stopped the wagon and briefly paid tribute to the corpse at the base of the column commemorating the revolution of July 1830, and a guard formed a circle with torches as the defenders passed by, placing a kiss on the brow of their commander while the drum beat. Wrapped in a red flag, the body continued to the cemetery, where his brothers, members of his staff, and a few hundred guards stood bareheaded.

Wednesday and Thursday

Sporadically, the rattle of firing squads broke the silence of the night, though the army had already begun to experiment with using the *mitrailleuse* for mass executions. The army's killings hardly stopped with any uniformed member of the National Guard taken, since any male of almost any age could be a potential enemy and too much was at stake not to take them into custody, and necessity required remaining unburdened by prisoners.

Parts of Paris burned furiously as of the morning of Wednesday, May 24. The Tuileries, in particular, actually had been torched, likely to clear the field before Communard defensive positions. More generally, though, the incendiary shelling had started fires in the western, more bourgeois neighborhoods of the city that the army first encountered.

The flames gave rise to the myth of Communard women *pétroleuses*, engaged in arson. US ambassador Washburne helped to spread the idiotic lie that 8,000 of these female Communard arsonists scurried through the shadows of the city in hopes of destroying civilization as we know it. Once this started, they murdered women caught not only with anything flammable, but even with olive oil—or nothing at all. Those with children posed a problem only in that the children, of whatever age, might have to be killed as well.

There had been noteworthy cases of mercy. Individual soldiers and groups of soldiers showed remarkable courage in protecting the unarmed and disarmed from their comrades. In one case, officers ordered a soldier shot for himself refusing to murder civilians. Clinchant and Ladmirault took measures to prevent the killing of prisoners, though corps commanders could not be everywhere and those with such homicidal underlings as Galliffet would find that humanity had little place left.[10] We know of cases where individual soldiers helped to hide a Communard or, in one case, prevented the murder of a dozen male prisoners aged twelve to seventeen taken in the west.

Such things were noteworthy because they were so rare. Everywhere, the soldiers captured Communards by the dozen, and shot them in batches numbering in the hundreds, alongside any unfortunate bystanders. Near the present wall of the Communards in Père Lachaise cemetery, one observer counted about 800 bodies in one trench grave and 300 in another, and he did not have time to count the other trenches in just that location.

Brooding over the harrowing stories of wholesale massacre, some of the local officials decided to act at around 7:20 a.m. on that earlier blanket authorization of the retaliatory killing of hostages. Some 300 of them were held at Mazas on the river. They chose half a dozen for execution in the exercise ground. "I am not the enemy of the Commune," stammered the Archbishop of Paris, Georges Darboy, who had attempted to facilitate his exchange for Auguste Blanqui. "I have done all I could," he added. "I have written twice to Versailles." The officer in charge of them informed them that they were not about to die at the hands of the Commune "but the *Versaillais*, who are shooting the prisoners."

At two o'clock, the Communard minister of war, Delescluze, gave a resounding speech to the remaining officials of the Commune. All was not lost, he said, and a great effort to hold out to the last might still turn the tide. When news of the execution of hostages reached him later, Delescluze simply continued to write. However, when alone with a friend who was working with him, he hid his face in his hands, "'What a war!' cried he, 'what a war!'"

The collapse of the Communard center was the single most important event of the day. Remarkably, defenders still held the Palais royal and protested the order to evacuate, only to have it repeated. After they fell back, the Commune abandoned the Hôtel de Ville, torching it, the police headquarters, and the courthouse. This loss of the Hôtel de Ville left the Commune pursuing its own purposes on either side of the river.

---

10   Merriman, *Massacre*, 203–4.

Resistance on the left bank collapsed in the course of the day. The army overwhelmed the *fédérés* on the Rue Vavin, just southwest of the Jardin du Luxembourg. It took two hours to overwhelm the barricade at the Place de l'Abbaye, near the Église de Saint Germain des Prés. Thereafter, the *Versaillais* poured through the Jardin du Luxembourg, though not in time to prevent the detonation of the city's magazine there. Cluseret's old friend, Eugène Varlin, the militant internationalist and bookbinder who had taken the organization to Le Creusot, had been fighting for hours before he showed up at the Panthéon, which had been so well defended in June 1848.

Storming through the Luxembourg, government columns streamed through the streets of the Latin Quarter into the Val-de-Grâce to the south of the Panthéon. They also reached the Boulevard St. Michel by the Rues Racine and École de Médecine, which women had defended. Up the street at the Panthéon, the defenders had raised barricades at the entrance of the Rue Soufflot, at its the center, and from the *mairie* of the Fifth Arrondissement to the Faculté de Droit. By four o'clock, though, the army was advancing against them from three sides, making the defenses untenable. The resistance apparently lasted long enough for Georges Ernest Boulanger—the future *Général Revanche*—to be wounded.[11]

The fall of the Panthéon mirrored that of Montmartre, as did the celebratory slaughter by the army. Near the Panthéon, the military arrested a well-known but rather moderate socialist. They took him to the Luxembourg, where General Cissey consulted a list and had a staff officer simply inform the prisoner that "the general had ordered that he was to be shot at the Panthéon, on his knees, to ask pardon of society for all the ill he had done." When the man refused, they knocked him to his knees. He shouted, "Vive l'humanité!" Then they killed him.

The simple murder of such civilians became not merely commonplace but general. The army executed two Polish emigrants, Adolf Rozwadowski and Michał Szeweycer, who had been involved in the revolutionary movement at home years earlier, but whose only crime in Paris had been

---

11   Peter M. Rutkoff, *Revanche and Revision: The Ligue des Patriotes and the Origins of the Radical Right in France, 1882–1900* (Athens: Ohio University Press, 1981); and William D. Irvine, *The Boulanger Affair Reconsidered: Royalism, Boulangism, and the Origins of the Radical Right in France* (Oxford: Oxford University Press, 1989).

to have a lantern in their window. The army saw it as a signal; so they were shot and killed, their bodies left in the streets for two days.

Wróblewski and his comrades provided the Commune its only real success of the day at the Butte-aux-Cailles. The *Versaillais* had launched their first assault at daybreak, and the *fédérés* rushed forward to meet them. The stubborn resistance left the soldiers temporarily unwilling to follow their officers into another assault. Nevertheless, the fall of the Panthéon left to army to their north and, indeed, to the east. This forced their line of communications with the rest of the defense across the Seine shifting to a barricade on the Austerlitz Bridge, opposite the Mazas.

When the battle around the Butte-aux-Cailles renewed on Thursday, much of the army had already bypassed it to launch attacks on the prison on the Avenue d'Italie, a kilometer east. The *fédérés* there cleared the prisoners—including a group of Dominicans—by turning them loose. Some of the priests were shot.

The forces at Butte-aux-Cailles simply ignored orders to retreat across the river into the Eleventh Arrondissement, and the army resumed its general attack on them around midday. The *Versaillais* had much more success behind it to the east, following the ramparts as far as the Avenue d'Italie and the Route de Choisy, defended by powerful barricades. Still, the fire raging in the tapestry works of the Gobelins made the barricade on Boulevard St. Marcel vulnerable. Meanwhile, a prolonged artillery barrage blasted the Butte-aux-Cailles.

At this point, Wróblewski finally drew his contingent back east toward the Place Jeanne d'Arc, finding an already strong army presence along those streets behind them and some barricades in government hands. Almost hemmed in on all sides, Wróblewski ordered them to fall back to the protection of Communard fire from the Austerlitz Bridge. In the end, he brought about thousand men and a cannon across the Seine, but the army rolled over the handful of *fédérés* serving as a rearguard.

The collapse of the Communard forces on the left bank late on Thursday left Vinoy to take his reserve across the Seine and advance toward the Place de la Bastille by the small streets that abut the Rue St. Antoine, as well as the quays on both sides of the river. Alongside them, Douay's corps pressed east along the Rues Charlot and de Saintonge.

Thursday had not gone well for the Communards on the right bank either. Within earshot of the butchery, their remaining leaders seized on the suggestion to get US ambassador Washburne to ask for the German negotiation of an armistice. They authorized a commission headed by Delescluze to accompany the American secretary to the Cité Vincennes. At three o'clock, they reached Vincennes, where the local *fédérés* thought they were escaping the city, until one of them recognized Delescluze.

The Germans brushed off that kind of intervention, but moved troops into territory held by the Commune. Around 5 p.m., thousands of Bavarians moved forward from Fontenay, Nogent, and Charenton, forming an impenetrable cordon from the Marne to Montreuil. Later, thousands more Germans moved into Vincennes, with eighty artillery pieces. At 9 p.m., they isolated the Château de Vincennes, disarming fédérés hoping to return to Paris and join the Commune's defense. The Germans actively set the stage for what would be the final chapter of the French government's butchery of its own citizens

Back from Vincennes, Delescluze found that other leaders of the Commune had become increasingly scarce. Leó Frankel, the member of German Social Democracy who had been assisting in the organization of the city's working women, fell at a barricade in the Faubourg St. Antoine. Though wounded herself, Élisabeth Dmitrieff rescued him and got him to safety. When Wróblewski and his forces joined them from the left bank, Delescluze offered him the late Zadlo-Dombrowski's field command. Wróblewski asked whether the right bank had a few thousand resolute soldiers operating under a centralized command and declined the offer when Delescluze replied that, at most, they had only a few hundred.

Most Communards yet under arms had done as they had repeatedly been instructed and looked to the defense of their neighborhoods. Over the day, the army had advanced toward the Place du Château-d'Eau (today the Place de la République), where a young woman of nineteen, dressed as a fusilier, had led a desperate resistance through the day. When an officer fell dead in front of their barricade; a fifteen-year-old dashed out amid a hail of bullets to retrieve the *képi* to the cheers of his companions. At 6:45 p.m., Delescluze himself gathered about a hundred *fédérés* and led them off in that direction.

There, gunfire felled Delescluze. With no clear alternative, no plans, and no resources to exploit, Varlin took charge as delegate of war.

The loss of this barricade opened the way to the Rue de Turbigo, thus enabling the *Versaillais* to occupy the whole upper part of the Third

Arrondissement, and to surround the Conservatoire des arts et métiers. After a rather long struggle, the *fédérés* slipped away, leaving behind them a single stubborn woman with a loaded *mitrailleuse*. As soon as the soldiers got within her view, she blasted away at them.

At a barricade of the Faubourg du Temple, the most indefatigable gunner was a boy. The army summarily murdered all its defenders except another child who pleaded for three minutes to hurry home and give his silver watch to his mother. Moved, the officer let him go, not thinking to see him again, but three minutes later the soldiers heard him announce his return as he walked to the wall to take his place over the bodies of his comrades.

By Thursday evening, the *versaillais* formed a broken line, roughly from the Gare de l'Est, through the Château d'Eau to the Bastille and the river beyond. The Commune retained but two arrondissements intact, the Nineteenth and Twentieth, with about half of the Eleventh and Twelfth.

The shades of night brought back the glare of the flames that raged through parts of the city.

Final Blows: Friday and the Weekend

By Friday, May 26, five days into the constant cannonades, the rains began to fall. One could hear the gunfire but the weather muffled it. Everybody outside wound up wet, and the rainfall made it even harder to recognize who was coming toward them through the street.

Archibald Forbes, the English newspaperman present in Saarbrücken at the war's start, now also witnessed its sonquinary postscript in Paris. After covering the first days of the assault on the city, he had left through the Prussian lines to personally deliver his copy to his London editor.[12] Forbes then returned to watch the last tragic days.

Most of Friday's work took place north of the Seine. Here and there, shots came from the pockets of resistance across the left bank, though many of these may have been merely the sound of executions. Resistance also continued behind the army's line, though these would soon exhaust their ammunition.

12 Archibald Forbes, *Memories and Studies of War and Peace*, 3rd edn (London, Paris, and Melbourne: Cassell and Company, 1895), 127–71.

Along the main line, Vinoy, Douay, and Clinchant resumed their assaults on the Commune. They easily overran the scattered outposts along the river. By 7 a.m. it faced what had become a pitched battle around the Communard barricade on the Place de la Bastille. The *fédérés* had rushed cannon to the position, and held it until 2 p.m. However, government troops had gotten to their east and scattered fighting had continued north, roughly along the line of the Canal Saint-Martin.

By Friday, little more than a shadow remained of whatever authority the Commune had ever had. The few remaining members of the council wandered the neighborhoods of the Eleventh, Nineteenth, and Twentieth Arrondissements still out of reach of the army. Just as whatever power they ever exercised flickered, the reenactors of Jacobinism among the communards insisted on declaring a revolutionary dictatorship over the city.

A few still clung to hope that a direct American intervention might end the massacre. They took a letter for Washburne to the Prussian outpost at the city wall. One officer after another palmed the problem off to another authority, and eventually sent the courier of the Commune back with assurances that the ambassador would get the document.

Meanwhile, the army bulled its way into a cluster of slaughterhouses in the basin of La Villette, itself only a few kilometers shy of German-occupied Aubervilliers, where Cluseret had made the case for the Commune. On Friday morning, the troops overran the barricade on the Rue de Flandre but the 269th, which had offered stubborn resistance for days, withstood the enemy and continued fighting from small enclaves around La Villette.

Leaving a few thousand men to secure the Bastille, Vinoy continued on in mid-afternoon. One column veered back to the river at Mazas and continued to the Gare de Lyon. Their artillery there helped reduce the barricade on the Rue de Reuilly that, nevertheless, held back the army for a few hours. Their movements converged on the Place du Trône. In sharp contrast, the decentralized defense of the Communards precluded an opportunity to concentrate their artillery.

On Friday night the government artillery raked the neighborhoods of Ménilmontant and Belleville in a way no German guns had done. Government shelling continued to pound Belleville, some landing as far as Bagnolet and wounding some of the Germans. Some of what was left of Communes defenders trickled into this small corner of the city it still held, and tried to shelter in the already overcrowded houses, some of which collapsed on them.

Most of the remaining Communards spent at least part of the night in the open air, many in the flickering glow as fire destroyed La Villette.

The city's defenders woke with a chill on Saturday morning. Around 7 a.m., the army occupied the Place du Trône and pressed on to locate the heart of the resistance there, around the *mairie* of the Eleventh Arrondissement. The *versaillais* concentrated half a dozen big guns against the barricade defended by two inexpertly handled cannons.

Government shells still overshooting Belleville landed to the east, driving more civilians from their homes. They rushed the city gate on the road leading to Les Lilas and Romainville. At one o'clock, one of the responsible Germans finally lowered the drawbridge to allow them to escape. At one point, though, the sergeant of the *gendarmerie* at Romainville attacked them and called out to the Germans there to open fire. One of them shot a woman, although, in hindsight, it is remarkable that they let anyone through. A few hours later, officers of the French Army approached the Germans at Romainville for permission to pursue the offending civilians. The Germans claimed that they lacked the authorization to do that and referred the French to the occupation authorities at St. Denis.

At nearly two o'clock, Communards in the Rue de Bellevue blocked the advance of several battalions of the army, who brought up artillery. From the Place du Marché five bare-armed artillerists without leaders or orders began firing three cannons, assisting those at the Place des Fêtes in defense of the Buttes Chaumont. The five continued without rest for three hours, when they ran out of ammunition and scurried off to rejoin the skirmishers on the barricades.

Around this time of the day, the army had cornered a few hundred *fédérés* in the walled high ground of the Père Lachaise cemetery. Five thousand soldiers with active artillery surrounded them. Although the defenders had no ammunition for their own cannons and did not have numbers enough to actually occupy the wall, the *versaillais* balked at entering until their guns had battered down the gate. Once they entered, the *fédérés* disputed them foot by foot, gravestone by gravestone. Surrounded by death, the fighting became desperate, usually ending with bayonets and knives.

To the southeast of there—around five o'clock—a column of *fédérés*

moved a line of captured soldiers up the Rue Haxo from a recently evacuated prison in which they had been held to the church at Belleville.
"Their arrival caused a fatal diversion. The people ran up to see them
pass, and the Place des Fêtes was dismantled." The defenders of the
buttes had to fall back to their last line. By 6:30 p.m., that column of
fédérés reached Vincennes with forty-eight gendarmes, ecclesiastics,
and civilians. Finding the gates of the chateau closed to them, they could
not deliver the hostages there. So they lined them against a trench at the
fool of a wall and leveled their rifles. A local official eager to delay any
execution warned them that they were near a powder-magazine.
Nevertheless, the guns flashed and the hostages tumbled to the ground.

Later in the day, a *versaillais* staff colonel approached the Château de
Vincennes to negotiate its evacuation by the 375 *fédérés* stranded there.
Their commander, Colonel Nicolas Faltot, was a veteran of the wars of
Poland and of Garibaldi and he had played a prominent role in the
mutiny of the troops at Montmartre, which detonated the insurrection.
At its close, he proved no less a formidable figure. He had commanded
the 82nd Battalion through the siege and won the Legion of Honor for
Buzenval. He had become identified with the Blanquists, as part of the
"revolutionary army." The army offered him safety in return for his
cooperation. Perhaps Faltot had just learned not to trust the government, but answered that his honor forbade his deserting his men.[13]

The colonel proved a tough negotiator, even when he had absolutely
nothing with which to bargain. He pointed out that, by virtue of their
position, they had taken no part in the battle against the *versaillais*.[14] He
demanded passes, not for himself, but for some of his officers of foreign
nationality, but Vinoy demanded an unconditional surrender. Faltot
appealed to the Germans under the articles of war. However, MacMahon
had already ensured the cooperation of the Prince of Saxony. The fate of
the chateau seemed unavoidable as the rest of the Commune was
pacified.

Developments back in Paris indicated that this would be only hours
away.

---

13 Johnson, *The Paradise of Association*, 85 n. 54. Mentioned by Eudes, Maurice
Dommanget, *Blanqui, la guerre de 1870–71 et la Commune* (Paris: Domat-Montchrestien,
1947), 115.

14 Lissagaray, *History of the Paris Commune*, 303.

Through the late afternoon, scattered survivors, refugees of the fighting across the city, had clustered in its northwestern corner. Wagons rumbled in beneath the continued whir of the shells. There the wounded found no doctors or medical supplies, nor even a mattress on which to die. The spent, the bloodied, the dying staggered into what remained of their vision of a city on the hill. Injured men, women, and children—and few remained uninjured in one sense or another—brought a cascade of news from the front, about the fall of this street, the loss of that barricade, and the massacres everywhere. People declared their rage and desperation with sobs, with shouts, with shrieks. Among them wandered Varlin and the last members of the elected council, exhausted and painfully aware of what awaited them all.

Around four o'clock the troops of Vinoy and Ladmirault made a relentless push along the ramparts from different directions, converging on the Romainville gate and ending the hope of any further German largess in saving civilian refugees. Over the next hour, other soldiers overran the barricade of the Rue Rebéval in the Boulevard de la Villette, and advanced on the strongest remaining defenses, along the Rue de Paris from the rear. At 8 p.m., the army took the *mairie* of the Twentieth Arrondissement. The commander of the 191st and the remaining half dozen of his men held one barricade until their ammunition was exhausted.

For all of their propagandistic whining about the hostages, none of the army bothered going nearby to the Prisons de la Roquette to release the prisoners, despite having secured the nearby Père Lachaise. Through most of Saturday, the still-incarcerated hostages had been left to their own devices, the few that had tried to escape having been shot. Not until 9 p.m. did the government send anyone to rescue them. "This delay of twelve hours sufficiently shows their contempt for the lives of the hostages."

By this time, the army had driven most of what was left of the resistance into a small square formed by the Rue du Faubourg du Temple, the Rue des Trois Bornes, the Rue des Trois Couronnes, and the Boulevard de Belleville. Two or three streets struggled on in the Twentieth Arrondissement, including the Rue Ramponeau. In a last heroic act, Varlin and other remaining leaders of the Commune tied red scarves around their waists and rallied those still capable of a coordinated resistance. With their *chassepots* slung over their shoulders, they marched down the Rue des Champs for the last fierce fight. "A gigantic Garibaldian" carried the red flag before them. They entered the Eleventh Arrondissement and continued to the barricade at the corner of the Rue du Faubourg du Temple and the Rue de la Fontaine au Roi.

By ten o'clock, the firing had begun to sputter away. The *fédérés* loaded their last cannon with double shot. It boomed from the Rue du Paris, as what Lissagaray called "the last sigh of the Paris Commune": "Their last cartridge spent, overwhelmed by shells, they threw themselves upon the muskets bristling around them."

There came to be several claims for the location of the last barricade. It was most likely somewhere around Belleville or in the Eleventh Arrondissement. Lissagaray recounted a romantic story that the last barricade had been in the Rue Ramponeau, where a single Communard held it for a quarter of an hour. Thrice his marksmanship broke the staff of the *versaillais* flag hoisted on the barricade of the Rue de Paris. He likely spent the last of his ammunition and slipped away in the darkness. Since the most probable source for the story would have been the individual in question, his survival can be assumed, and we can but hope that the story was true.

That said, scattered neighborhood shooting continued well into the night.

Reprisals continued the following day, Sunday, May 28. Famously some 147 Communards were taken to a wall at the edge of the Père-Lachaise. The Mur des Fédérés remains one of the most visible remaining sites in the city associated with the Commune.

A priest fingered Varlin, who was captured by soldiers. They took him through the streets, where they permitted the heroes and heroines of the bourgeoisie to beat him about the head and face until his left eye dangled from the socket and he had become unrecognizable. They dragged him to the spot on the Rue des Rosiers where other soldiers had earlier killed Lecomte and Clément-Thomas, and murdered him there. In case this human sacrifice would not be sufficient, they marched forty-two men, three women, and four children to the location and told them to kneel bare-headed before the wall. One woman, grasping her child in her arms, refused, and urged her companions "to die 'upright.' "

So played out the justice of the republic, not so differently than had been that of the empire.

Only the Château de Vincennes was left for Sunday. Vinoy also had contact with "a few disreputable individuals" who offered to ensure its surrender by quietly taking the most intractably radical defenders out of the picture. One of these, a sergeant named Merlet, familiar with explosives, had already taken measures to blow the place up rather than surrender it. The magazine held 1,000 kilograms of powder and 400,000 cartridges that could still be of use to the insurrection.

On the morning of Sunday, May 28, at 8 a.m., the sound of a gunshot from Merlet's chamber brought in his comrades at a rush to find him shot in the head. Later a Captain Bayard of the 99th admitted to having shot Merlet to prevent his using an electrical detonator to explode the magazine.[15] He and another government agent opened the gates of the fort on Monday. By mid-afternoon, the army had occupied and shuttled its disarmed defenders to Versailles, except for nine of the officers, for whom an actual trial might prove troublesome.

Instead they held a council of war and condemned all nine. In the early hours of Wednesday, May 31, the authorities took the nine captured officers to the ditches. Another of them, one Delorme, possibly the individual who had been with Garibaldi in Burgundy, turned to the commanding officer of the *versaillais* with the words, "Feel my pulse. See if I am afraid."[16] At 3:30 a.m., the firing squad performed one of its last acts of the patriotic butchery.

The government turned the preeminent metropolis of Western civilization into a slaughterhouse. The army transformed its soldiers into brigands engaged in the murder, rape, and robbery of the people they had ritually sworn to defend. Their work eclipsed the St. Bartholomew's Day massacre, the Reign of Terror in the French Revolution, the insurrectionary clashes of 1830 and 1848.

Repression of the Commune continued far from Paris. In Brussels, Victor Hugo's denunciation of the Belgian government for failing to offer refuge to the Communards resulted in the mobbing of his home.

---

15 John Sutton, "Le château de Vincennes aux mains des communards," at commune1871.org.

16 On May 30, 1946, a commemorative plaque was placed at Vincennes.

On the border, officials regularly detained anyone trying to cross who struck them as suspicious. An English tourist briefly held there indicated that they had shot some of them.[17]

The army had arranged for the burial of 17,000 Communards. However, it simply threw many bodies into makeshift pyres in the streets or onto the flaming ruins around them. Many were pushed into mass graves without their identities or paperwork, such as the hundreds Georges Clemenceau saw near Père Lachaise cemetery. Reasonable estimates generally run to 17,000 or more.

Nor did the killing actually stop with the military reoccupation of the capital. The army officially took 43,522 prisoners, over a thousand of them women, and 615 under the age of sixteen. It marched them to Versailles or the Camp de Satory, stopping for roadside executions along the way and confining the survivors in notoriously crowded and unsanitary conditions until they could be processed. In the end, they did not bring to trial more than half, while unrecorded numbers of the rest were variously dispatched. The military courts that tried them convicted 13,500 of the 15,895 brought to trial. They sentenced ninety-five to death, over 250 to forced labor, nearly 2,400 to prison, and the rest to deportation, most to New Caledonia.

The "republic" had chosen to destroy Paris in order to save it. It also destroyed the old idea of a republic itself.

---

17   Appleton, *Reminiscences of a Visit to the Battle Fields*, 13–14.

Conclusion
The Final Conflict

New Views of Revolution

A modern Western world emerged from the events of 1870–1. The management of mass warfare institutionalized not only the mechanisms necessary for more and larger conflicts but also the means for the repression of internal opposition. It set us on the path to where old terms like "militarism" or "the merchants of death" would fade in importance with their normalization as defense and national security. Yet, in the decades since the Commune, revolution has been a recurring response for reasons that recall the disaster of 1871.

The ordeal of Paris and its people became a fitting demonstration that war, on this new scale, would write its own rules and follow its own logic. The level of human suffering inflicted on the people of Europe's most celebrated city, in the heart of the triumphalist West, remains mind-boggling, though its unpracticed nineteenth-century character allowed many to escape the carnage. The Communards who survived the subjugation of Paris experienced widely diverse fates. The authorities sought particularly to make an example of Louis Rossel, the officer who had turned on the army, and executed him in November.[1] The working-class Garibaldian from Le Creusot, Adolphe Assi, never returned from his exile to New Caledonia, though Louise Michel did. Nadar escaped

---

1   Lissagaray, *History of the Paris Commune*, 260.

exile, but his photography business dried up, which drove him from Paris. Minna Puccinelli had lost her husband in the combat before Dijon, and she joined the International in Belgium before making her way to Spain at the time of the revolts there.

Not a few Communards escaped the bloodbath in the city. Perhaps because he had tried to save the lives of the archbishop and other hostages, local clergy hid Gustave Cluseret for several months before he escaped to Switzerland. Those who had politically opposed him in the insurrection reechoed the slanders against him by the government, one amused newspaper writer describing him as "not only a villain of the commune, but a villain of the Crimean War, a villain of the Garibaldian army, and a villain of Fenianism." Assi's old comrade, Jean-Baptiste Dumay, escaped the military occupation of Le Creusot and found refuge in a Geneva machine shop.[2] So did Sainte Suzanne Melvil-Bloncourt, the Afro-Caribbean member of the Commune. Others found their way to London or to the United States, where the former commander at Fort Issy, Edmond Mégy, spent most of the rest of his life, though he died in Panama. Even in its repression, the Commune contributed to the internationalizing of the movement against capitalism.

Many uninvolved in the Commune came back to a Paris reeking of burned ruins, carnage, and institutionalized arrogance. Auguste Bartholdi returned to Paris on May 30, within hours of the final slaughter, to find his house occupied by troops, and his republican hopes for France sufficiently dashed to send him off to America. Louis Lartet also returned to Paris, likely to take his dead father's place among the leading scientific lights of the capital, but his war experience pushed him into a quiet professorship at Toulouse, where he passed his life. Jules Verne buried his skepticism about nationalism in *Les cinq cents millions de la Begum*, a popular vilification of the Germans with a catastrophic vision of a great city's vulnerability that owed much to the war and the Commune. Clara Barton, who had been through the horrors of the American Civil War and the wartime

---

2   "The Villains of the Commune," *Liberty*, 8 (May 21, 1892), 2; Noel, *Dictionary of the Commune*; Jean-Baptiste Dumay, *A Capitalist Stronghold: Creusot* (s.l.: s.n., 1882); Jean-Baptiste Dumay, *Memories of a Working Militant of Creusot (1841–1905)* (intr. and notes Pierre Ponsot), Maspero (Grenoble: University Presses of Grenoble, 1976). For material on the subject covered in this section see Molis, *Les francs-tireurs et les Garibaldi*, 237–8.

casualties of Alsace, sought to bring her medical experience to the aid of the city, but the conditions of its people collapsed her into what was described as a nervous exhaustion that left her temporarily blinded.[3] Like Berlin after its military subjugation in World War II, the recovery of Paris required a massive replacement of the earlier population, and that took a generation.

Inspired by the disasters at home, Bartholdi embarked on his monumental work *Liberty Enlightening the World*, as a gift to the American people. Emma Lazarus, the Jewish feminist, socialist, and poetess, would describe her as "a mighty woman with a torch" rather than a "brazen giant . . . with conquering limbs astride from land to land." She envisioned an inclusive nation built on the will of "the wretched refuse" of the old order—the tired, the poor, and the "huddled masses yearning to breathe free." In doing so, Lazarus did not misrepresent the purposes of Bartholdi, who later praised the American socialist leader Eugene V. Debs, the son of Bartholdi's schoolteacher friend from Colmar.[4]

Before Lady Liberty, however, emigrated the mythical *pétroleuse*. On October 7, 1871, George Francis Train warned a Chicago audience that an impending disaster awaited them should they fail to address "the social problem." When the great Chicago fire broke out a few days later, some publications cited Train's warning as proof that foreigners of the mysterious International sought to burn American cities as well.[5] The fictional character of such idiocy aside, the institutions of power in

---

3 Émile Cartailhac, "Éloge de M. Louis Lartet, membre libre de la Société archéologique du Midi de la France prononcé à la séance du mardi 43 février 1900," *Mémoires de la Société archéologique du Midi de la France*, 16 (1908), 13–14; "The Catastrophic Imaginary of the Paris Commune in Jules Verne's *Les 500 Millions de la Bégum*," *Journal Neophilologus*, 90 (October 2006), 535–53.

4 See also Esther Schor, *Emma Lazarus* (New York: Schocken, 2006); and "Ironies: Race, Gender and the Deception of 'Freedom,'" at xroads.virginia.edu. On the Bartholdi–Debs connection, see my introduction to the *Eugene V. Debs Reader: Socialism and the Class Struggle*, ed. William A. Pelz (London: Merlin Press, 2014).

5 "Desperate Conspirators: The Real Leaders of the Commune and Instigators of the Conflagration of Paris—A Plot to Burn Other European Cities," *New York Times*, June 3, 1871, 1; and also *New York Herald*, June 3, 1871, 5; "The International Society," *New York Times*, October 16, 1871, 4; Paul Bennie, *The Great Chicago Fire of 1871* (New York: Chelsea House, 2008), 7. Train did launch the Lafayette Association of American Capitalists to raise money to arm France, but he seems to have recruited nobody. "George Francis Train," *Freeman Journal*, January 19, 1871, 2.

republican America squealed their giddy approval as heartily as the most antiquated despotisms in Europe.

American officialdom readily endorsed the claim that the French republic had been engaged in a great crusade against an invisible enemy so cunning it never gave away its existence with anything so paltry as evidence. Clearly, Thiers was never alone in blaming the Commune on an all-powerful, secret revolutionary International. And those who had led the German Confederation into war returned infected with a serious dose of that most pathological French disease. It was a delusion cherished through the ages by all reactionaries.

What had all this death and destruction achieved?

The international anticapitalist movement drew some obvious conclusions. The fetishized obsession with "Jacobin" politics among most of the Commune leaders led to a strangely nostalgic predisposition to reenact a revolution that was ultimately neither democratic nor successful. So, too, the fate of Blanqui and his efforts certainly discredited the persistent Babouvist illusion that a carefully scheduled armed insurrection could impose an effective revolutionary challenge to the power of the state.

Then, too, a toxic utopian dogma left the Commune's leaders with a tragic agency in the shaping of their destiny. In particular, that fetishized insistence on decentralization and a suspicion of older military doctrines predisposed the Commune to leave it to the neighborhoods to look to their own defenses, even as the army overran them piecemeal. Most basically, commune movements emerged in local communities, where they faced isolation and repression by the national power of the old order. Cluseret—and many others—rightly ascribed their defeat to a stubborn obsession with decentralization. While hardly decentralized internally, the isolation of the Russian Revolution and its leadership fostered similar assumptions.[6]

Although often misidentified with democratic values, such values do not mandate decisions that incline us to self-defeat. On the other hand, success required a thoroughly democratically movement capable of defending itself, which the early Bolsheviks well understood, translating and printing Cluseret's discussion of street fighting.

From this perspective, though, revolution represents ultimately

6   Cluseret, *Mémoires*, vol. 1, 4.

defensive measures by the people. Indeed, these aim less at dissolving state power than at providing a viable alternative when state power effectively begins to dissolve itself.

The emergent Left, then, acquired ideas, while the established institutions made more tangible gains.

Still, the war resolved absolutely nothing of the issue that had caused it, the crisis of the monarchy in Spain, which exploded into revolts similar to those in France. The Spanish volunteers with Garibaldi's army balked when the French authorities sought to disarm them, declaring that they wanted to carry their weapons back over the Pyrenees to fight against the tyranny at home. In the end, the abdication of King Amadeo in February 1873—like Bonaparte's departure from France—left Spain something of a republic by default under essentially the same old rulers. Advocates of a decentralized federal state soon challenged those "republicans" who favored replicating the imperial model without a monarchy. On July 9, anarchists in the IWA led a rising against authoritarian employers at Alcoy, detonating cantonal revolts at Murcia, Cartagena, and elsewhere across Spain. They expressed concerns similar to those of the commune movements in France, and the press even reported panicked sightings of Cluseret in Spain.[7] After looking into that abyss of popular rule, the "First Republic" saw less risk in an alliance with the military, the Church, and, ultimately, a monarchy.

The war did establish a new German national state, but victory and defeat are elusive questions over time. In the end, the presence of a strong Reich dominating Central Europe would foster emulation in self-defense by potential rivals. In its aftermath, all the great powers began modernizing their military and naval forces, at unprecedented expense and yielding unprecedented profit to their contractors. It created a dynamic where war would increasingly become the solution of first resort. So they all got much better at it.

Many civilized rulers over many of the Western nations recoiled in horror when Otto von Bismarck mockingly observed that history owed less to the resolutions of majorities and the will of the people than to what he called "blood and iron." Yet their own subsequent history

---

7   Socci, *Da Firenze a Digione*, 266; Bookchin, *The Spanish Anarchists*, 84–6. For Spanish republican interest in Garibaldi's activities, see Emilio Castelar, *Garibaldi* (Florence: Coi tipi dei Successori Le Monnier, 1882).

demonstrated the legitimacy of Bismarck's observation, and validated the faith he shared with Thiers. The demands of the capitalist market and the institutions necessary to protect it mediated and redefined every promise of republicanism. With the rise of industrialized warfare, the Schneiders in France, the Krupps in Germany, and their peers around the world made unprecedented fortunes as what a more straightforward world called "merchants of death." In turn they bankrolled the institutions and careers that assured them of greater profit.

Less than half a century after the founding of the *Kaiserreich*, the practice of war reached a staggering crescendo. Its founding victims nurtured an anguished desire for *revanche*, politically organized by characters such as Georges Boulanger and Paul Déroulède. The German rulers learned nothing about the pitfalls of their confiscation of Napoleonic arrogance, and the legacy bequeathed to Helmuth von Moltke's nephew became an unalloyed curse.

Global disaster resulted. Among the Germans, Alfred Graf von Schlieffen reduced the raw experience of 1870 into a formulaic ritual for conquering France. In the 1914 effort to demonstrate this, the generalship of Paul von Hindenburg and the airships of Ferdinand von Zeppelin supplied some of its more memorable features. Most directly, participants delivered and suffered injury or death at the front mostly by a bolt from the blue delivered from unprecedented distances—the horrific legacy of the Krupp artillery of the Franco-Prussian War. The French nurtured the national *union sacrée*, giving rise to the prime ministry of one of its chief architects, Georges Clemenceau. More substantively, the mystique of Verdun's defense inspired a prolonged and ultimately pointless clash of arms that ultimately claimed around a million lives. A similar number died around the corner of the Western Front along the Somme, centered in the area of the prehistoric Butte de Warlencourt.

With the epidemics and related deaths, the estimated human cost of the so-called Great War ran to between 50,000,000 and 100,000,000 lives, and a Second World War took a similar toll not long after. And while governments have since avoided global conflicts on this scale, they have managed to generalize mass death over entire regions of the earth.

The scale of conflict could not have been anything less than international. Developments beyond Europe during these years certainly demonstrated how the project of nation building required the blood and bones of one's own people. China struggled toward a new national existence freed from its imperial past, a conflict in which the governments of the Western heartland of both republicanism and Christianity actively aided its brutal repression of the people. In the crushing of the Taiping Rebellion, the reprisals, the plagues, and the famine, China had lost an estimated 30 million people by 1864. That same year, Bonapartist-inspired megalomania took Paraguay to war with Brazil, then Argentina and Uruguay, which ended the lives over the half the people in Paraguay and virtually exterminated the male population of military age.

The course of these wars forever dissolved the assumption that nation-building required republican bricks. A Bartholdi or a Garibaldi or a Lincoln had increasingly thought of "republican" politics as centered on the considered will of the people, and expected a representative system defined by the state of society in general. They believed, or came increasingly to believe, that national unity, republican government, and egalitarian social reform would form a common, mutually interdependent republican society. That republic would be essential rather than superficial, substantial rather than formalistic, and constitutional rather than legalistic. They thought it would naturally be promulgated in good faith.

Assemblies, parliaments, congresses, and *Reichstags* of the later nineteenth century neither grew from nor cultivated a genuinely representative civic culture, but became mechanisms through which self-interested elites exercised power. This required twisting the most fundamental features of the older republican ideology, such as rooting the legitimacy of a social contract in the consent of the governed. It translated "consent" into a mere periodic electoral ritual in which voters choose between preselected political figures and parties already committed to the structure of power and the stream of profit. And those of "the governed" permitted to participate even in this ritual had to be those deemed responsible, while excluding those deemed unworthy of participation because of race, gender, or class.

The process inherently marginalized the entire population other than the self-interested elites and their retainers. Bismarck's new state redefined Germans hesitant about Prussian policies as "fatherless" bastards without a country. Thiers's butchers talked of the Communards as savages, barbarians, and bandits, comparing them to the Arabs and even the "Red Indians" they had gloriously exterminated in Mexico. The

American preservation of the Union may have required the destruction of slavery, but, in its aftermath, the institutionalized victors joined former slaveholders in decrying "Red Republicanism" or "Black Republicanism," the racial implications of both terms being quite straightforward. The US repudiation of its affinity for republican governments (however racially specific) also became evident in the unapologetic affinity of US ambassador Elihu B. Washburne with the autocrats of Europe as opposed to the people of Paris.[8] The new nation-states freely exercised their power to make themselves the official arbiters of inclusion, and freely excluded those who lacked power, wealth or an ability to contribute much to either.

So it is that officeholders with strong monarchist inclinations, such as Thiers, simply turned the language of republicanism to rationalize fundamentally imperial priorities. What they would call their state mattered little, so long as the hierarchic nature of power survived and revolution was averted.

The danger here turned less on policies than on power. Mass military mobilizations subjected vastly larger sections of the population to the stresses of modern war, which weighed most severely on those in uniform. An ongoing individual discontent in uniform assumes a collective presence, perhaps assuming a mass scale and, ultimately, open mutiny.

English and American papers watched with interest the pioneering efforts of the emerging German state to contain the socialist threat within the army. With the raising of mass armies, it "can also no longer be denied that the Social Democratic influence has even extended to the military." The authorities tried secretly to prevent this. "Domiciliary searches have taken place in the barracks and lodgings of soldiers for Social Democratic newspapers and pamphlets, and any further reading of such publications, as well as frequenting places in which these destructive principles are propagated, is strictly forbidden." Paradoxically, though, the government gave military training to the working-class and peasant youth that might be turned against them, "such as happened in Paris during the Commune."[9]

---

8   Robin Blackburn, *An Unfinished Revolution: Karl Marx and Abraham Lincoln* (London: Verso, 2011), provides a solid introduction to these problems in the US.

9   "Social Democracy in the German Army" (from the *Pall Mall Gazette*), *Evening Post* (New York), July 19, 1876, 1.

The aspirations of radicals came into sharper focus in response. For some decades, both radicals and their critics in various Western countries began to distinguish between the established practice of a republic and that utopian idea of a "social republic." Around mid-century, socialism and anarchism emerged from the cocoon of representative ideologies.[10] For some years after the Commune, socialists continued to look toward electoral politics. Even an increasingly skeptical Marx talked about the possibilities of the workers voting socialism into power, where they could participate in the free and fair elections he imagined were taking place in Britain, Holland, Belgium, and the United States.

Social democracy represented one response to the lessons of the Commune that the ruling class would never allow working people to come to power by the same route that they, the bourgeoisie, had used against the feudal nobility. Already, groups of capitalists in the new industries—such as the Krupp works at Essen—had adopted, funded and institutionalized the mutual aid practices already pioneered by specific smaller groups of workers.[11] The national embrace of such an approach by the government of Bismarck merged with the more minimal expectation of Ferdinand Lassalle's version of socialism.

Nevertheless, the German comrades set to work in the wake of the war on what became the largest socialist party in the world. Wilhelm Hasenclever returned from the army to a long career in the Reichstag. More importantly, he assumed the presidency of the ADAV, which he led into a regrouping with the SDAP to form the Sozialistische Arbeiterpartei Deutschlands (the SAP). It became the cornerstone for a revived International, the Second or Socialist International, founded in 1889.

Veterans of the commune movements in France also threw their lives

10   See Mark Bevir, "Republicanism, Socialism, and Democracy in Britain: The Origins of the Radical Left," *Journal of Social History*, 34 (Winter 2000), 341–68; and B. H. Moss, "Republican Socialism and the Making of the Working Class in Britain, France, and the United States: A Critique of Thompsonian Culturalism," *Comparative Studies in Society and History*, 35 (April 1993), 390–413.

11   Werner Ettelt and Hans-Dieter Krause, *Der Kampf um eine marxistische Gewerkschaftspolitik in der deutschen Arbeiterbewegung, 1868 bis 1878* (Berlin: Verlag Tribüne, 1975), 253. Also W. F. Willoughby, "Chapter IV. Iron and Steel Works of Friedrich Krupp, Essen, Germany," *Bulletin of the Department of Labor*, 1 (November 1895–November 1896), 508–16.

behind these projects. After Cluseret returned from Switzerland in 1884, he won election to the National Assembly as a socialist deputy in the Parti ouvrier français. When Dumay returned, he launched a general trade union federation in Saône-et-Loire before moving to Paris, where he became an early leader of the party and the new Socialist International, while also serving in the National Assembly. Leó Frankel returned to his native Hungary and attempted to start a socialist party there. Depressed and exiled in New Jersey, Eugène Pottier had poured his Communard soul into his poem L'Internationale.[12] He returned to die penniless and largely forgotten, but his poem, set to music, became and remains the anthem of the world movement to abolish capitalism.

Those efforts and those of their successors won electoral and legislative victories in terms of policy but never took these countries closer to the abolition of capitalism in terms of its most essential feature, that of class power. To avoid that question, the dominant powers have been willing to offer massive material concessions as readily as bloody repression, and the rise of the West to exploit the rest of the planet created more wealth to do so.

Karl Marx and the International may well have been correct that capitalism created its own gravediggers, but it would neither cooperatively tumble itself into its grave nor consent to be put there without taking with it as much of human civilization as it could. Rather than bringing to birth a new world, subsequent generations witnessed a globalized system of exploitation with wars of unprecedented scale, endemic mass starvation, and the systemic rationalized destruction of the biosphere, while the established order cultivated the mass capacity for unreasoning delusions, habitual deference, and socially sanctioned cruelty necessary to sustain the more dysfunctional features of the dominant institutions and prevalent ideologies.

They even offered their own version of a United States of Europe.

The Western world cultivated a mechanism that legitimated and rationalized itself. It carefully crafted illusions of an ever-expanding prosperity, and the kind of gradual linear progress toward a more just and inclusive society. Despite a few not inconsequential hiccups, such as 1968, the Commune came be rendered as an unfortunate misunderstanding and a kind of scaled-up, best-forgotten incidence of

---

12   Ernest Museux, Eugène Pottier (Paris: H. Fabre, 1910), 43–4.

domestic violence. In the more recent phase, the eruption of social media began to bury it all in packed layers of ash.

Under those circumstances, any lessons to be drawn from that past became the domain of academic specialists. Nevertheless, several quite obvious conclusions confront historically minded radicals.

Matters may look grim on the 150th anniversary of the Commune, but a balanced view is more complex. By the later twentieth century, the much-touted celebratory parade of neoliberalism became a forced march back to the eighteenth century, creating a historically unprecedented polarization of wealth. This exaggerated inequalities of all sorts, until a series of economic crises and environmental realizations began jolting the Western world.

While some responded with the well-exercised superstitions of race and nationality, legions went into motion against corruption and for a more fair society. Even in the US, still terrified by the ever-invisible *pétroleuses*, young people have begun to repudiate the capitalist economic and social order. In Paris, *gilets jaunes* took back from the authorities the same streets that had been torn in bloody strife from the hands of Communards.

Armed with the unfulfilled promise of past revolutions, the specter of the Commune has now returned to haunt Europe and the world like that proverbial fearful hobgoblin that has made repeated appearances. In the end, time has not cheapened those lessons learned at such a high price in 1870–1.

Acknowledgments

This study grew slowly but had deep roots in undergraduate and graduate school interests, with an appropriately long and entangled indebtedness. The project had active encouragement, advice, and consultation over years and decades, essential for an Americanist venturing into the very different standards and norms of European history. A long line of specialists in the field whose work has always kept me interested provided encouragement that proved decisive to my pursuit of the project. These include Michel Cordillot and David Jordan, whose courses in French history remain vivid after more than forty years. Institutionally, I am extremely grateful to the Charles P. Taft Memorial Fund and the Department of History at the University of Cincinnati, which made possible a prolonged research trip to the military archives at Château de Vincennes, the superbly knowledgeable and patient professionals at that institution, and the excellent staff at Verso. My wife, Katherine Allen, has been, as ever, patient and supportive in my work. Finally, I would like to thank old friends who gave long, if skeptical, encouragement as I ventured into their fields: Janine Hartman, a historian in UC's Romance Language and Literature Department; the late Bill Pelz, a German historian; and Andrew Villalon, an Iberacist of exceptionally cosmopolitan interests. I dedicate this work to them.

Still, however much I relied on their sound advice and solid insights, the responsibility for errors or shortcomings in this work are entirely my own.

A Note on Sources

Readers interested in pursuing the subjects addressed in *Soldiers of Revolution* are addressed to specific citations in the notes, but may find useful studies that contribute in a general way. While naturally intended for English-language readers, this work has relied heavily on consulting the online resources of the Bibliothèque nationale de France (Gallica) and the Deutsche digitale Bibliothek, with some similar regional and local projects, and many available through Google Books and the Internet Archives. In several insightful essays, David H. Pinkney once mused about the very real frustrations of being an American student of French history, offering practical advice on its pursuit. While much of this still applies, the digitalization of newspapers and archival material, as well as of published works, has placed so much before the world that serious research in some areas has become practical to an extent that Pinkney could not have imagined.

The Franco-Prussian War

Standard accounts include Michael E. Howard, *The Franco-Prussian War: The German Invasion of France, 1870–1871* (New York: Macmillan, 1961); and Geoffrey Wawro, *The Franco-Prussian War: The German Conquest of France in 1870–1871* (Cambridge and New York: Cambridge University Press, 2003); as well as Quinton Barry's more expansive military history

The Franco-Prussian War 1870–71, vol. 1, *The Campaign of Sedan: Helmuth von Moltke and the Overthrow of the Second Empire* (Solihull: Helion & Co. Ltd., 2009), vol. 2, *After Sedan: Helmuth von Moltke and the Defeat of the Government of National Defence* (Solihull: Helion & Co. Ltd., 2009); and his *The Somme 1870–1: The Winter Campaign in Picardy* (Solihull: Helion & Company, 2014), and *The Last Throw of the dice: Bourbaki and Werder in Eastern France 1870–71* (Solihull: Helion & Company, 2018). See also Douglas Fermer's *Sedan 1870: The Eclipse of France* (Barnsley: Pen & Sword Military, 2008), *France at Bay, 1870–1871: The Struggle for Paris* (Barnsley: Pen & Sword Military, 2011), and *Three German Invasions of France* (Barnsley: Pen & Sword, 2014).

Documentary sources are massive and often very repetitive on certain points. However, they are readily available online. Moltke and the German General Staff published a compilation on *Der deutsch–französische Krieg, 1870–71, und das Generalstabswerk*, also included in the Grosser Generalstab, ed., *Moltkes Gesammelte Schriften und Denkwürdigkeiten*, 8 vols. (Berlin: E. S. Mittler, 1892). The French version of the war simply translated the German documents with the addition of their own select documents as *Guerre Franco-Allemande de 1870–71*, trans. E. Costa de Serda (Berlin and Paris: Ernest Siegfried Mittler and J. Dumaine, 1872), and *Guerre franco-allemande: Résumé et commentaires de l'ouvrage du grand état-major prussien*, ed. Felix Bonnet, 3 vols. (Paris: Librairie Militaire de J. Dumaine, 1878–83). English translations by Clara Bell, Henry W. Fischer, and Archibald Forbes appeared in various editions in the wake of the war, particularly *The Franco-German War of 1870–71 by Generals and Other Officers*, trans. and ed. Major-General J. F. Maurice, Wilfred J. Long, and A. Sonnenscheins (London: Swan Sonnenschein and Co., Ltd, 1900); and the United States General Staff School, *Franco- German War of 1870: Source Book* (Fort Leavenworth, KS: The General Service School, 1922). In addition to sources cited in the text, with more anecdotal material is the compilation by Georges Hardouin (writing as Dick de Lonlay), *Francais et allemands histoire anecdotique de la guerre de 1870–1871*, 5 vols. (Paris: Garnier Fréres, 1887–91). Also relevant in these comparative studies might be Philip M. Katz, *From Appomattox to Montmartre: Americans and the Paris Commune* (Cambridge, MA: Harvard University Press, 1998).

More recent work has focused on the conflict in the context of the emergence of modern institutions. Stig Förster and Jorg Nagler, eds., *On the Road to Total War: The American Civil War and the German Wars of Unification* (Washington, DC and Cambridge: German Historical Institute and Cambridge University Press, 1997), underscores the rise of the modern state and national identities. Manfred F. Boemeke, Roger Chickering, and Stig Förster, eds., *Anticipating Total War: The German and American Experiences, 1871-1914* (Washington, DC and Cambridge: German Historical Institute and Cambridge University Press, 1999), combines the experience of both Germany and the United States.

Society

A few of the more useful items on social classes informed the approach of this study. For the sensibilities of the majorities of the populations of France and German regarding the war see Richard J. Evans and W. R. Lee, eds., *The German Peasantry: Conflict and Community from the Eighteenth to the Twentieth Centuries* (New York: St. Martin's Press 1985); and Eugen Weber, *Peasants into Frenchmen: The Modernization of Rural France, 1870-1914* (Stanford, CA: Stanford University Press, 2007); as well as David A. J. Macey, *Government and Peasant in Russia, 1861-1906: The Pre-history of the Stolypin Reforms* (DeKalb: Northern Illinois University Press, 1987). On the artisans, a vital group for understanding the core of activists, see Cynthia Maria Truant, *The Rites of Labor: Brotherhoods of Compagnonnage in Old and New Regime France* (Ithaca, NY: Cornell University Press, 1994); and for their importance in the making of the workers' movement, see Michael P. Hanagan, *The Logic of Solidarity: Artisans and Industrial Workers in Three French Towns, 1871-1914* (Urbana: University of Illinois Press, 1980); and, almost classically at this point, Joan Wallach Scott, *The Glassworkers of Carmaux: French Craftsmen and Political Action in a Nineteenth-century City* (Cambridge, MA: Harvard University Press, 1974).

The Contemporary Left

See Mike Rapport, *1848: Year of Revolution* (New York: Basic Books, 2010). On the aftermath, see Sabine Freitag, *Exiles from European Revolutions* (New York: Berghahn Books, 2003); Roman Koropeckyj,

Adam Mickiewicz: The Life of a Romantic (Ithaca, NY: Cornell University Press, 2008); Patrick H. Hutton, *The Cult of the Revolutionary Tradition: The Blanquists in French Politics, 1864–1893* (Berkeley: University of California Press, 1981); and Doug Greene's well-informed exploration of whether 1871 was a "Missing Victory? Blanqui and the Commune," *Cosmonaut* (posted October 13, 2018), at cosmonaut.blog.

For recent work on Garibaldi, see Lucy Riall, *Garibaldi: Invention of a Hero* (New Haven and London: Yale University Press, 2007); and Alfonso Scirocco, *Garibaldi* (Bari: Laterza, 2001), reissued in various editions, the most prominent in English being *Garibaldi: Citizen of the World* (Princeton: Princeton University Press, 2007). A bit older, but still very useful, are Andrea Viotti, *Garibaldi: The Revolutionary and His Men* (Poole: Blandford Press, 1979); Jasper Ridley, *Garibaldi* (New York: Viking Press, 1974); and Anthony P. Campanella, *Garibaldi e la tradizione garibaldina: Una bibliografia dal 1807 al 1970*, 2 vols. (Grand Saconnex and Geneva: Comitato dell'Istituto internazionale di studi Garibaldini, 1971).

For Garibaldi's international legions, see Anne-Claire Ignac, "French Volunteers in Italy, 1848–49: A Collective Incarnation of the Fraternity of the Peoples and of the Tradition of French Military Engagement in Italy and Europe," *Journal of Modern Italian Studies*, 14 (November 2009), 445–60; Gilles Pécout, "The International Armed Volunteers: Pilgrims of a Transnational Risorgimento," *Journal of Modern Italian Studies*, 14(4) (2009), 413–26; Simon Sarlin, "Fighting the Risorgimento: Foreign Volunteers in Southern Italy (1860–63)," *Journal of Modern Italian Studies*, 14(4) (November 2009), 476–90; and Ferdinand Boyer, "Les volontaires français avec Garibaldi en 1860," *Revue d'histoire moderne et contemporaine*, 7 (April–June 1960), 123–48.

The footnotes have covered Cluseret in terms of the work by Florence Braka and his own memoirs. Unusually, M.W.H. wrote a review long enough to be serialized, two under "Some New Books. Gen. Cluseret's Memoirs—The Truth about the Paris Commune," *New York Sun*, August 21, 1887, 4, *New York Sun*, September 4, 1887, 4, and another as "Some New Books. Minister Washburne's Recollections," *New York Sun*, October 16, 1887, 4. The *New York Sun* was the paper of the former socialist Charles A. Dana, run with the help of the ever-unrepentant socialist John Swinton. See also Alban Bargain-Villeger, "Gustave Cluseret and the Socialist Lefts, 1848–1900," *Socialist History*, 46 (2014),

13–32, and some rather superficial pieces by Lowell L. Blaisdell, "Cluseret and the Fremont Campaign of 1864," *Mid-America*, 46 (October 1964), 252–68, and "A French Civil War Adventurer: Fact and Fancy," *Civil War History*, 12 (September 1966), 246–57. A curio of the period is A. Landy's "A French Adventurer and American Expansionism after the Civil War," *Science and Society*, 14 (Fall 1951), 313–33. A national officer of the Communist Party of the US writing at the height of the Cold War, Landy ignores evidence about Cluseret's abolitionism to rather bizarrely reduce his interest in the abolition of slavery in Cuba as nascent US imperialism, and ignores the irrefutable evidence about the hostility of the US government to his activities in Europe to describe them as those of an American secret agent. Very recent but remarkably insufficient is William J. Phalen's *The Democratic Soldier: The Life of General Gustave P. Cluseret* (New Delhi: Vij Books India Pvt Ltd, 2016).

On the "First International," see Fabrice Bensimon, Quentin Deluermoz, and Jeanne Moisand, *"Arise Ye Wretched of the Earth": The First International in a Global Perspective* (Studies in Global Social History) (Leiden and Boston: Brill, 2018); Marcello Musto, *Workers unite! The International 150 Years Later* (New York: Bloomsbury Academic, 2014); Boris I. Nicolaevsky, *The Revolution Is Not a Masonic Affair: Boris Nicolaevsky's Study of "Secret Societies in the First International"* (London: Unpopular Books, 1997); and Henryk Katz, *The Emancipation of Labor: A History of the First International* (Westport, CT: Greenwood Press, 1992); Peter Brook, "The Polish Revolutionary Commune in London," *Slavonic and East European Review*, 35 (December 1956), 116–28; and Samuel Bernstein, *The Beginnings of Marxian Socialism in France* (New York: Russell, 1965). See also Michel Cordillot, *Aux origines du socialisme moderne: Le première internationale, la commune de Paris, L'Exil: Recherches et travaux* (Paris: Éditions de l'Atelier, 2010); Timothy Messer-Kruse, *The Yankee International: Marxism and the American Reform Tradition, 1848–1876* (Chapel Hill and London: University of North Carolina Press, 1998); and Woodford McClellan, *Revolutionary Exiles: The Russians in the First International and the Paris Commune* (London and Totowa, NJ: Cass, 1979). Older accounts also usefully include G. M. Stekloff, *History of the First International*, trans. Eden Paul and Cedar Paul (New York: International Publishers, 1928) and I. A. Bakh, *Die Erste Internationale, 1864–1876* (Moscow: Progress, 1981).

For documentary evidence, see *Documents sur l'Association internationale des travailleurs (1re Internationale) de 1864 à 1870* (Paris: Centre d'études et de recherches sur les mouvements trotskyste et révolutionnaires internationaux, 1993); and Thierry Drapeau and Pierre Beaudet, eds., *L'Internationale sera le genre humain! De l'Association internationale des travailleurs à aujourd'hui* (Saint-Joseph-du-Lac, Québec: M Éditeur, 2015). The vast literature revisiting the schism between the followers of Marx and of Mikhail Bakunin is almost universally too abstract for historical uses, boiling down largely to a fight over abstractions and vocabulary.

The Paris Commune

The library on the Commune continues to grow at a rapid pace. Demonstrating this, even as this work moved to print, we have Quintin Deleurmoz, *Commune(s), 1870–1871: Une traversée des mondes au XIXe siècle* (Paris: Seuil, 2020), framing the importance of the rise in global influence, particularly in its treatment of the Commune's influence in the *Outre-Mer*, and areas heavily influenced by France at the time, such as Mexico. The massive and monumental new *La Commune de Paris 1871: Les acteurs, l'événement, les lieux*, ed. Michel Cordillot (Ivry-sur-Seine: Les Éditions de l'atelier/Éditions ouvrières, 2021) will surely supersede others as the basic reference work on the subject. The narrative in the closing three chapters draws on some excellent general accounts available in English, particularly the latest by John Merriman, but also those by Rupert Christiansen, Stewart Edwards, Alistair Horne, Frank Jellinek, and Robert Tombs, but rather than offer what will only become rather quickly outdated compilation, it seems more useful to point readers to the ever-expanding online resources available from the Amies et Amis de la Commune de Paris 1871.

Primary sources are themselves available at that site and elsewhere. Online, those interested will find various editions of Prosper Olivier Lissagaray, *Histoire de la Commune de 1871* (Bruxelles: H. Kistemaeckers, 1876), going into English as *History of the Commune of 1871*, trans. Eleanor Marx Aveling (London: Reeves and Turner, 1886), with numerous other translations and editions. Many of these had a fleeting presence on my shelf before being passed along. Then, too, there are a number of online versions, including those available from Google, Gallica, Guttenberg, the Internet Archives, and the Marxist Internet Archives. Pagination for these various editions vary, or, in some online versions, are simply non-existent. For this study, I simply used the edition that happened to be on the shelf at the time, which was the *History of the Commune of 1871* (London: New Park Publications, 1976). Similarly accessible is Karl Marx's *The Civil War in France*. Gallica has digital versions of the *Journal officiel de la République française sous la Commune* and copies of the more popularly read papers of the Commune have been available on the site of the Amies et Amis de la Commune de Paris 1871; see also Mitchell Abidor, trans., *Communards: The Story of the Paris Commune of 1871 as Told by Those Who Fought for It* (Pacifica, CA: Marxists Internet Archive, 2010); and Abidor's *Voices of the Paris Commune* (Oakland, CA: Revolutionary Pocketbooks—PM Press, 2015).

The French sources on the Commune are expanding rapidly, particularly as we have gone through the sesquicentennial. For the most up-to-date discussions of ongoing research on the subject, see the website of Les Amies et Amis de la Commune de Paris 1871, at commune1871.org, particularly the one on "Bibliographie." Even this long after the event, new details are coming to light, providing us with a granular sense of the experience of the working-class neighborhoods of the city. Recent work on the regional outbreaks outside of Paris and on the role of foreigners in the Commune, particularly that of Michel Cordillot and his colleagues, permit an increasingly sharp focus on the nature of the Commune and its connections, as well as the experience of the Communard beneath the manifestos from the Hôtel de Ville.

Maps

There are numerous sites available online with good maps of the Franco-Prussian War, Wikipedia having pulled together useful maps of campaigns and battles in the public domain. For maps of Paris, particularly the movements during Bloody Week, see the following: "Chronocartography of the 1871 Paris Commune," thefunambulist.net; Mark Jacobsen, "The War of the Paris Commune, 1871," at clausewitz.com; and Fosco Lucarelli, "Mapping the 'Bloody Week': the Last Days of the Paris Commune in a Cartographic Narrative," January 29, 2014, socks-studio.com, as well as the "Left in Paris," locating the sites of 1871 in maps of the modern city, leftinparis.org.

Index

Scotland, 9

Secret society tradition, x, 14–15, 22, 31, 32–3, 133, 263

Sedan, 54, 131, 188, 266; 94, 95–6, 103–8, *passim* 110–19, 188, 219, 220, 260; capture transforms the war, 125, 127, 135; impact on Paris, 148, 172

Serraillier, August, 33, 154.

Socci, Ettore. 180, 186.

socialism and means of cooptation, 252; Socialist International, 253–4

Sozialdemokratische Arbeiterpartei (SDAP—Social Democratic Workers Party). 39, 59, 60, 253

Spain and Spaniards, 7, 9, 10, 17, 52, 160; Cantonal revolt in Spain, 249; as Communards, 218; dynastic crisis, 46–47; in French army, 132, 169, 176, 180; and international organization, 30, 32–3; prospects of rebellion, 180

Spicheren (Aug. 6, 1870), 76, 77, 81, 88

Steinmetz, Karl Friedrich vpn, 56, 76–7, 78, 83, 88, 89

Stephens, James, 18, 19

Strasbourg (Aug. 14–Sept. 28, 1870), 25, 53, 54, 56, 69, 79, 83; surrender of 121, 127, 140

Struve, Gustav von, 42, 43

Sweden and Swedes, 10; as Communards, 218

Switzerland and the Swiss, 10, 37; as Communards, 218; in final campaign of the war, 172, 173, 177, 179; individuals fighting for France, 133; internationalist networks, 32, 120; as neutral haven for refugees, 43, 142, 193, 220, 246, 253

the Saar, 57, 58, 68, 78

Thiers, Marie Joseph Louis Adolphe, 111; crushing of the Commune, 215, 227, 248, 249, 252; hostility to Paris, 186, 188, 189, 194, 197

Thionville, 54, 83, 121

Toul (Aug. 16–Sept. 23, 1870). 83, 131

Toulouse, 25, 181, 193, 194, 246

Tournachon, Gaspard-Félix (a.k.a. Nadar), 21, 215, 246

Tours, 91, 113, 122, 129, 148, 181

Train, George Francis, 19; adventurism in Marseilles 141–2, 143, 147–9; Fenian and Cluseret connections 19; Garibaldian connection 16; and the

pétroleuse, 247

Trochu, Louis Jules, 80, 220; commanding the defense of Paris, 111, 112, 157, 177, 199; on nature of preparations for war, 47–8

Turcos, 65–6, 72, 74, 75, 96, 150, 172; Blacks among, 66; former slaves in North Africa, 65–6; no quarter to, 71–2; *tirailleurs algériens*, 12, 64, 71, 73, 74, 76, 106; *see also* North Africa and Africans; Africa and Africans

United States of America; *see* America and Americans

universal republic, 13; 15, 24, 29, 32, 129, 152, 186; United States of Europe, 13, 31, 46, 254; United States of South America, 18

Varlin, Eugene; at Le Creusot, 35; Communard, 188, 234, 237, 241–2, 243

Vendôme, 166, the column 215

Venice, 15, 29

Verdun. 54, 79, 82, 83–4, 85, 86, 91–2, 101; failure of the Prussian attempt to capture, 93–4, 110, 121

Verne, Jules, 113, 141, 215, 246

Versailles, 112; base for the suppression of Paris, 185, 188–91, 193, 195–7, 200, 201, 203, 204, 212, 213, 214, 216, 223, 224, 229, 230, 233, 243, 244; capital moved there from Bordeaux, 187; German empire established in the Hall of Mirrors, 181

Victoria (Queen of the United Kingdom), 55, 156.

Vilification of the underclass, 251

Villersexel (Jan. 9, 1871), 162, 171, 172

Vincennes, Cité et Château de, 112, 215, 236, 240, 243

Vinoy, Joseph, 80; and the Commune, 188, 231, 235–6, 238, 240, 241, 243; defense of Paris, 112, 154; operations near Sedan, 104, 106

Vizetelly, Edward H., 130–1

War, its normalization and globalization in the age of the Franco-Prussian conflict, 245, 249–50; Paraguayan War, 251; roots of the Great War, 250; Taiping rebellion, 250–1

Washburne, Elihu B., 148; hostility to the